The library of the heart will hold this book with special meaning. In the style of treasured classics this well-worded book feeds the contemporary appetite with the solid food of good literature and involves the reader in the heartwarming account of survival under pressure. The characters entered my life, and my life is enriched by their experience.

—JEANNETTE CLIFT GEORGE
SPEAKER, AUTHOR, FOUNDER/DIRECTOR OF
A.D. PLAYERS CHRISTIAN THEATER COMPANY
STAR OF *THE HIDING PLACE* IN THE ROLE OF CORRIE TEN BOOM

I was instantly enthralled by Sharon Schuller Kiser's clear and captivating way, her engaging style, refreshing humor, and above all her compassion for her characters. She writes, I suspect, with a tear in her eye and a heart broken open.

—CHERYL ANNE PORTER
MULTI-PUBLISHED AUTHOR
SPEAKER, HUMOR COLUMNIST AND AUTHOR OF *JESSIE'S OUTLAW*
CHOSEN BY THE LIBRARY OF CONGRESS FOR ITS RARE BOOK COLLECTION
AND NATIONAL READER'S CHOICE AWARD WINNER

Sharon Schuller Kiser's rich, descriptive language creates a poignantly warm coming-of-age story that captures the powerful message of forgiveness and acceptance.

—MELANIE DUFORD
PUBLICATIONS COORDINATOR
MISSIONARY VENTURES INTERNATIONAL

As compelling as Beverly Lewis's Amish books, Sharon Schuller Kiser's tale of orphans discovering their hidden selves will, I predict, take lovers of fiction by storm. *THAT End of Lilac Lane* will resonate with you—we are all trying to find out who we are and what we will be. The dramatic ending will stay with you forever as Sarah Emily learns life's most important lesson—the key to her future, not the secret of her past. Sharon Schuller Kiser is a gifted storyteller with her picturesque language and lilting style. She, like her enchanting character Sarah Emily, has "special in her blood!"

—KRISTY DYKES
MULTI-PUBLISHED, AWARD-WINNING AUTHOR AND SPEAKER
CO-AUTHOR OF *AMERICAN DREAM, SWEET LIBERTY* AND
CHURCH IN THE WILDWOOD

After reading the book, I immediately said, "Where's the sequel?" I reread the book a second time just to savor the beauty of the story and immerse myself in the clear, concise images. Sharon Schuller Kiser's joy in the Lord shines through on every page and so the story's effervescence will literally bubble in your spirit. Through the story of Sarah Emily, you will not only excitedly move from one chapter to the next with anticipation, but also grow spiritually in the awareness of your own importance and standing with God, our Heavenly Father, as the gospel message unfolds effortlessly within the story. THAT End of Lilac Lane will inspire a study group or make an excellent gift for your favorite friend.

—REV. DR. BETTY HARRISON
EPISCOPAL MINISTER, RETIRED PROFESSOR

In her new book, THAT End of Lilac Lane, Sharon Schuller Kiser captures her vivid imagination and creative abilities as she aptly details each scene, bringing this intriguing and captivating plot to life before your very eyes. The light humor coupled with suspense makes it irresistible. This is a work of art.

—JOYCE M. TANNER
WOMEN'S MINISTRIES DIRECTOR
PENINSULAR FLORIDA DISTRICT ASSEMBLIES OF GOD

Sharon Schuller Kiser delves deep into the heart of the reader and gives us the assurance of a loving Father, no matter what our circumstances are. Her great attention to detail gives a glimpse into the desperate search we all have for our identity. That identity, the child of a loving Heavenly Father, is mine.

—JAMIE BROWN
FREELANCE COLUMNIST
THE LEDGER, A NEW YORK TIMES SUBSIDIARY

THAT End of Lilac Lane does an excellent job of reminding us all, male and female, young and old, that as human beings our sense of who we are (our identity) comes from God and from God's Word. Oftentimes we look to the culture or self-help books for a definition of self, which only serves to confuse us or lead us astray. In a touching and inspirational way, THAT End of Lilac Lane calls us back to seeing ourselves as God sees us, made in God's image.

—REV. LINDA McMILLAN SMITH
PASTOR, NEW FRIENDSHIP PRESBYTERIAN CHURCH (USA)
HUNTERSVILLE, NORTH CAROLINA

If life is a journey of discovery and learning, Sharon Schuller Kiser has captured much life as she writes of Sarah Emily's ordeal and trials. What makes the story so riveting is the sense that the themes of Sarah Emily's story could be, in some sense, each of our stories of self discovery and dawning awareness that life is more than circumstances and of others' perceptions of who we are. Redemption triumphs!

—BARRY LOOP
PASTOR, FIRST MENNONITE CHURCH
RICHMOND, VIRGINIA

THAT
END OF
LILAC LANE

SHARON SCHULLER KISER

CREATION
HOUSE PRESS
A STRANG COMPANY

THAT END OF LILAC LANE by Sharon Schuller Kiser
Published by Creation House Press
A Strang Company
600 Rinehart Road
Lake Mary, Florida 32746
www.creationhouse.com

Cover design by Terry Clifton

Library of Congress Catalog Card Number: 2003108995
International Standard Book Number: 1-59185-280-3

03 04 05 06   8 7 6 5 4 3 2 1
Printed in the United States of America

If I were to count my blessings, I could happily and contentedly stop with:

> *My husband, Don, who has been the love of my life for thirty-four years,*
> *My sister, Cynthia, who is my dearest friend,*
> *My children, Lisa and Andrew, who are the joys of my life,*
> *And Don's parents, Ralph and Hilda, who have always treated me like a daughter.*

And my counting would still be in numbers too high for the mortal brain to tally because the wonder and delight of having them in my life goes on and on and . . .

Prologue

1869, Lander, Illinois

He shoved the mahogany box into her tiny hands so hard they stung. "Here, your mother loved this. I guess you should have it." Then he left—left *her*, a four-year-old, all alone.

Desperate to pull him back, she shouted, "Wait, you've forgotten me. Please, Pa, please don't leave me." But he was gone, disappearing as quickly and completely as the sun behind a swollen cloud.

"I don't know where I am," spilled from her and was lost in the hot frightened tears splashing onto her mother's mahogany box. "This isn't where I live. I don't belong here." The box began to shake in her hands as the quaking she felt inside exploded out.

The air was split by honking geese flying overhead, and the door of the reddish-brown brick building where her pa had left her in front was banging open. She turned to the building, swiping tears out of the way, to see a boy come bolting out, his face tilted up to the sky, running at top speed, following the birds.

He skidded on his heels to a sharp stop only a fingertip away from smacking into her. The dust from his skid boiled up, huffed and sank back down with the resignation of knowing where it belonged. "I heard the geese and came out to see them," he offered as a reason for the near-trampling. "Why are you crying?"

She didn't answer, only stared. There was a thin skin of dirt stuck to the skin of his face. It didn't take him long to start circling her, his arms and legs moving as loosely and easily as if he had just oiled them. He studied her from shiny eyes the color of the pecans she picked up from beneath the tree in her grandmother's yard.

He raked a hand through brown jagged clumps of hair and slid his hands into the pockets of overalls that were too short for his legs. "What's your name?" he asked, his gaze inspecting from the top of her long hair all the way down to her polished black shoes. "Doesn't anybody cut your hair off?"

She pivoted, examining him examine her. Right away, she saw that his eyes didn't go with his face. Even at four years old, she somehow knew they were old eyes that had seen things, knew things, felt things she hadn't.

"Are you an orphan?"

She pondered this question, pulling the box closer to her chest and sniffing back the last tears. After a long minute of thinking, she realized she had no idea what being an orphan meant. And what kind of thing was that to ask about her hair? No one had ever spoken to her of cutting it. Her grandmother always fixed it as it was now, brushed from her face and held in place on either side with hair clasps. As far as her name went, she did know that. It was Sarah Emily Butler, but she was still too terrified to speak.

"I'm Timothy, and I'm six years old," he said, evidently giving up on pelting questions at her since she hadn't answered even one. They made the final dual loop, eyeing each other. Then his lips stretched into a lopsided smile big enough to reveal spaces where two top teeth had once been. The smile cracked the dirt skin into fine lines around his eyes and mouth, lines as fine as the sharp tip of a knife would carve.

That gawky smile and those old but shiny eyes had her fright melting away. She smiled back. Something about this bundle of boy made her feel safe.

At that moment, another cluster of the squawking geese flew

over. This time, Sarah Emily looked up. They were flying in the shape of her grandmother's perfume bottle, a triangle she had called it.

"Some day I'm going to know what makes them fly away when it gets cold and know where to come back to when it gets warm again," Timothy said, staring up at the disappearing birds. Then he looked at her. "We're about to eat. I can show you where if you're hungry."

She was hungry. She didn't know why or where she was, and, surely, Pa would be back soon to get her. But food, in the meantime, sounded good. Slowly, she nodded her answer.

"Good. Come with me," he said, wrapping a grimy hand around her wrist while she continued to cradle the box in both hands. He guided her toward the front door as if he had a puppy by the collar—a lost puppy that he seemed to sense needed him. Ever so gently, he coaxed the puppy inside her new home.

Chapter 1

September 1881, Lander, Illinois

he bristly rope burned Sarah Emily's hands, yanking her along with the other eight orphans tethered to the headmistress. The burning, though, didn't bring on so much as a twitch because her concentration was fixed on only one thing. And that was craning her neck back to where her attention had snagged on two young mothers chatting at the corner of Lilac Lane. She even disregarded the jolt of her toe catching a root from the unrelenting forward drag of the rope. By twisting her head around toward the mothers, she managed to catch a snatch of their conversation.

"Look at your sweet baby," one mother stood cooing to the other, clasping her gloved hands in delight and bending over a pristine white pram. "I certainly can tell she belongs to you. Her mouth, why, it's just like yours."

The thrill of those words shot straight into Sarah Emily. Their target was the vast cavernous hole right in the center of her being. As soon as the mother's words sunk in, for the first second, they turned her bones to butter. But then just as quickly, they restored her solid. *It's who you look like. That's how you know who you are.*

She crimped her eyes shut, crushed her lips together and held her breath making sure the wonderful revelation couldn't escape.

At last, she had it—the answer to the secret of how to squirm out of the clumsy, ill-fitting, plain brown wrapper of being an orphan. It was a wrapper that got about as much notice as yesterday's soggy coffee grounds and was every bit as easy to throw away.

That ordinary paper shroud could encase a mundane chunk of yeast or mound of salt. And those sorts of things weren't known to stir an ounce of excitement in anyone.

But then, there were those special times, times when the coarse string was untied, and a new, delicately smooth china cup and saucer for the headmistress gleamed up from the crinkled pile of brown paper.

For the merest fraction of time, Sarah Emily indulged herself in the exhilarating feeling of peeling back the orphan paper and finding out that all along she was the exquisite china. The second that ridiculous thought veered off to reflecting on how Timothy saw her, she swooped it up and out. *Be sensible,* thumped at her thoughts. Timothy saw her for the orphan she was, the lump of yeast, common and unexceptional.

Still, she had nurtured the dream for such a long time of leaving the orphan wrapper behind like a snake sheds its old, used-up skin, never to wear it again. Now, right on the street, out in the open, casually, as if everyone knew how to make that happen, the clue was tossed into the air as delicately and almost imperceptibly as a dandelion puff.

And she grabbed it.

It's who you look like. That's how you know who you are.

The rope jerked harder, wrenching her head forward. Her twisting around must have caused them to proceed slower than the headmistress' swift steps. Sarah Emily was all too aware of the single-minded aim of the scrawny woman to get home and be soothed and warmed by a cup of hot tea. It was a ritual Miss Percy regarded and protected as her favorite companion.

Sarah Emily opened her eyes, but kept her lips pressed together.

It was silly, she knew, but she feared losing the valuable gift from the mothers. It had come so unexpectedly, without warning, she feared it might disappear as suddenly. She hurriedly looked for Timothy in the group not bound together on the rope. Her hope was that he had heard too.

If he had, he would be every bit as excited as she at finally unraveling the baffling mystery, relieved just to put the wonderings to rest. His eyes would be searching for hers, snapping like lightening bugs. He would be grinning his all-out grin, the wide one that rode a little higher on the right. It would be the same smile—except with all its teeth—that had eased her fear the day she had been left at the orphan asylum twelve years ago.

Timothy hadn't heard. A twinge of disappointment clipped her, popping her mouth open to relieve her bursting lungs. She saw he was preoccupied listening to Ben, who was walking backward so that he faced Timothy, waving his hand over his head and babbling nonstop, his gangly boniness accentuating his pointy bobbing chin.

Oh well, all was not lost, she assured herself, gulping down air. She would tell Timothy everything the second they got back, and she could let go of this miserable rope.

Anger banged in her chest at being dragged from the unexpected source of the long-sought-after, all-important information. Although she felt much older, having been thrust into becoming an adult long before she could button her own shoes, it was only twenty-nine days until she would be sixteen, old enough to be hired out for work, even old enough to be married. But, for right now, being sixteen meant she wouldn't have to hold on to a gnarly knot of that thick rope ever again. Sarah Emily gritted her teeth. Not ever again.

Refusing to let anger or even the regret of Timothy not hearing what she had heard distract her in this glorious moment, she forced her jaw to relax and swung her gaze to the corner once more. She wanted to get one last look and maybe hear one last word. She didn't give a fresh fig, not even an entire basket of fresh figs, if it delayed the headmistress from her precious cup of tea.

But when she caught sight of the mothers again, they had started crossing the street, pushing their prams with only their backs visible and their talking gone garbled and muffled. Every instinct in her itched to dump the rope and race after them, arms windmilling to stop them so she could try to beg even one to tell her more. Truth be known, they probably hadn't been aware of the rumpled pack of orphans. It was an odd thing, but most of the town had the ability to avert their eyes, rendering the orphans invisible and thereby no intrusion on their collective conscience or lives.

It didn't matter; she brushed the preposterous fantasy of talking to the mothers aside. It was true, she hadn't heard much, but she had heard enough—enough to send her mind and heart sprinting and darting like a colt turned loose in a fresh, green pasture. She glanced at Timothy, imagining how excited he would be too. Sarah Emily inhaled a deep breath of supreme satisfaction, angling her face a smidge higher than usual.

It's who you look like. She let the new thought bounce around several times. Each time it landed, she savored the way it felt. It felt good, better than good. It was an eruption of bright light, tickling laughter, a wild sense of release. If it wouldn't draw the ire of Miss Percy, Sarah Emily would whoop out loud, as loud and far and long as she could with the sheer joy of being freed from the thick, suffocating swaddling of not knowing. How long had she hunted, grasping blindly for the way of discovering and identifying who she was? How long had she tried to identify that part far beyond her name, far beyond the color of her eyes, the size of her feet or her slightly crooked side top tooth—all the way down to the unseen part, the deep and hidden part?

Now she had it. *It's who you look like.* Her heart jubilantly jumped and tumbled before settling back into place.

She defiantly twisted around again as far as she could while keeping one hand clamped on the rope that tugged her farther down the street, to smile and silently thank the disappearing mothers for unsuspectingly giving her this treasure. And the long, contented sigh she had been saving for this very moment, she allowed to slide out on the tiniest squeal of delight. Thankfully, she was the tail of the rope today. That position, along with the scuffling feet of those on the rope with her and the clacking wagons on the street, muted her tiny squeal so no one bothered to look her way or ask for any explanation.

The rope tugged Sarah Emily to the left. She faced forward just as she and the unkempt band of orphans trudged down the dusty walk that passed under the sharp-pointed, black iron letters ORPHAN ASYLUM OF LANDER.

"Halt." The headmistress gave a brusque double clap of her hands.

The nine gripping the rope and the seven walking a wiggly, single file beside them immediately stopped.

"Timothy." Miss Percy's lips squashed together like a drawstring purse, her back stiff and straight as if she had been seamed together with steel.

Not Timothy. Not today. Sarah Emily had the urge to fling her hand in the air, batting at the irritating voice that called Timothy's name.

"Yes, Miss Percy?" Timothy spoke up from those not holding onto the rope, at once throwing back his shoulders and jerking his hands out of the pockets of his overworn overalls, exchanging his relaxed stance for one of guarded apprehension.

"Leash. Shed," Miss Percy said, stingy as usual with the amount of words she used to talk to them. Being orphans, they weren't worthy of a full sentence from her, rounded out to civility with the usual in between words. As often as possible, her edicts to them were as bare and bony as a carcass picked clean by vultures.

Leash. Sarah Emily's mind tightened around the word trying to squeeze it out of her ears where it doggedly clung, roaring and jeering. It was only a word, she told herself, and she had heard it at least a thousand and ten times. But even so, every time it pricked as real and sharp as backing into a cactus. Miss Percy loved to call the rope a leash so they would feel like dogs—mangy, unwanted dogs that people shoo and swat off their porches and out of their yards with flailing brooms. *But next month, in precisely twenty-nine days . . .*

From the beginning, it had seemed a ridiculous notion to Sarah Emily that Miss Percy thought the rope would keep them from running away. If Miss Percy thought that, she should make the older ones do more than just hang it back on the bent nail at the shed. She should make them march down the street clutching it too. After all, they were the ones who mostly tried to escape.

"Attention." Miss Percy again clapped twice. "Drop."

Sarah Emily heaved an agitated groan and, along with the others, let go of the hated rope. It landed on the ground with a dull thud. She scrubbed her stinging palms on her apron and looked at Miss Percy's taut, thin lips and hard, gray eyes. Sarah Emily decided it wasn't worth another speck of her time right now to figure out Miss Percy or her reasons for anything.

In all the years, Sarah Emily had never been able to come up with an inkling of an idea as to why Miss Percy kicked and poked at kindness like it was something alive, sapping all her energy to keep the beast beaten back.

Today, since overhearing those mothers, something much more exciting to figure out tempted Sarah Emily like a ripe berry dangling on the vine—even if it was dangling near the back of the bush surrounded by a tangle of briars and sharp thorns. She would get it. She would find out whose face *her* face favored.

She only wished today of all days it wasn't Timothy's turn to put the rope away. While she watched him, she chewed on her bottom lip, torn by whether or not to go with him to the shed.

Timothy dutifully left the muddle of older boys he had been standing with to gather up the rope. After loosely bunching the prickly rope in his hands, he sucked a breath deep inside and seemed to use that extra air to expand his shoulders and straighten his long, lean back. Propelling his legs into quicker, heavier steps than his normal gait, he started toward the dreaded shed.

Miss Percy was already making her way to the front door, leaning toward it as she walked, anxious to sip her hot tea, her new black coat flapping and flouncing around her heels.

In the other direction, Sarah Emily heard the crunching of the thick cover of pumpkin and wheat-colored leaves scattering under the rushing feet of everyone heading to the side yard to enjoy those last free minutes before supper.

Standing there, the sweet hint of autumn apples blew by her from a tree at the rich folks' end of Lilac Lane. On the same breeze came the pungent smell of tonight's supper at the orphan asylum—reheated, reheated soup.

She glanced in the direction of the shed just as Timothy was about to disappear into the raspy thicket. Sarah Emily didn't give herself one second longer to contemplate. If she did, no question, she would go with Timothy. She set off, instead, toward the main building, racing up the chipped, brick steps and through the heavy, bruised front door. She blinked her eyes to adjust to the dim front entry. The only sunlight in the windowless entry hall had to sneak and squirm and squeeze in under and around the closed doors of the adjacent rooms.

She hurried on, the enticing words of the mothers still lodged in her heart, even though guilt clamored to squash her excitement. The last time she had the chore of putting the rope away, Timothy so willingly went with her. And she should be going with him now. Even if Timothy wouldn't admit it, and he wouldn't, she knew no one wanted to go alone near the eerie shed with weeds tangling themselves around the door and scraggily oak limbs hanging low, creating grotesque shadows that would dive and lunge with the wind. And those critters you can't see, rustling about, sounding just like a giant, slithering snake or who knows what manner of monster. Shivers nettled across her scalp and bolted down her spine.

But today, sorry as she was, Sarah Emily couldn't go with Timothy. She had to see the photograph. She was convinced the faster she could determine who she looked like, the faster she would be on her way to becoming a *real* someone—not just an orphan. And once armed with that, she argued, laboring to justify her decision to abandon Timothy, she could explain all this even better to him.

"It's who you look like," she breathed between barely moving lips. "It's who you look like. It's who you look like." Down the gray hall, up the stairs and around the corner to the girls' dormitory, she ran as quickly as she dared without risking irritating Miss Percy and her ever-present black leather strap.

Once in the dormitory, she dove under the bed, accidentally clunking her head on the iron frame. She grimaced, but didn't stop until she had what she came for. She wriggled out, took the tattered top off the cardboard container and set it on the scratchy, wool blanket. She swatted back an annoying straggly strand of hair that flopped in her eye. Then lovingly, she lifted out her mahogany box.

As always, she was struck by the beauty of the rich raspberry-brown wood, the tiny gold clasp and the four perfectly round feet. It truly was her most special possession.

She eased herself onto the bed, which creaked like the stairs at midnight as she settled on its edge. She opened the hinged lid of the mahogany box and pulled out a tin photograph. Her heart beat faster.

Do I look like them? Her eyes wouldn't move off the people she held in her hand—her parents. Surely she resembled one of them. What about her mouth—like the mother and baby on the street corner? Maybe it was her nose. People always commented on her upturned nose. But, try as she did, she couldn't see how she looked like either of them.

Before today, Sarah Emily had focused only on the sense of affection she saw in the picture between her parents. Although her father sat very straight and his left arm had a sharp bend at the elbow, her mother's hand rested on it with a softness that melted right into him. And the tenderness in his eyes...

His eyes. Her father didn't look at her with tenderness the day he had brought her—a four-year-old—to the orphan asylum. His eyes had been fierce and full of anger. The spiky teeth of that memory gnawed into her, and she quickly reached for the box to get the photograph put away, out of sight.

Then another thought latched on with dog-and-bone tenacity. She wasn't a child anymore. She was nearly sixteen. "Yes! Nearly a woman," she shouted. Leaping off the bed, she clamped the photograph to her chest under crossed hands.

The tinny clang of the supper bell jarred her. Without hesitating another moment, she slipped the photograph into her frayed apron pocket, slid her precious box back under the bed and hurried to search for Timothy among the hungry crowd rushing to the dining room. It didn't take long to spot him. Since he was close to eighteen, his head bobbed above the other boys, a giraffe among ponies. He was talking to James but glanced around. At the sight of her, he motioned for James to go on ahead, and his face loosened into the tipped, bright smile that always set her world straight.

She caught up next to him. "I sure am sorry I didn't go to the shed with you, but there was something I had to see."

"That's okay. I saw you traveling on a lightning bolt. What was going on?"

Aware at how close to throbbing, actually nearer to giddy, she was in her eagerness to tell him the news, she tried to slow her breathing before cupping one hand around her words so only he could hear. "I found out how a person knows who they are."

His steps slowed, and he turned to her. "What?" he said, brown eyes rounding with interest.

"Thought you'd want to know." She paced her steps to match his and leaned in closer. "How much will you pay me if I tell you?"

"Oh, come on, Sarah Em, quit your fooling around." He had stopped walking to stare at her. "What's the secret?"

It was impossible to tease him any longer. "Did you hear those ladies talking on the corner this afternoon after we left Doc Werther's office?" her words came bursting and popping out.

"What ladies? I couldn't have heard anything even if I'd plowed square into them. I was walking behind Ben, and he kept turning around and running his mouth about the two inches Doc said he'd grown since last year's checkup."

"I didn't think you did." She tried to slow the pounding haste within herself to properly deliver the choice morsel. "It's who you look like," she said with certainty, and for authority, she added a nod of her head.

For that valuable information, he gave her his pained, pointed look. It started with rolling his eyes; next he pinched them shut, then sprang them open as wide as he could, feigning an attempt to get a better look at her since, of course, he must have misunderstood what she had said. She couldn't be serious.

It was a look she had seen before, many times before. It would emerge when she tried to convince him of a new speculation she had or to persuade him of the value of one of her frequent plans. Schemes, he liked to call them. Schemes, he said one day, rolled out of her as effortlessly as marbles out of a bag. He always meant the look to be funny, and she usually found it just that. But today, it only annoyed her.

"Oh, Timothy Marshall, what don't you understand? Do you have to take until the end of time to cogitate on this like you do everything? It's plain and simple. It's who you look like." She sent her thoughts careening to find the perfect explanation, soon realizing that an uncomplicated, actually quite straightforward explanation would do nicely. "You need to know whose nose or mouth or eyes yours are like. That's how a body knows how they'll turn out. You know, who you'll be." It was simply that simple, easily that easy. She waited for him to be duly impressed or grateful she had told him, but mostly she wanted him to be eager to learn more.

"Somehow that doesn't sound right," was all he said flatly, keeping his eyes pinned on her. *Explain* was their clear message.

She mentally elbowed back the urge to give in to exasperation. "Then listen to this." She launched into an enthusiastic, nonstop, detailed account of every word she had overheard the mothers say on the street corner. Just to make sure he understood, she repeated it all again. Replacing her spent breath, she looked at him, expectancy swelling in her. "Now, do you believe me?"

"Sarah Em, that can't be the way it is. No. That just can't be."

"Yes it can. Why do you have to waste so much time thinking about everything? Just because you haven't read it in a book, doesn't make it untrue." She shoved her hands into her apron pockets and started again toward the dining room, deflating as fast as yesterday's soapsuds.

When they reached the massive staircase, Timothy waved her into the slanted ceiling alcove under the rise. In the small space, she could smell leftover traces of the rubbing alcohol and winter-green oil from Doc Werther's office. Between Timothy's eyes, a pair of questioning, anxious creases were forming.

"No matter what you say, I want you to know, I don't view thinking as wasted time," he said. "And some people don't know who they look like. You've got a photograph of your folks, but you told me yourself you don't really recollect them. So, even if you look like one of them, what good will it do you? Knowing what someone looks like doesn't tell you anything about what's in here." He thumped his fingers on his chest, rousing a stronger whiff of the minty wintergreen. "And you've no idea why your pa left you after your ma died or why he doesn't ever come to see you."

"I know," she said, slumping with defeat. "I know." Could Timothy be right? Maybe this wasn't the way to figure out your hidden self that was covered up in that plain paper wrapper. What if being an orphan meant never unearthing those parts of you that were buried beneath the drudgery of orphan life, or even worse, never knowing your purpose for living and being?

"Come on you two," Ben panted, racing by the alcove. "You'll be late. Miss Percy's on her way to the dining room."

"Yeah, we're coming," Timothy called out, then laid a hand on her shoulder. "Sarah Em," his voice gentled while tenderness smoothed out the creases around his eyes. "Sarah Em, I think there's got to be another way of identifying who a person is and who they'll be."

For a long minute, she stared at him, too frustrated to speak. She was sure, so totally sure, of what she had heard the mothers say, and she had been just as sure Timothy would understand. Up until this very moment, they had been like two people rowing a boat. On the subject of wanting to know who they were, they had been rowing together in perfect rhythm, stroke for stroke. Now, when they had discovered which direction to row, he was tossing his oar in the water.

Disappointed, she ducked her head under the low opening of the alcove, stepped into the hall and trailed the stragglers to supper.

Timothy came after her, hanging on to her elbow until she gave in and stood still. "You know, I've got no way of knowing who I look like. And I sure don't know why I got put here." He drew an audible breath and kicked at an invisible something on the floor. "I don't even know if my folks are dead or alive." He suddenly looked up, unflinching. "But I do know I want to be a special man."

"A special man—whatever that means." Sarah Emily all but hooted and her resolve to follow her new information returned with a gush. "First you've got to know if you've got 'special' in your blood, Timothy Marshall. And you can be sure I'm going to find out what's inside of me." She wasn't about to give up on what she had learned that afternoon, not even for Timothy.

Deep down, she was usually glad Timothy didn't make hasty conclusions like she often did. But *this* was different. This had to be the answer to the secret everyone struggled to know...the secret to what made your own hidden thoughts in the night when black was pressing against the window...the secret that made one orphan able to hold his head high when he walked down the rich folks' end of Lilac Lane and another hang his head like shame was riding heavily on his back...the secret that made some ask everyday if they were going to live with a family, while others let large chunks of the calendar go by without ever mentioning leaving the orphan asylum.

It was, by far, the most important, the most elusive, the most sought-after secret of all. Surely, Sarah Emily thought, it must be so even for those without the burdensome misfortune of being an orphan. It was the secret of who you really are—inside—where no one else can see.

She wasn't a child anymore. And she longed—no, she *had*—to have the answer. She had to know who she looked like.

She was going to show Timothy the photograph, even though he had seen it plenty of times before, and ask him if he could tell who she favored. But since he felt like it wasn't a true test, she decided against it. Later, after he had a chance to think about what the mothers had said, she would show him.

Entering the noisy dining room alongside Timothy, she saw Miss Percy standing in the center, briskly patting the sides of her head, pressing her black hair that was stretched from her forehead and temples and cinched at the back in a tight bun. Seeing that, Sarah Emily was reminded that everything about Miss Percy, including her disposition, was spun up in a tense, tight knot.

Sarah Emily forced herself to focus on the new girl standing next to Miss Percy. The girl had huddled herself into as small a package as possible. The fright and despair at being an orphan were as visible and recognizable on her as claw marks would be if she had been mauled by a bear.

Miss Percy clapped her sharp, double clap, and the new girl flinched.

Sarah Emily wiggled her hand into her pocket and fingered the photograph that was hidden there.

Chapter 2

"Attention." Miss Percy clapped her brown-speckled hands together again, and, as always, an explosive double clap resounded. Instant, total silence fell on the dining room. "Betsy Howard," Miss Percy said, the words flicking off her tongue as if they were stray slivers of fish bone. A quick pivot, and the head-mistress rushed from the dining room, leaving the frightened Betsy Howard to fend for herself.

Immediately, the noise erupted to where it had left off. Sarah Emily watched the new girl's terrified gaze dart around the room while she inched backward to the wall and then flattened herself against it.

"Just look at her, Timothy. She looks to be about my age and acts like a scared mouse searching for a hole to crawl into. How can Miss Percy be so cruel?"

"Aw, Sarah Em, I don't know why that always surprises you. She always acts likes there's a burr caught under her corset. You notice, as usual, she didn't even tell that new girl how to go through the food line."

Sarah Emily sighed with the terrible truth of Timothy's words and nibbled one side of her bottom lip. The tired smell of leftover soup and the sharp scent of vinegar the floor had been scrubbed with stung her nose. Never moving her gaze from the girl plastered to the wall, Sarah Emily said, "Timothy, you go on ahead. She's pushing so hard she's going to punch a hole right through the brick wall. I can't leave her alone."

"I didn't figure you would. As soon as you started chewing on your lip, I knew you were studying on something. Go on, we can finish our talk later. But you'll still be wrong about needing to know who you look like."

She snapped her head around to look at him, but before she could wedge in a word of dispute, he grinned, an easy hope-we're-through-arguing-grin. Then he headed for a nest of boys swarming to get in line.

The corners of her mouth went up, seemingly of their own volition, almost like her mouth knew she couldn't stay mad at him and wanted to go ahead and get it over with.

He turned, still grinning, and caught her smile. He tossed her a quick nod just as Ben came alongside.

"You getting in line or what?" Ben playfully thumped Timothy on the shoulder.

"Yeah, right in front of you." Timothy landed a pretend punch on Ben and they tussled like long-armed monkeys all the way to the food line.

Sarah Emily moved toward the bewildered-looking girl with hair that hung in curls the way shavings spiral from a wood plane. It was the most cared-for part of her. The lemony-yellow hair had been carefully brushed and fluffed. *Exuberant hair.* Sarah Emily had never seen such gorgeous hair. Yes, *definitely exuberant hair* she would call it.

"Hi, my name's Sarah Emily," she spoke up so she'd be heard amidst the clamor of dishes and voices. "Don't pay any mind to Miss Percy," Sarah Emily said with a wave of dismissal. "She never gives help to anyone new." Though Betsy's only response was a slight lift of one eyebrow, Sarah Emily asked, "Want to come with me?"

Relief washed across Betsy's face. "Yes. Thanks," came her answer, barely loud enough to be heard as she peeled herself off the wall and followed Sarah Emily.

At the food line, Sarah Emily made sure Betsy did exactly as she did—picking up a thick bowl and a spoon and putting it on the tray, then holding it at arms length allowing Cook to ladle in the brothy soup.

"Welcome, Betsy," Cook said. "Now you just try and make yourself at home, child." Cook's velvety voice remained slow and kind despite shouts of irritation at the delay from a couple of hungry boys waiting near the end of the line.

Up on tiptoes Cook rose, her neck stretched to get a direct look at the complaining boys, wisps of black hair tufting from the edge of her tightly tied blue kerchief like stuffing escaping from a pillow. "Boys," she calmly said.

It only took from her that gentle, one-word reprimand to have them responding at once with, "Sorry," and repentant smiles.

Cook smiled back. "Thank you, boys," she said, lowering herself and turning again to Betsy. "Are you hungry?"

Betsy nodded, and for a second her eyelids trembled shut.

"Law, Child, just let me know if you want more when you finish this."

After they walked away with their bowls full, Sarah Emily told Betsy, "Even though Cook won't ever say much about Miss Percy and her doings, what Cook does for us is way better than words any old time. You'll see."

"Oh," was all Betsy said, but she stayed right on Sarah Emily's heels as they threaded their way between the rows of long, brown tables flanked by hard benches.

Sarah Emily made a quick search for Timothy since they usually ate together. He was already seated at a table too full of boys for them to cram in. She knew he would presume that she would eat with Betsy. It was probably better, she thought, when she heard Ben trying to convince James that he actually had grown two inches, for Betsy to be with only girls tonight anyway.

Sarah Emily stopped at a table near the back of the room that had two empty places. "Hey, everybody!" she raised her voice above the girls' chatter. "Say hello to Betsy."

Some looked up eagerly and greeted Betsy with friendly smiles and hellos while others kept eating, never bothering to lift their heads.

In return, Betsy gave a weak but fearful smile, her face paling to the pasty white of boiled potatoes.

When Sarah Emily saw Betsy's reaction, she thought Betsy might be more comfortable at a table not so crowded. She motioned with her tray to one where only a few girls bunched together at the other end. "Let's sit here."

No sooner had they sat down across from each other than Betsy started fidgeting with a long strand of that exuberant yellow hair. Her eyes, like a clock pendulum, swung from the food on her tray to Sarah Emily and back.

Clinking dishes, chatter, arguing, laughing, scuffling feet, all collided together into a lumpy wall of racket. The sounds were so familiar to Sarah Emily that she realized she didn't hear them anymore. But she was certain Betsy was struggling to hear her own thoughts.

"You can start eating whenever you want," Sarah Emily told Betsy, who with a single sling of her finger unwound her hair and picked up her spoon. For a few minutes, the two ate in silence, then Sarah Emily asked, "You've never lived in an orphan asylum before, have you?"

Spoon suspended between bowl and mouth, Betsy shook her head.

"I didn't think so." Sarah Emily smiled, but felt awful for the noticeable fear Betsy was straining to keep under control. Sarah Emily had seen too many others come, and usually, if someone came from an orphan asylum, they weren't so scared, or wouldn't let it show anyway. "You'll get used to living here. Won't like it, but you'll get used to it." Sarah Emily lied, and her stomach winced. It was what Doc Werther did two years ago when she had that dreadful toothache, and he had told her it wouldn't hurt when he stuck the needle in her gum. He had said it to keep her from being so afraid. And she knew that. But she also knew it would hurt. And it did. She felt just as certain Betsy knew she would never get used to living there either. But what good would it do to say it out loud?

Sarah Emily reached for the breadbasket and tilted it to see if any was left. "Empty. Marjorie, how about sending that bread down here?"

Marjorie never stopped eating, only grunted, batting the basket with the knuckles of her left hand, sending it sliding down the center of the table. Two girls lifted their milk cups to make way.

Sarah Emily snagged the basket and held it out to Betsy, saying, "Here, have some."

Betsy reached in, grasping as many slices as her hand would hold. She swerved nervous eyes around the table, then let one piece drop by her bowl, and the others she laid in her lap.

That was different. Sarah Emily had seen hungry new orphans pull their food close and hunch over it like a starving dog. She had seen some stuff extra bread in their pockets for later. She had even seen one boy trade everything special he had come with—a marble, a broken arrowhead, a three-legged petrified frog—for extra food. But she had never seen bread in the lap.

"Just stand up here and let's see who's taller," Ben said, his voice punching through the wall of racket.

"Soon you'll learn who everybody is." Sarah Emily took a slice of bread and talked on, wanting to make Betsy feel at ease while she ate. "When you know who everybody is, that'll help you not to feel so strange. Like I told you, Miss Percy never gives directions to anyone new. I know it would mean a lot if she'd tell you what's going on when you first get here, but she's not exactly the motherly type."

In one great gulp, Betsy swallowed her mouthful. "Motherly?" she croaked in a hoarse whisper.

Sarah Emily blinked at Betsy's sudden reaction and hopeful face. "*Not* the motherly type," she repeated.

Ben and James scuffled out of the bench and stood back-to-back. "See, what did I tell you?" James said, slashing another hole in the wall. "I knew you weren't taller than me."

"Oh. I misunderstood you," Betsy said, cutting her eyes to look at the boys. They sat down and the holes they had punched closed up and the wall became solid, indistinguishable racket again. "Sorry, I only heard *motherly*," Betsy said, her eyes clouded, and she returned to eating.

Sarah Emily could have kicked herself for saying that word. Everyone wanted a mother, but that was a desire, around there, best not voiced, just kept in one's dreams. Mothers seemed about as scarce as—Sarah Emily tugged the slipping shoulder of her too big dress back up to where it belonged—about as scarce as a dress that fit.

Could it have been what she had seen and heard that afternoon that made her say motherly? Sarah Emily pushed the question out of the way, sensing Betsy's letdown. "Cook's the closest thing we have to a mother." That was certainly true, and she wanted Betsy to believe at least that much.

Betsy's mouth lifted at the corners, just barely.

It looked like a brave attempt at a smile, and Sarah Emily returned it, hoping hers appeared more confident. Wanting to get away from the subject of mothers, she started rattling on about school between bites, while Betsy slurped the hot liquid into her mouth almost quicker than she could swallow. The only time Betsy looked up from her soup was to pluck another slice of bread from her lap.

When her spoon scraped the dry bottom, Betsy lifted the heavy, mud-colored bowl to her mouth. Her tongue flicked and licked, latching onto every clinging morsel.

"You want some more?"

"Can I?" Betsy set the bowl down, leaning forward, her hair cascading forward with her. She pushed all but one tendril away from her face and twisted it round and round her finger.

"Oh sure, remember, Cook said so. And besides, we've been eating this for three days now. On the third day, Cook always tries to get rid of it. So long as there's some in the pot, you can have more."

"If you're certain it wouldn't be a bother to nobody." Without any lost motion, Betsy twirled her finger, loosing it from her hair, and scooped up the bowl, clutching it in both hands. "How do I get it?" Her eyes begged even stronger than her words.

Sarah Emily stood, reaching for the bowl. "I'll get it for you. Be right back." She made her way across the dining room, lamenting the fact that Betsy's long hair would be gone by this time tomorrow.

At the food line, she held Betsy's bowl out to Cook. "This is for that new girl, and she's mighty hungry. She needs something besides broth. Could you scoop down to the bottom of the pot and see if there's anything solid left?"

Cook glanced over at Betsy. "Law, that poor child," she said softly, drawing in a caring breath, causing her heavy, sloped chest to rise and fall. When she pushed the ladle deep into the tall kettle, only brown broth came up. She poured it back and tried again. This time, up came some rice and a few specks of carrots floating in the liquid.

"That looks a bit more stomach-satisfying. Thanks."

"Surely hope that makes her feel some better," Cook said, looking at Betsy again.

"I've been meaning to ask you how your dress fund is coming." Sarah Emily dabbed at a stray drop of soup that trickled down the side of the bowl. "Seems like it's going on months and months that you've been saving to have it made."

"All in due time. Yes, in due time." Cook's smile inched up until her padded cheeks lifted about as high as they could go. She leaned the ladle against the edge of the soup pot, wiped her hands on her apron and reached into her pocket. From deep inside, she produced and held up a green scrap of fabric, no wider or longer than two fingers.

"Green? I thought you were getting blue. Did you change your mind?" Before Cook could answer, the richness of the color and the plumpness of the weave drew Sarah Emily to it like a magnet, pulling her forward, lifting her heels from the floor.

Even Cook's earlier best description of new fabric hadn't pre-pared Sarah Emily for the beauty of that little scrap of cloth. To keep the soup from sloshing out, she set Betsy's bowl down. "I'd forgotten green cloth could be so green. Most dresses around here have been washed and worn so many times they're thinner than an eggshell and the color's long been beat out of them." Sarah Emily pulled at her own dress sleeve as evidence. "I'm not sure if this dress started out yellow or gray, but it's about the color of dirty dishwater now."

"I know, child, and it's a shame. No, more like an abomination, for a girl not to have a new dress at least every now and again. But tell me, do you really like this color?"

"Oh, yes," was all Sarah Emily could manage, and that came out on a wisp of an admiring breath as she stared at the swatch.

"Mrs. Mitchell gave me this today when I went to the mercantile. Said she'd never seen no one come to visit bolts of fabric more than me." Cook rubbed the slip of fabric against Sarah Emily's cheek. "Ever feel anything so fine?"

"Never," Sarah Emily murmured, her eyes closed, one hand keeping Cook's and the green sliver pressed to her cheek. Just then, she felt a tap low on her back, just above her apron tie.

"I saw you helping the new girl," Cora's voice rang out behind Sarah Emily.

Letting go of Cook's hand, Sarah Emily turned to Cora. A length of yellowed lace circled her neck with its long tails slung over her shoulder.

"Well, don't you look lovely? Very dramatic," Sarah Emily said, smiling at Cora's fondness for dressing up with a grand flourish. "Where did you get that?"

"Miss Percy was gathering things for the ragman—next week is his time to come—and this lace was attached to that old brown shawl of hers. I ripped it off 'cause I thought it was pretty."

"Did Miss Percy see you?"

"No, but I left the shawl, that's the heaviest part." Cora pulled one of the long tails to the front and tossed it in the air. "This doesn't weigh enough to matter. But listen, I wanted to tell you I've been watching you with that new girl, and it made me remember when I first came and how you were kind to me too."

"My goodness, I'm surprised you remember. You were no bigger than a shirt button."

"I remember," Cora said somberly.

"Yes, I suppose you do. Unless you come when you're so little you don't even know your own name yet, you remember the day you were left here. Everyone does." Then she giggled and threw the lace end back over Cora's shoulder. "But with the spunk you've got, you would've done just fine without me."

"Skunk?"

"Spunk."

"Cora, you spunky skunk," Cook said and pushed her fabric fragment into her pocket, laughing her hearty laugh that always sounded like music and felt like a hug. "Show Sarah Emily what you showed me right before supper."

Cora brightened, stretched her mouth open and jiggled a loose front tooth with her tongue.

Sarah Emily bent down. "Well, I'll be. Looks like you're about to lose another baby tooth. Don't swallow it like you did the last one, you hear me? Be careful." She winked.

Cora flashed her snaggledy grin as she lifted her bowl to Cook for a refill. "I will."

"Good. Well, I've got soup to deliver." Sarah Emily picked up Betsy's bowl. "I really do love your lace collar. But you remember now, teeth aren't for snacking." She smiled at Cora, then said to Cook, "You know, I'll be wanting to see that new dress as soon as you get it."

"Don't think I'll be keeping it hidden away," Cook said as though amused with herself. "You'll be knowin' about it."

On the way back to Betsy, she glanced around scouting for any bread left on the other tables. Seeing a basket with some next to Ben, she whisked it off as she sailed by, catching Timothy's approving gaze.

"Hey, I was still eating that," Ben yelled.

"You're through now." Sarah Emily glared back over her shoulder and narrowed her eyes at him. At the table, she set the bread and soup in front of Betsy who looked up, startled, from her lap where her hands were tightly clenched.

Seeing the food, Betsy instantly snapped back from wherever her faraway thoughts had taken her and thrust her bony hand into the breadbasket, snatching out four slices. Just as before, she dropped one by her bowl and the others in her lap. Then grabbing her spoon, she dug into the soup with the enthusiasm of a miner in a newfound gold strike.

Sarah Emily sat quietly until Betsy gulped the last bite, pushed aside the empty bowl and swiped the back of her hand across her mouth. "You sure were hungry," Sarah Emily said, stacking her bowl on Betsy's and setting them aside.

"I guess so. It's been a while since I had much to eat." And she slipped away, off again into silent thoughts.

Sarah Emily had no difficulty recognizing the sadness etched on Betsy's face and was curious about what had happened to her folks. Just then the mothers on the street corner dashed across Sarah Emily's mind. Does Betsy know if she looks like either of her parents? She thought she probably should, at least, let Betsy get settled in before she asks. "Come on, I'll show you the girls' dormitory before everyone gets there."

The second Sarah Emily pushed open the door to the huge, gray room, Betsy gasped and her body stiffened. Betsy gripped the doorframe with one hand and wrapped a finger of her other in a coiling shank of hair.

Sarah Emily couldn't help but wonder if all the curls in Betsy's hair were from her all but constant twirling and winding of it.

"That's a lot of beds," Betsy said, her gaze sweeping the room.

"Yeah, I know. The reason is because all the girls sleep in here," Sarah Emily said, wrinkling her nose at the sour, oniony smell of supper that had found its way upstairs. She waved at the scuffed wood floor. "The kitchen is right below us, so this dormitory usually smells like whatever's cooking. The only good thing about that is in the morning it smells like cinnamon buns."

"Cinnamon buns? Do we get cinnamon buns for breakfast?"

Betsy untangled her finger, and a hint of a smile pinked her cheeks.

"No. Miss Percy has Cook make them every morning just for her. We have oat porridge."

"Oh."

"But she can't stop us from enjoying the smell." Sarah Emily grinned. "Now, let me show you where your things go. Miss Percy's real particular about us keeping everything in its place." She walked across the room, then looked back for Betsy.

Betsy hadn't moved.

Sarah Emily went to Betsy and touched her arm. "It's scary at first, but you'll be okay. I just know it."

Betsy breathed in a short gulp, let go of the doorframe and followed.

Sarah Emily led her past five rows of iron beds—four beds in each row—dominating the center of the dormitory. They stopped at the wall lined with muslin nightgowns, dangling in columns from hooks. Sarah Emily pointed to an empty rusty one. "Here's where you'll hang your dress and apron at night and your nightgown in the morning."

Betsy nodded.

Then Sarah Emily took her to the opposite side of the room where three tall, black wardrobes hid the entire wall. Opening the double doors on one, she touched an empty shelf. "This is where you'll keep your extra dress and underpinnings and anything else you've got."

For a second, Betsy glanced at a small olive green canvas satchel that squatted in a misshapen lump on the floor. "When Miss Percy took me to the dining room, she told the lady who brought me to bring it up here. I ain't got much," she said with a glance back at the beat-up satchel. "Only one special thing."

"That's okay." Sarah Emily shrugged. "None of the rest of us have much either. Easier to keep it all tidy." She hoisted Betsy's satchel to the shelf. "You can unpack later." She tapped the wardrobe door; it swung in and clicked shut.

With Betsy staying close, Sarah Emily made her way to a long table holding ten washbowls and pitchers. Hanging above the table were dingy towels, limply clinging to more hooks. Sarah Emily laid her palm flat on the scarred table. "Now, this is where you wash up each morning. We have to share the basins. And usually, about once every other week or so, depending on the weather, we get a bath in the washtub downstairs."

Betsy's tired gaze skittered down the length of the table. And then with a wary touch, she fingered the chipped edge of the white basin nearest her, crazed with a dense web of fine lines.

"Don't worry. You'll figure out how to lean over and not cut your arms." Sarah Emily answered Betsy's unasked question and went on. "We take turns emptying the water and bringing up fresh. But you'll get a list of chores later from Miss Percy. Right now, what we need to do is find you a bed." Sarah Emily turned to the center of the dormitory, surveyed the room and pointed. "That one at the end of the first row doesn't belong to anybody."

"Where's yours?"

"Over here." Sarah Emily pulled the sagging shoulder of her dress back up to where it belonged, walked to the middle of the fourth row and stopped beside her bed. She watched Betsy's eyes measuring how far apart theirs would be.

"You know," Sarah Emily tapped a finger to her mouth, then waved it at the beds, "maybe we could make a switch and get you closer to mine."

"That'd be nice," Betsy said evenly, in spite of her expression exploding with enormous relief.

"Anyway, Ophelia's bed is too close to that first one I showed you. She gets so goosey and overwrought at the least little thing. She makes a nervous gnat seem calm. Let's see, Marjorie sleeps here." Sarah Emily gestured to the bed in the third row next to hers and rolled her eyes. "There's not much use asking Marjorie for hers, though. She's been here all her life—seventeen years— and she doesn't have much concern for anybody else. And, by the way, if you don't want to get into trouble, stay clear of Marjorie."

Sarah Emily weaved her way to the last row and sat down on the bed across from her own. "This is Nettie's. She's real sweet and has only been here about six months. I figure she'll know what you must be feeling. We'll ask if you can have hers."

"I don't want to put nobody out." Betsy walked to the bed in question and sat down beside Sarah Emily. "But it would be nice to be next to someone I know—at least a bit."

❧

Two hours later, when the big clock in the hall banged eight times, Miss Percy charged into the girls' dormitory carrying a burning candle in a tarnished brass candlestick.

Sarah Emily got the photograph of her parents back into her mahogany box. She scrambled out from under her bed just as Miss Percy turned down the wick in the oil lamp suspended from thin wires in the middle of the ceiling.

The intense look on Miss Percy's face and the resolute click of her heels signaled that tonight wouldn't be one of her rapid bed checks, ending with her leaving just as quickly without so much as a weak "good night" flung back to them.

Ever since Sarah Emily had gotten into her nightgown, the minty scent of wintergreen rose freely from her chest. It hung heavy in the dormitory air from all the girls who'd had their checkups that day, giving her an almost dizzy feeling. Although Doc Werther's office also smelled of rubbing alcohol and carbolic soap, it was the wintergreen oil he used to wipe off his stethoscope that lingered the strongest. While aimlessly wondering if he used it to mask the other bitter medicinal smells, she was suddenly aware of how heavy she felt, how droopingly tired she was.

Today, besides her regular chores and school, there'd been going to Doc Werther's, over-hearing the mothers, and the new girl. But it was the scene on the street corner earlier that day that kept flying to her mind like birds to fat worms. *I wonder who Miss Percy looks like and why she turned out the way she did.* In the candlelight and with unusual interest, Sarah Emily studied Miss Percy's needle-sharp nose. Then, sleepily, she let her eyes roam down Miss Percy's stick frame studded with knobs: knuckles, knees and elbows. Sharp and hard, nose to toes, that was Miss Percy.

Sarah Emily settled under the covers and from under limp, drooping eyelids her attention was drawn, as it so often was, to the flower-shaped jeweled brooch Miss Percy always wore precisely three inches down from her left shoulder. The red petals were rubies with diamond centers, and a row of emeralds formed the stem with more emeralds shaping the two leaves. That night, the candlelight sent especially dazzling sparks from the stones.

"Into bed, you orphan brats."

Abruptly, Sarah Emily was wide awake.

Miss Percy marched up and down and around the rows of metal beds, striking her black leather strap against one foot rail and then another, making a terrible crack, leaving the beds buzzing and vibrating. Even her shadow cast a fear-provoking sight with her black hair firmly attached into its bun at the back of her neck and her bony face little more than sharp angles and dark hollows.

Soft is what Sarah Emily imagined a mother would be. Sarah Emily wormed her way deeper in the bed and brought the blanket to her chin, thinking, *soft, a mother would be soft, only soft . . . hair with fluffy soft curls that bounced when she laughed . . . lips that were pillow soft and left sweet as molasses kisses on your cheek . . . eyes so soft that love seeped out even when you were being scolded . . . hands as soft as bird's wings that touched your back when you crossed the street together.*

Yes, especially hands that touched your back. She had once seen a mother and daughter crossing the street. The two leaned in close, laughing, while the mother laid a hand on her daughter's back protectively guiding her. That had to be the perfect picture of soft mother's love, Sarah Emily was certain.

"Orphan brats, all of you," Miss Percy snarled, evaporating Sarah Emily's soft mother pictures. She wondered if they would ever be more than a mirage scooting away at Miss Percy's snarlings.

"You've given me a headache again today." Miss Percy kept at her pacing. "No one wants you. But here I am, trying to give you a home, and you give me a headache." She stopped, then waved the flickering candle toward Betsy as if it were a pointer. "And like we aren't crowded enough, I have a new orphan brat to house and feed." She whipped the leather strap through the air, leaving a shrill, piercing whistle to settle over all the girls.

Ophelia squealed. Nettie clamped her eyes closed. Cora glared. Marjorie yawned.

In the pale, yellow candlelight, Sarah Emily saw Betsy's face twist with fear. That sight twisted Sarah Emily's heart with anger. *Miss Percy enjoys frightening us. It's plain from the way she does the new ones, even before they've done something wrong.*

Whack! The strap came down hard on the rail of Betsy's bed, causing ferocious shaking of the whole iron frame. Betsy became a heap of trembles and jerked the rough blanket over her head.

Sarah Emily scrunched the sheet in her fist and braced herself. *Here it comes—Miss Percy's warning about the shed. Why didn't I remember to tell Betsy about this so she wouldn't be scared?*

And just as she feared, at that moment, Miss Percy whacked the foot rail again. The black strap quivering at her side, the candlestick held just above her head, Miss Percy leaned over the covered mass of Betsy. "Tomorrow I take you to the shed. I want to show you where bad orphans go." With that, Miss Percy left, slamming the door.

And the frightful, thick blackness of the room was a relief.

Immediately, Sarah Emily scooted out of bed, felt for Betsy and slid the blanket off her face. But Betsy didn't budge from the tight knot she had wound herself in.

"It's hard when you first come, but you'll get used to it, really you will. I just know it." Sarah Emily lied again, wishing that somehow, *poof,* she could make those words happen while she stroked Betsy's head. But knowing that would never happen, she said softly, "Straighten out so you can sleep."

Betsy unfolded her legs, the spring squeaked under the lumpy mattress. "I am awful tired." And that was borne out by her wispy, weary voice that trailed off. Then, as though hit by something worthy of mustering her last bit of waning energy, she clasped Sarah Emily's hand. "I do want to thank you for helping me settle in—and especially for getting me the bed next to yours."

"You can thank Nettie for that. She was nice about it, wasn't she? Now you've got to get to sleep."

"First, will you tell me what Miss Percy was meaning about going to a shed?"

Sarah Emily's chest tightened. "We'll talk about that come morning. Best be quiet now or Miss Percy's liable to come back with her strap."

"Yeah," Marjorie's throaty whisper came through the darkness, "you two better hush or we'll all be in trouble."

"I know," Sarah Emily said back to the voice. "But she's new."

"Okay, morning then," Betsy's words wobbled, weariness and fear obviously getting the best of her. "I don't want to get everyone in trouble."

Sarah Emily pulled the worn blanket over Betsy's arms. "Yes, morning's best." Standing there, she could hear Betsy's ragged breaths and knew she must be as scared as a hen locked in a fox house. How could she be anything but scared being in a new place and Miss Percy not offering any comfort, only fearful words?

Silence filled the room except for the slight rustle Sarah Emily made climbing back into bed. *It can't be fair that we have to live with Miss Percy.* She quickly snatched up her angry thoughts and stuffed them into a set-aside section on the floor of her heart.

Reaching through the darkness to the next bed, Sarah Emily found Betsy's trembling hand, held it tight, closed her eyes…

…and dreaded tomorrow.

Chapter 3

he next morning, Sarah Emily awoke before any of the other girls even began to think about giving up sleep. But just to make sure, she quietly eased up on one elbow to peek at Betsy, whose cheek was mashed into a tangle of curls. Asleep—that was good. Sarah Emily needed to talk to Mr. Wilbur before Betsy got up.

Still propped on her elbow, Sarah Emily tilted her head back and took a second to breathe in the delicious, yeasty-sweet aroma of cinnamon buns dancing up from the kitchen. Filling herself so full she thought her skin might tear, she licked her lips and, for the slightest moment, for the millionth time, tried to imagine what they must taste like. She exhaled reluctantly. Every morning that scrumptious scent pushed away the musty odor of damp towels mingled with yesterday's meals. She breathed again. Then, careful not to cause a sound, she inched out of bed, dressed, grabbed a shawl, pushed back the annoying hank of floppy hair and ran downstairs. Opening the massive front door, she was relieved to see the caretaker sitting beside the lilac bushes, his usual early morning place until the weather would blow too cold.

"Morning, Mr. Wilbur."

He turned toward her with his welcoming smile that crinkled the eyes and wrinkled the nose that held a pair of gold, wire-rimmed spectacles. He patted the empty place beside him on the bench. "Come sit with me. And tell me, how's the Sarah Emily Girl on this grand morning?"

Grand morning? She looked at the sun on its way up in a lazy, pink-tinged sky and then at the dear man she was talking to. Besides being with Timothy, being with Mr. Wilbur was the safest feeling she knew. And if for nothing but that, she could agree, it was a grand morning. A comfortable feeling floated through her. "I'm fine," she said, smiling. "Yes, I'm just fine." And she sat down.

"With that birthday of yours coming up next month, maybe I shouldn't be calling you Sarah Emily Girl. Should it be Sarah Emily Young Lady? Or maybe just Sarah Emily? You remember last year Franny and Judith both ran away to get married the instant they turned sixteen." His expression teased.

"Can't say I haven't ever thought about running away. But to get married? I don't think so."

"I hope thinking about running away is all you do." His teasing expression dissolved into a serious one. "You know that's not a good choice."

"I know, and anyway, I couldn't leave you or Cook or Cora and Nettie...or Timothy..." she swallowed hard, mostly to swallow the sudden Timothy-sized lump that rose up in her throat at even a playful mention of leaving him. For some time she had been attempting to prepare herself for the day Timothy turned eighteen and couldn't live at the orphan asylum anymore. So far, it had been an unsuccessful attempt because most of the time she couldn't bring herself to think about that dreaded day. And the idea of *her* purposefully leaving before him was even more unthinkable.

Neither did she and Timothy talk about it often. It was nearly impossible for either of them to imagine, let alone discuss easily. They had been together, best friends, for twelve years. That upcoming day in March hung over them like a heavy broken limb, ready to fall. But, when one of them did haltingly, hesitatingly bring it up, Timothy always assured her he wouldn't go far. He would get a job close by so he would still see her everyday. But the reality was he'd have to go wherever someone would be willing to hire a person branded with the shame of being an orphan. No matter what distance that was, she knew that, and that knowing always caused a sucking apprehension in her chest.

To recover, she found and returned Mr. Wilbur's gaze. She adored the affectionate name of Sarah Emily Girl, and his being like a grandfather. Whenever she talked to him, even when she was younger and bombarded him with silly chatter or questions, he always said her name without any trace of impatience in a way that made her feel important. The name made her feel like a lily sprouting in a field of weeds. The name was a prized treasure. The name was hers. "I'll never be too old. Not when I'm sixteen or eighty-six," she told him emphatically. "You've been calling me that as long as I can remember—and I love it. You've got to promise me you'll never quit."

His beaming eyes and wide smile suggested he'd hoped for that. "All right then," he said as he took off his green work cap. "Sarah Emily Girl it stays."

Although she didn't say anything, she noticed, as she had for several days now, that his gray hair wasn't being held in its usual neat way with hair tonic. His piney-scented hair tonic fused with the scent of wood from the projects he was always working on and the outdoors that he loved. From the day she'd come, the scent encircling him had made her think of him as a tree, a wonderfully strong, tall tree.

She'd spent the first weeks—she couldn't remember how many—sitting on the front steps, her arms clamped around her up-drawn knees, her chin resting there, waiting, certain Pa would come for her. Mr. Wilbur would pass by, the faint scent of pine coming with him, and ruffle her hair and smile. If he had time, he'd sit, too, sometimes talking, sometimes just sitting. She had found that piney scent somehow comforting while everything else around her swirled in confusion. Since then she'd always known him to smell of his tall-tree hair tonic.

Now, in their early morning conversation, Mr. Wilbur waved

his cap back and forth, reeling her thoughts back as he said, "The lilacs from up and down the street are sure making a great cloud of perfume this morning. They've bloomed longer than I've ever known them to." With the cap dangling in his hand, he scratched the top of his head with two work-worn fingers, seemingly unaware of his ruffled hair. "Imagine—lilacs still blooming this time of year. They act like they just don't want to quit. But with cold weather coming, I expect these have to be the last."

"All the lilac bushes on this street might be mingling their goodness together, but the two ends of Lilac Lane sure don't mingle anything else."

"That's the sad truth." Mr. Wilbur sighed and nodded and slid his head back into his cap.

The weight of what Sarah Emily came to talk to Mr. Wilbur about pressed down on her, and she didn't want to tell him why she was there. With their backs to the orphan asylum, a nearly square box of reddish-brown bricks stacked three stories high, she could forget it stood naked, except for the few elderly lilac bushes planted in better days and a scraggly old sycamore tree on the other side of the walkway. Whatever grass was there was as worn down as old velvet. Sitting with Mr. Wilbur, all wrapped up in his sympathizing smiles and the sweetness of the lilacs, she pretended this was her grandfather, and they were laughing and sharing stories in his beautiful front yard.

She swung her feet, kicking at a swell of rust and ruby sycamore leaves, and a pleasant daydream began. She usually didn't allow herself much time for daydreams, but sometimes one about a family just couldn't be stopped, especially this familiar one where a kindly faced grandmother would call from the front door, "Breakfast is ready. Bacon and eggs on the table."

What a perfect kitchen looked like popped up clearly in Sarah Emily's mind. There were enormous windows with tumbling, sprawling plants lining the sills. A breeze lifted the crisp curtains. In the middle of the table, a tall, creamy-white pitcher over-flowed with colorful fresh-picked wildflowers. A huge platter held hot, fluffy scrambled eggs and crispy, thick bacon strips. Next to the platter, a red strawberry-shaped jar was filled with Grandmother's fresh preserves. A big basket lined with a red and white checked napkin was piled with giant cloud-like biscuits. And another was brimming with hot cinnamon buns. And best of all, the kitchen smelled of love.

"Now tell me, why are you up so early?" Mr. Wilbur asked.

The sound of his voice gave her a start and she scolded herself for letting her mind wander off so much this morning. She released a quick breath and pulled herself up straight as she unwillingly shifted her thoughts from the cheerful imaginary kitchen and a family of her own, back to the seriousness of present business. "A new orphan—Betsy's her name—came yesterday about supper time."

"Oh," escaped along the rough edge of a heavy sigh. He plunked a knuckly, work-gnarled hand over each knee and slouched forward a bit. "I didn't know. I was in River Bend most of the day on errands. When I finally got back, I was bone tired, so I took my supper in my room."

"I knew you weren't there when we ate. That's why I wanted to tell you about her first thing this morning. Mr. Wilbur, this one's scared and frail. I don't think she can make it through the day."

Mr. Wilbur reached back and patted her hand. "You know Miss Percy wants the new ones to understand she's boss." Dismay spilled from his voice and the slow deliberate shake of his head. "But I'll do what I can."

"I know you will." Of that, she was positive. Standing and facing him, she was eager to tell him about the mothers she'd seen and heard while coming back from Doc Werther's yesterday. Surely, Mr. Wilbur could explain about looking like someone and how that made you turn out a certain way. Maybe he could even explain it to Timothy since she certainly hadn't gotten anywhere. Much as she hated to wait, though, she'd have to ask him later. Right now, she needed to check on the terrified new girl. "I best be getting back upstairs. I want to be there when Betsy wakes up."

Mr. Wilbur adjusted his cap and stood to his feet. "I see you really like this new girl, don't you?"

"Yes." She thought a moment. "There's something real sweet about her."

"And there's something real sweet about you too, Sarah Emily Girl."

She smiled at him with warmth kindled from his words as they walked toward the front door.

Out of nowhere, clouds huddled like wads of dirty dust. "Not a storm, not today." She lifted her face to the fickle sky and turned in a circle. A nasty wind whirled, sending sand and bits of crushed, dried leaves into her hair and eyes. She cringed.

"Now, where did that come from?" Mr. Wilson bunched his forehead and studied the weather.

"This is going to make bad things even worse."

"I know," he said. "Let me work on Miss Percy to see what I can do about—did you say her name was Betsy?"

Sarah Emily nodded.

"Let me see what I can do about Betsy. Now get on upstairs, and I'll see you at breakfast. Try not to worry," he called as they parted.

She stole one more look at the ugly sky and then, undetected, slinked through the front door and crept back upstairs to the girls' dormitory. She knelt beside Betsy's bed just as the wake-up bell greeted the new day with its annoying wail.

"Good morning," she said as Betsy rolled over, opened her eyes, gave Sarah Emily a half-smile, and watched the other girls stretch and yawn. It didn't take long before the room broke into the morning-routine frenzy with all its noise and commotion.

"How ya doing?" Sarah Emily asked but didn't wait for an answer, just skimmed the dingy wool blanket off Betsy. "Get up and dressed as fast as you can. If we aren't in the dining room on time, Miss Percy won't let us eat."

"Okay." Betsy sat up and swung her legs over the side of the bed, moving a mass of long tousled curls off her face. "But now will you tell me what Miss Percy meant when she said I was going to the shed today? Wondering about that kept waking me up last night."

"Oh, that." Sarah Emily picked at the frayed edge of the blanket. "We'll talk about the shed at breakfast," she said, trying to push some brightness into her voice. "Now, don't you be scared. Just get dressed."

"You promise to tell me at breakfast?"

"Promise." The word came out a lot weaker than Sarah Emily had planned.

While Betsy washed her face and put on the same faded brown dress she'd come in yesterday, Sarah Emily quickly made her own bed. When that was finished, she turned to find Betsy standing in front of the wardrobe, reaching into her satchel and bringing out a beautiful hairbrush. Its ornate silver back and handle gleamed in the morning light. Sarah Emily stared at what, undoubtedly, must be the one special thing Betsy said she had. Not only was Sarah Emily captivated by the loveliest brush she'd ever seen, but also by the luxurious way Betsy was pulling it through her hair, leaving a pile of loose curls resting on each shoulder.

"Betsy, how beautiful!" Nettie swooned, lightly touching Betsy's curls and then the brush.

"Let me see." Cora crowded in, wearing her lace neck wrap. Today she had it tied in a bow on the side, one tail flipped over her shoulder, the other dangling down the front of her dress. Sarah Emily marveled again at how such a little thing as a scrap of tattered old lace could please Cora—and how creative at just six-years-old she could be with it.

"Oh, do my hair," Cora said as soon as she saw the brush and swung around so her back was to Betsy, "so I'll look perfect with my new scarf." Cora's smile couldn't have been brighter.

Betsy ran the bristles through the short shreds of Cora's hair. "That feels like a good itch for a scratch." Cora giggled as other girls gathered around to gush over the exquisite silver-backed brush.

Marjorie hurried past. "You're all going to be late," she said, breezing out the door.

The throng of girls separated like threads on a skein of yarn, each to finish her own chores. Betsy replaced the brush in the satchel, shutting it with a *thwump* as the cracked leather latch settled in place.

By the time Sarah Emily had pulled up Betsy's blanket, Betsy moved quickly to help smooth out the wrinkles.

Sarah Emily told her, "We have to have our beds made before breakfast. You'll get used to jumping up, spreading up the bed, washing your face and getting dressed lickety-split."

"There's a lot I have to get used to," Betsy said, swooping up her satchel and putting it back on the shelf.

"And you will." Sarah Emily gave the pillow a final pat. That task finished, she linked arms with Betsy and swiveled her toward the door. "Let's go get breakfast," she said. What she didn't say was how much she desperately hoped Mr. Wilbur had found Miss Percy and was distracting her from her intended plans.

As soon as they arrived in the nearly full dining room, Sarah Emily saw that Timothy was eating. Then she looked around and found Mr. Wilbur talking to Miss Percy. Good! Sarah Emily relaxed a little.

Sarah Emily showed Betsy where to get the oat porridge that was always breakfast. While Cook asked Betsy how she had slept and commented on her pretty hair, Sarah Emily kept watching Mr. Wilbur and Miss Percy. Sarah Emily would have liked to introduce Betsy to Timothy, but she first had to find out what Miss Percy had in mind. Once breakfast was over they could meet, if, that is, Betsy wasn't dragged away to the shed.

With bowls full, Sarah Emily maneuvered Betsy to a table close enough to hear what Mr. Wilbur and Miss Percy were saying. After a sideways glance at Betsy, Sarah Emily was relieved to see Betsy's attention was only on her food.

"I really need us to go out back so you can show me where you want that fence moved," Mr. Wilbur said matter-of-factly, flapping his work gloves in that direction. "You know, Mildred, some of those old posts are about to fall down. Now, before winter sets in and the ground freezes up, would be a great time to do it."

That was the moment Cora crossed the dining room balancing her breakfast tray, the flimsy lace tail over her shoulder puffing up and floating down with each step she took.

"Cora, halt," Miss Percy demanded.

The room went silent and turned as one toward Cora.

Cora stopped so fast, her oatmeal bowl skidded back against her, sloshing out goopy cereal.

"Lace?" Miss Percy angrily questioned in her sparse word way.

Sarah Emily watched, while a sick lump grew in her stomach.

"Out of the rag pile," Cora spoke up, her spunk front and center. "I took it off your old shawl, but I left the shawl because I knew it weighed more, and you'd want the ragman to buy that."

"Mildred," Mr. Wilbur touched her arm, "let her have it. I'll pay you whatever you think the ragman would give you for that scrap she's got."

"If you have extra money for such foolishness as this, then obviously you're being paid too much." Miss Percy whirled around to Cora. "Give," she said and held out her hand.

Cora's response of a defiant glare was enough to rattle any enemy.

Miss Percy paused for a split second as if to reassemble herself. Then her thin mouth thinned even more from the visual challenge.

After a tense stare-off between the two, Cora slammed her tray down on the nearest table. More oatmeal splashed up and splattered on the top of Cora's apron along with the length of lace swinging in front. And on Miss Percy. It looked to Sarah Emily like Cora was going to refuse to take the lace off.

Miss Percy raised her strap. *Whack.* The leather strap slapping against the edge of the table caused everyone to jump. The sick lump in Sarah Emily's stomach doubled.

After one final scornful glare at Miss Percy, Cora unwrapped the scarf from her neck, letting the ends drag through the oatmeal on the tray before slapping it into Miss Percy's hand. Even Cora knew that ultimately Miss Percy would win. But it did thrill Sarah Emily to see oatmeal oozing between those veiny fingers.

Miss Percy whacked the strap on the table again. "My office. After breakfast." She threw the lace on the table and wiped her hand on a napkin. Then she scooped up the lace in the soiled napkin, furiously balling them both together.

That kind of callousness could not come naturally like breathing and swallowing did. Sarah Emily was sure that Miss Percy must have to work at it.

Then she heard Miss Percy telling Mr. Wilbur, "I've already made it clear, I don't want to check the fence this morning. We've more than enough time before winter. And haven't you noticed, there's going to be a terrible storm? You can't work on fences today." She gave a grunt of impatience and drew her lips into the way she had of producing a wrinkled pucker, like a bitter pill was crushed between them.

Sarah Emily watched in frustration. Dear, sweet Mr. Wilbur had tried to help Cora, but Miss Percy had total authority. Sarah Emily had often questioned Mr. Wilbur why he stayed on at the orphan asylum. His abilities far exceeded even the best all-around handy man and could have gotten him a job anywhere. His answer always came with a wink, "And just where is it you'd like me to go?" Sarah Emily had the feeling that behind the scenes, he and Cook saved them from more Miss Percy wrath than they knew.

For now, though, Mr. Wilbur would pick up where they had left off, just like everyone else in the dining room, where eating and talking were back to normal. Except for Betsy, whose eyes were so wide, her eyelids looked pinned to her forehead.

Mr. Wilbur was trying to get Miss Percy to listen, tapping his work gloves on his thigh. "Well then, if there's going to be a storm, let's take a quick look so I'll know where to put it when the weather's favorable."

"I said, not today. I have a new orphan, and I've got to get her to the shed."

Hope plummeted to the tattered soles of Sarah Emily's shoes.

"And I," Miss Percy thunked her hand on her chest, "certainly don't want to get soaked taking her out there. And whatever, Jenkins Wilbur, is wrong with your hair? It looks like a tornado combed it." With all that said, she strode away, wadded napkin and lace in one hand, her black leather strap dangling from the other.

Mr. Wilbur immediately tried to mash and flatten his flyaway hair. Then he gave a solemn look in Sarah Emily's direction, pressed his lips together and slowly shook his head. *I tried, but she isn't budging,* his face said.

The time for stalling had run out. "Betsy?" Sarah Emily hooked one foot under her other leg and twisted on the bench until she faced Betsy. "Let's talk about the shed."

Betsy put her spoon down. She, too, turned and faced Sarah Emily.

"After breakfast, Miss Percy is going to take you to the shed." Sarah Emily wanted to look away but forced her eyes to stay steady. "It's where she keeps the leash."

"A leash?"

"That's what Miss Percy calls it. It's a rope that has big knots tied about every ten inches. It's an absurd thing, but until you're sixteen, she makes you hold on to a knot when we go somewhere, you know, so we all stay together. She thinks it keeps us from running away. Those older than sixteen walk along beside the ones on the rope. Anyway, it hangs on a nail outside a tumbled-down old shed. And just so we never forget how scary the shed is, she makes one of us get the rope when we leave and another put it away when we get back."

"Is she going to make me get the rope?"

"No." Sarah Emily breathed deeply, wishing that was all it was while she searched for the right words to prepare Betsy for what really was going to happen. A tightening sensation crept around her neck when she realized there weren't any right words for this explanation—not any she knew. She would simply have to say it. "Miss Percy recently started making all the new orphans spend a day inside the shed. It's so from now on you'll mind her. Because if you don't, that's where you go for punishment."

"Have...have you been put in there?" Betsy's face never changed; her only movement was a twisting finger disappearing into a tendril of long hair.

Sarah Emily shook her head. "I'm not new. And I've tried not to rile her so much as to make me go. I admit, I've come pretty close a couple of times. One day, though, she took us all out there and made us, one at a time, go inside. But it's some of the ones who've been locked in who told me what that was like."

"What did they say?" Betsy's finger kept twirling the shank of hair, coiling it tighter.

"Well, it's dirty and kind of spooky..." Sarah Emily swung around and rested her forearm on the table, mindlessly stirring the mushy, gray oats in her bowl. She just couldn't go on explaining to Betsy about the most dreaded place in the orphan asylum. The eye-popping tales from the others who had been locked inside were enough to terrify her.

She didn't want to tell Betsy how it was dark and cold. Or about the huge rats and other critters that lived in and around the shed. Or how the roof was full of holes. Or how the wind howled right through and moaned like death was coming to snatch a body. Or how shadows caused creepy figures to swirl around like demons. Or how James, the toughest boy in the orphan asylum, screamed himself hoarse the day he was put in the shed just for sneaking into the kitchen and eating one of Miss Percy's cinnamon buns.

"I'll be okay," Betsy said, her fingers lightly resting on Sarah Emily's arm. "Really, I will."

"What?" At Betsy's words and touch, Sarah Emily snatched herself back from the grim thoughts she had been sorting through. "You'll be what?"

"Okay—in the shed. I'll be okay in there."

"But Betsy, you don't know what it's like." As soon as those words were out of her mouth, Sarah Emily saw Miss Percy coming directly toward them, her steps swift and determined, her lips already stirring with the decree. Suddenly an idea to keep Betsy out of that torture spread like a paper fan in Sarah Emily's mind. "Help me on this," she whispered and sprang from the bench.

Rolling her eyes back, Sarah Emily began to flail her arms, while shaking her head back and forth and howling, trying to sound akin to a sick wolf.

"Miss Percy," Ophelia shrieked and jumped up from the table. "Sarah Emily's having a fit. Her brain's plumb twisted itself into a kink. It's just like those daft people in the crazy house. We're going to have to chain her to her bed."

Spoons clattered into bowls, milk cups thudded down on the table, benches scraped backward and everyone scuffled to their feet.

"What's the matter with Sarah Emily?" Cora hopped up onto the bench, stretching to see over taller ones as they all gathered around to watch the spectacle of someone "titched" in the head.

Nettie quickly moved beside Cora, taking hold of Cora's apron tie so she wouldn't topple forward.

Mr. Wilbur loudly swallowed the last of his coffee and clapped the cup on the table as Timothy sidled up next to him.

"Let me see." Ben pushed his way through.

Pleased with the ruckus she was creating, Sarah Emily slumped to the floor, contorting and howling. She stretched her eyes wide and tried not to blink so she would look even wilder. It was then that she saw Timothy and Mr. Wilbur look at one another and exchange winks.

"Get out of my way, Ophelia." Miss Percy pushed aside the unstrung girl, dropped to her knees and lunged, making a grab for Sarah Emily.

"Careful, Miss Percy," Ophelia squawked. "When a person's brain gets unbuttoned, they might bite."

Miss Percy jerked her hands back and stared at Sarah Emily writhing on the floor.

"Get away, everyone," Betsy spoke up. "I know what to do when a body's got a cracked brain."

Sarah Emily bit her tongue to keep her smile from sliding out. Her hopes mounted. Her plan just might work. At least, it had a chance since it was going even better than she had dared expect. She never dreamed Betsy would catch on and play a part so readily and with such ease.

Tall, gangly Ophelia scrunched and wrung her dress. "You'd better be careful."

"I will." Betsy brushed past Ophelia. "Just step back." She quickly sat down on the floor, crossing her legs behind Sarah Emily's head.

By now, Sarah Emily was quieting her howls into gurgles as she slowed her twitching and thrashing on the floor. She felt Betsy take hold of her head. Pulling Sarah Emily's head into her lap, Betsy gently rubbed Sarah Emily's temples and began a soft humming.

I like the sound of that tune, Sarah Emily thought while Betsy continued to rub and hum. The room grew silent, except for Betsy's gentle music.

Sarah Emily saw Mr. Wilbur and Timothy straining to contain their laughter, hands over their mouths and stomachs jiggling. Cook lifted the hem of her apron to cover her mouth, her eyes dancing. There was Miss Percy bent over and speechless, her black eyebrows wrinkled together. Ophelia paced back and forth, befuddled and jittery. And the other orphans lined up like crows on a fence.

"I'd say Betsy has just made you and Sarah Emily a trio of mischief," Mr. Wilbur said in a low whisper to Timothy.

"Yeah," Timothy whispered back. "Sarah Emily's a never-ending stream of schemes. Where they all come from, I'll never know or understand."

When she heard their whispering, Sarah Emily flicked her eyes at Miss Percy to see if she heard too. Thankfully, she hadn't. But it was time to start calming down, Sarah Emily decided, before Miss Percy did catch on to her trick.

As if on cue, Betsy said, "We'd best get her to bed."

Miss Percy's cold hand covered Sarah Emily's forehead. "Can I get you anything?"

Although shocked at Miss Percy's uncharacteristic compassion, Sarah Emily felt encouraged by Miss Percy's reaction and Betsy's participation. Confident, Sarah Emily continued her plan. "I...I need..." She swallowed hard. *Slow. Now, act like it's difficult to concentrate,* Sarah Emily silently coached herself. *Okay, be real pitiful.* She blinked several times pretending to corral her senses. "It would be nice if Betsy could sit with me so she can keep rubbing my head," she said in a tiny little voice, ending with a tiny little sigh.

As if struck by a lightning bolt, Miss Percy stiffened so fast her brooch jiggled. "I should have known," she spat through gritted teeth. "You've caused this whole show so Betsy wouldn't have to go to the shed. Well, have I got a surprise for you, Miss Theatrics, you'll be the one going to the shed today."

Betsy bounded to her feet.

Sarah Emily's head clunked on the floor. "Ouch!" she yowled, rubbing the throbbing spot. But even worse than the head thunk was the terrible fright of Miss Percy's words spinning in her head. *You'll be the one going to the shed today. You'll be the one...*

"No!" Betsy shouted. "I'll take my turn in the shed. Sarah Emily don't need to go."

For only the quickest flash of time, Miss Percy gawked with surprise at Betsy's offer, then stood and bumped her aside. Towering over Sarah Emily, Miss Percy slapped her hands to her hips, striking a threatening pose. "Get up. And I mean right now, you orphan brat."

Mr. Wilbur stepped between Miss Percy and Sarah Emily. "You can see everyone is terrified. Let me take Betsy to the shed and show it to her, but don't make her stay." He dropped his voice. "Please, Mildred."

"Yes. Take me." Betsy elbowed in between Miss Percy and Mr. Wilbur, nearly toppling the headmistress out of her shoes. "I'm the new one. I should go," Betsy said with confidant boldness.

Somehow Sarah Emily managed to get up, even with the tangle of legs squeezed around her. *Did Betsy say she'd take my place? This same Betsy who just yesterday was so scared she trembled?* It was one thing for Betsy to join Sarah Emily in her scheme, but quite another to offer to go to the shed. Sarah Emily was completely confused in the midst of the confusion she had concocted.

"I'm the one who should go to the shed," Betsy pleaded again.

"Absolutely not. I said Sarah Emily is going." Miss Percy spoke as if she were fastening each word down with a nail. She then sent a scorching glare around the room and snapped at the scared-still group, "School. Now!" They took off like chickens in a storm. "Cora, my office."

Cora stopped just short of going out the door.

Miss Percy snatched a fistful of fabric at the neck of Sarah Emily's dress and dragged her through the dining room. Spending far more words than usual, she again made herself clear. "This one is spending the day in the shed."

Chapter 4

Timothy didn't follow Miss Percy's order to get to school. Instead, he stood frozen at the sight of Sarah Emily being dragged out, a lump leaping to his throat and rage slicing through his body. Then, only his hands moved, curling into fighter fists while his mind played out a secret wish. He saw himself running toward Miss Percy and with one swift and solid punch, he knocked the heartless woman to the ground. Rescuing Sarah Emily, he took her by the hand, and the two of them ran far, far away from this dreadful place.

Timothy's protective fantasy vanished when others jostled past him in their haste to obey the headmistress.

"With the fury Miss Percy's got stirred up, you better get moving," Nettie said, scooting around him.

Timothy slowly unclenched his fists. *There's going to come a time when I won't ever let anybody hurt Sarah Emily again, not Sarah Emily—my Sarah Emily.* He jumped. *My Sarah Emily* echoed in his head with such thunderous roaring that he thought he heard himself say it out loud. Had he? He swung around to see if anyone was looking at him. No one was. *My Sarah Emily* continued to spin through his brain with a roar, but in his heart it purred.

Everyone had left the dining room except Betsy, and he saw her snatch two pieces of bread off the table and cram them into her pocket.

Letting out a sigh of relief that he had kept his thoughts to himself, he walked toward her, saying, "School building's right next door. I saw you and Sarah Emily—"

"Are you her friend?" Betsy broke in, her eyes narrowing.

"Yeah. I'm Timothy. I've been her friend since the day she came here."

For several seconds, her eyes stayed crimped while she appeared to judge his sincerity. Evidently satisfied, she said, "Then we've got to do something real quick for her."

Timothy held the door open to reveal the school, a squat structure crouching behind the main one. Its face was bare of porches, overhangs and shutters, as vertically smooth as if a knife had made a clean slice in a loaf of bread. "Let's talk on our way to class," he said.

"It's a dreadful thing to be so plum sceert a body's blood turns to cold jelly." Betsy kept talking fast, getting it all out in one breath as they made their way on the path that linked the school to the main building. "And that's what's going to happen to Sarah Emily if she's never been alone in a place like the shed," Betsy said just before reaching the school. "So how can we get to her?"

"Meet me at recess," Timothy whispered as they entered the classroom.

Along with the others, he scrambled to his seat in the green wooden schoolhouse. He remembered the day he and Sarah Emily decided that the shade of green it was painted inside and out was the exact shade of mold. Now, Timothy looked to the back of the mold-green room and saw Betsy standing alone in front of the bookcase, shifting from one foot to the other, looping and relooping her hair around a finger.

The teacher sat at her desk as straight as a broomstick and not nearly as pretty. Miss Dickens looked up from her book, pulled her glasses midway down her nose, and squinted over the top rim.

"You must be the new one," she said in a voice flat as glass.

"I guess I am. Yes, ma'am."

"Well, sit down. Don't just stand there." Miss Dickens pushed her glasses to the top of her nose and went back to her book.

Betsy started toward the only empty desk.

"Can't sit there." Marjorie held out her arm, and as if proud for being difficult, snaked a smirk of malicious delight across her mouth. "That's where Sarah Emily sits."

Betsy backed away.

Timothy glared at Marjorie. She was positively the most irksome girl. Why couldn't she let Betsy sit there for today? She knew that Betsy must be feeling about as awkward as a pig in a parlor. "Miss Dickens?" he said.

Up came her head. Down came her glasses. Her dull, pale eyes stared back at him.

"Miss Dickens, there isn't an empty seat for Betsy."

"So go to the storeroom and get a desk and chair. Just what I need, another orphan," she said, ending with a loud, long sigh.

Once in the storeroom, Timothy quickly found the needed items and carried out the chair first and then the desk. He put them on the side of the room with the window, near Sarah Emily's seat, sure that tomorrow when Sarah Emily was back, she would like that.

Betsy sat down, and Miss Dickens stood up. With a long pointy finger, she slid her glasses down to the center of her milky-white nose.

Her skin is so ghostly white, her face looks like it is set for her funeral, Timothy thought, as he glanced over to see how Betsy was doing.

Then in her droning voice, Miss Dickens began the morning's lesson about nouns.

He tried to focus, grateful for another day in school. He missed so much school with Miss Percy hiring him out to the town's people as often as she could. She would say to him, "Until you leave, may as well make yourself useful to me earning some money. You've had more schooling now than you'll ever need. Besides, it won't be that much longer 'til you're eighteen and the state won't allow you to stay any longer. You'll be out on your own."

It irritated him that this subject was important enough for her to construct entire sentences. But, even so, Miss Percy was right; the six months until March 17 would pass fast, too fast. The thought of that formed a solid block of ice inside him. There were only two things that had kept him from running away before now. Leaving Sarah Emily, by far, was the main reason. From the moment she had arrived, he'd had a special relationship with her. And recently, she'd changed from a girl to a woman almost without a jolt, as far as he could tell. That was confusing, but nice. He mentally prodded himself from dwelling on Sarah Emily because he could get lost in those thoughts, thinking about her and nothing else.

The other reason he was still there was this very schoolroom and what he could learn. It was a fact that Miss Dickens wasn't the most dedicated teacher, but once he left the orphan asylum, schooling for him would be a thing of the past. Even access to books would probably be over for him.

He and Sarah Emily had spent hours reading the books in the tall bookcase at the back of the room, trying to learn everything possible from them. Some of the books he had read more times than he remembered. In those books, he learned facts, experienced a bigger world and traveled far with his back propped against the bookcase. A band of anger cinched his chest and he forced his thoughts away from the day he would have to leave those books. And Sarah Emily.

However, he had to admit, this notion Sarah Emily had come up with of who you will become frustrated him. He had been thinking about what he'd like to do with his life, and if he studied hard and learned what he could and worked for it...anyway, he didn't know what his parents looked like.

His gaze and attention scooted out the window to Sarah Emily in the shed. Timothy saw the sky getting darker and meaner, and worried about her all alone with such a fierce storm on its way. He glanced at Betsy whose gaze also kept darting out the window.

Finally, the big clock on the back wall clanged ten times and chair legs scraped across the wooden floor as the students made a hasty dash out for morning break.

Outside the classroom door, Timothy only had to wait a second for Betsy to find him.

"Which way is the shed?" she whispered.

"Follow me." Timothy ran with Betsy by his side. Lightening gashed crossways into the murky sky. "With the storm so near, Miss Dickens won't be coming outside, so she'll never miss us."

"Good," Betsy said, matching Timothy's pace. "Sarah Emily's been alone in that shed nearly two hours. We need to get to her—fast."

"Sarah Emily?"

"Timothy! I'm here," she shouted back the second she heard his voice above his pounding, running footsteps. She rushed to a hole in the wall of the rickety shed, calling, "I'm here. I'm here," and peered out into the ragged thicket.

As soon as Timothy came into view, fanning his arms to make a path through drooping, clingy vines, she let out a huge breath and sucked in another, suddenly aware that until she saw Timothy, she hadn't been breathing regularly. Then he stepped aside, holding back the spiny branches, and Betsy appeared. Sarah Emily couldn't believe it. But there was Betsy as well, batting at a wall of cobwebs and kicking through tangled, dense brush.

In a rush of gratitude, Sarah Emily said, "Am I ever glad to see you two." Only, she knew they couldn't possibly understand how extremely glad she was. Just their presence caused the tenseness in Sarah Emily's shoulders to loosen despite the darkening sky and the whipping wind.

Timothy had dropped forward, pressing his palms to his knees. "We wanted to see 'bout you," he huffed like a winded mule.

"You okay, Sarah Emily?" Betsy asked, gulping to catch her breath.

"Yeah, now that you're here." A crack of lightening chased thunder directly above the shed.

"We've got to get this rock away from the door." Betsy was hurriedly swiping her fingers across her dress to knock off the stuck cobweb strings. Then she bent over, firmly placing her hands on the heavy rock.

"Be careful. Rats are everywhere," Sarah Emily called out to her.

"I'm not afraid of rats."

That wasn't how Sarah Emily felt, but she didn't say anything, just watched Timothy and Betsy grimace and heave and shove on the rock. As she watched Timothy bear the brunt of moving the rock, an odd sensation of tingling took over her right toes. *What in the world?* she thought, trying to stop it by squeezing and unsqueezing her toes.

Recently, there were times, and this was one of them, when Sarah Emily would catch a glimpse of Timothy and almost not recognize him. It was a confusing feeling because she had seen him every day of her life since she had been left at the Orphan Asylum of Lander. And it was more than his getting taller. They had both been doing that all along. It seemed, in the middle of the night, new proportions had sneaked up on Timothy. He had become a man. His shoulders had widened, his arms had hardened, his face had taken on a distinct angular shape—quite handsome, she had to admit. How had all that happened without her noticing?

When her tingling toes were more or less under control, she said from her peephole, "Miss Percy put that there so I couldn't get out. You should have seen the determined scrunch she had on her face to do it."

"I always knew she was determined, but that mosquito-limbed woman must be stronger than she looks if she put it here all by herself." Timothy gave a final thrust, freed the door and slung it open.

The second he and Betsy rushed in, Sarah Emily clutched them both to her in a firm hug.

"Hey," Timothy yelped. "You're squeezing tighter than a garter on a fat lady's leg."

"And just what do you know about a fat lady's garter, Timothy Marshall?" Sarah Emily said as she let go and playfully thumped his chest. Then she stood back and grinned. "Am I ever glad to see you. I was scared—really scared. You'd think I was a child, the way, after Miss Percy left, I've been standing in one place with my apron pulled over my eyes." That was when it dawned on her that Timothy and Betsy shouldn't be there. "Just how is it that you two got away with coming here? Is it morning break?"

"Yes. Don't worry," Timothy said. "We'll be back before Miss Dickens misses us."

"You'd better, because you sure don't want her mad," Sarah Emily said, but already she was dreading the moment they'd have to leave. She got busy kicking musty clutter out of the way and motioned for them to sit down.

They all settled on the ground, under a shaft of light coming from a jagged hole in the roof with no one mentioning the sickening smell or the wind sounding like a thousand screams.

"Quick, we don't have much time." Betsy started talking the moment she sat down. "Let me tell you what to do. Rats make nests in the corners, so find a spot in the middle. And move around. At least move your legs or arms or something every once in a while. Don't get yourself all huddled up and still. That's when the rats will try to chew on you."

Rats the size of goats skulked across Sarah Emily's mind. She shivered. At the same time, Timothy's eyes grew as big as hens' eggs, and his mouth gaped open as if trying to insert one whole.

"It'll get scary," Betsy continued, appearing intent on saying everything she needed to without wasting time acknowledging their reactions or by using sugared words. "And when it gets so scary you think fright is going to bust your heart right out of your chest, that's the time you say part of the Lord's Prayer."

"The Lord's Prayer?" Timothy's forehead puckered.

"What's that?" Sarah Emily asked so quickly, her words nearly overlapped his.

"You don't know the Lord's Prayer? Are you heathens?"

Sarah Emily and Timothy looked at each other, shrugged their shoulders and looked back at Betsy.

"Oh, never mind now. Don't worry, I'm sure you ain't heathen, neither of you." Betsy flapped her hand, erasing the very idea out of the air and with it any need to explain. "Let me teach you what to say when you're so scared you think you'll die. Listen now: Yea, though I walk through the valley of the shadow of death, I will fear no evil, for thou art with me. Now, you say it too."

"Yea," Sarah Emily dutifully parroted Betsy, "though I walk through the valley of the shadow of death, I will fear no evil, for thou art with me."

"*Who* art with her?" Timothy aimed a thumb toward Sarah Emily.

"God," Betsy said.

"Oh." Sarah Emily wondered why this God hadn't been with her before now.

"How do you know so much about all this, Betsy?" Timothy asked.

She looked at the floor and swallowed so hard Sarah Emily heard it. Betsy poked a bony finger into a long shank of her hair and twisted and untwisted. "Mama died when I was born. And Papa took care of me and my older sister, Faith."

"You have a big sister? How wonderful!" Sarah Emily leaned closer, suddenly far more interested in a sister than how to survive the shed.

"Well...Faith...she's dead now."

Sarah Emily saw the ache sweep over Betsy's eyes, heard the tremble in her words and was about to tell Betsy she didn't have to talk about that right now.

But before Sarah Emily could tell her, Betsy raced on, seeming to set aside her own grief and regain the purpose for their conversation. "My Papa, he used to put us in a basement hole when he thought we was bad. It was dark as pitch and cold as ice, even in the summer. He'd leave us there all day and sometimes into the night. Faith, she taught me what to do. Just like I'm telling you how to stay away from the rats and what to say from the Bible. Once, Papa put Faith in the basement hole and then he got to drinking and must have lost track of time. After a few days passed, when I thought he was too drunk to know what I was doing, I opened the hatch so Faith could come up, but Papa saw me and slammed it back down. Then he locked me in the smokehouse and wandered off. It was days later 'fore he come back. I had food in the smoke-house and a big barrel of rainwater outside the window. But, Faith..." Tears splattered down Betsy's cheeks, and she turned her face away.

"You're safe here with us," Timothy said.

Sarah Emily covered Betsy's hand with hers.

"My papa felt real bad," Betsy said, staring at a spider at work on a web. "He learned his lesson, because after that, he never left me in the basement hole long enough to die."

The three sat silent. Sarah Emily wanted to respond to Betsy, but her throat tightened. Only the scurrying rats' feet spoke.

Betsy wiggled her hand free from Sarah Emily's. "Now Papa's dead. He got drunk and fell down the basement hole. I was so used to him going off for several days at a spell, I didn't know he was down there laying dead. The doctor said he probably died as soon as his head met with the floor, but he don't know that for sure. I'll never know if I could 'a saved him." She reached for a limp string of hair that dangled at her cheek and began winding it mindlessly tighter and tighter around her finger. "Papa and Faith, both dead in the basement hole," each word got softer and softer, swirling to silence.

After a long moment, Sarah Emily whispered, "Is that why you came to live here?"

Betsy nodded. "A neighbor woman, Mrs. Clay, came to see if Papa had some extra corn meal to sell. When she learned what happened, she brought me here. I begged her not to. I told her I could take care of myself. I'm plenty old enough. Been doing it the two months since Papa died. But she wouldn't give me a chance to prove I could keep it up." One shiny tear slid from the corner of her eye. "I ain't never been away from home before—not without Faith. That's why I was so scared when I got here yesterday." Betsy pulled her finger from the tangle of hair, swiped away the tear and looked Sarah Emily straight in the eyes. "But I do know how to survive a place like this shed. Now, just take mind of what I told you. This shed ain't going to swallow you up in a day's time."

The clang of the school bell rumbled eerily on the fast-moving wind. A spindle of alarm shot through Sarah Emily. Betsy and Timothy had to leave. She wanted to plead with them to stay longer, but she wouldn't. No telling what Miss Percy would do if they got caught out here.

They all hurried to their feet, and started for the door.

Timothy lightly skimmed Sarah Emily's arm with his hand, and said, "I'll check on you later."

After digging in her apron pocket, Betsy handed Sarah Emily two slices of slightly squished bread. "I took these from the table for you this morning. This should keep you from being too awful hungry. Just be careful, 'cause the rats will smell it."

"I will. Thank you." Sarah Emily hugged Betsy and a kinship took root in her heart. Then she watched from the hole in the wall while Timothy and Betsy pushed the rock back in front of the door. A quick waggling wave from them, and they took off toward the school building through the beginning rain, leaving her behind—alone in the dreadful shed.

Chapter 5

lone again, hard, stinging drops of rain pelted Sarah Emily from a gaping gash in the roof, but she stood still. The hand she'd lifted for a goodbye wave held her bread and stayed that way long after Timothy and Betsy were out of sight. She felt the bread getting soggy and slipped it into her apron pocket.

Her thoughts skipped from Timothy's saying he would be back later, to Betsy's bringing the bread, to hoping they hadn't been caught coming out there. Then her thoughts zeroed in on Betsy and the ordeal she would be enduring that afternoon when Miss Percy got hold of her hair. Sarah Emily wished she could be with Betsy when that happened. Knowing that wasn't possible, she pressed a hand to her ribcage and forced herself to take a deep breath, trying to be brave for Betsy and herself. She moved away from her hole in the wall to look for a drier place.

Her newfound bravery shrank. Her insides began to quiver, and she locked her arms around herself. Her mouth went dry. A thousand sharp needles jabbed at the back of her neck. Icy fingers squeezed her heart. How would she get through the rest of the day? She fought to control her rising panic, allowing her eyes to cautiously explore the shed for a hiding place. Although the holes in the roof were letting in rain, she was grateful for the little pricks of light they also let in. She slowly unwrapped her arms. It was then that she heard a noise. It sounded like a whimpering—a weak whimpering. *It's just the wind,* she decided, while edging forward. Her foot struck something hard. She twirled around while rubbing her toes. "That old trunk! I didn't see it." She realized the sound of her own voice made the shed not quite so menacing, and more than that, it gave her a sense of power. "That old trunk," she said again, even louder this time.

As soon as her foot quit throbbing, she lifted the dusty trunk lid, and the sweet scent of rosewater drifted out. For a moment, it displaced the putrid shed scent. Recognizing Miss Percy's old things, she dug around, bringing up a green felt hat with a turned up brim. She bent the brim down and set it on her head. Twisting the hat, she pulled it as low over her ears as it would go and gave it a saucy little pat. *That'll help keep the rain off my head.* Next, she tugged out a corset and studied the hard bones of the rigid garment. "No wonder Miss Percy's mean as a snake with this thing cutting off her breathing," Sarah Emily said, shoving it back into the trunk.

She slammed the lid closed and moved a little farther, tripping over a box of old pots and pans. The clattering sent rats scooting and scurrying in every direction. Gasping shallow breaths and clutching her chest, she dashed to the opposite side of the shed. There, she got tangled in the huge web the spider was still weaving.

"Now, I'm getting all riled up instead of just purely terrified." She picked wiggling bugs and dangling webs from her hat, face and apron. "How can it be lawful for Miss Percy to lock us in this horrid place?" She thrust out her tongue and blew a strand of web from her mouth.

A speck of light from another hole in the ceiling called her attention to a nearly thigh-high pile of rags. It was the length of a body, giving it the appearance of a hunkered-down beast. The beast was musty and withered from all the moisture that collected in the shed. This pile of used clothing and rags Miss Percy was accumulating for the ragman to buy next week was huge, much larger than usual. She had convinced the Ladies' Aid Society to donate all their castoffs to the orphan asylum to sell, and she had been quite pleased with the major acquisition. That flimsy piece Cora had wouldn't have made a one-penny difference in the amount Miss Percy would get from this heavy stash. Sarah Emily's memory spun back to the last time the ragman came.

Well hidden in the overgrown thicket, she and Timothy had watched Miss Percy plead with the ragman, her voice all sweet and drippy. "Now give me the best price you can. It'll help feed the orphans, you know." Then, when he had paid her, she took the money, thanked him, and when he left, she had counted it greedily. "Good," she'd said to herself. "Enough to buy that exquisite rose-patterned china cup and saucer with the lovely scalloped edge I've been admiring at the mercantile." Miss Percy had neatly and precisely folded the money, unbuttoned the first three buttons of her high-collared dress, and stashed the wad into her underpinnings.

Seething with that memory, Sarah Emily jammed a hand onto her hip. "Listen here, you spooky old building, you aren't going to bumfuzzle me. If Betsy can make it in the basement hole, I can make it in this shed. I just know it. Miss Percy is not going to undo me." She kicked at the rag monster.

"Ouch! Not again!" She shook her foot and then dropped to her knees to see what she had kicked this time. Pushing the rags away, she uncovered five wooden boxes. Each one was marked *Orphan Asylum Records* in bold, black letters. She twisted one box around to better catch the light and saw the letters *N through Q* written in the same bold black.

Alphabetical order? she thought, shoving each box under the skinny shaft of light until she found one marked *A through F.* Her breaths came short and quick. Could there be information about her family and why she lived at the orphan asylum? She threw off the lid from the musty container, and despite her trembling fingers, plucked through the folders until she came to *Butler, Sarah Emily; Born October 26, 1865.* She focused on each word and number. "Butler, Sarah Emily," she read again, aloud this time. "Born October 26, 1865."

She slumped back on her heels. Questions churned in her mind. What if she found out something she didn't want to know, like, what if her pa just up and decided he didn't want her anymore after her ma died? Suddenly, curiosity grabbed hold and shook her so hard she had to know what the papers could tell her—no matter what.

Perched up on her knees again, she opened the folder with her name at the top. Out fell yellowed, bug-eaten papers. She held a thin, crisp sheet to the light and tried to make out the writing, but the ink was so faded it was impossible to read. She held up another. It was the same. Yanking out more folders, she found the papers in them just as ruined. She opened the next box. The folders in it were damp and fell apart when she touched them. In fiery determination, she ripped the top off each box and searched for a shred of paper that was still readable—nothing, not one.

Sarah Emily stood, clenched hands at her side. "These papers had information about me, Timothy and all of us." She lowered her voice. "They told who I am—the things that would make me a real person, not just an orphan."

For several minutes, she stood stiff. Then deep sobs ripped through her broken spirit, and she collapsed like an empty sock back into the pile of foul-smelling rags. "Was I born just to be forgotten?"

Bitter tears splashed off her cheeks and drizzled into her ears. She cried so long and hard, she felt her eyes swell to puffy slits. She wilted and sank deeper into the moldy rags. *There are such a few solid things I know about my life. Now, how am I ever going to find out anything more?*

"Orphans have feelings. Orphans have hearts." She yanked the worn, green hat down lower on her head and stuffed her angry thoughts into that ever-filling part at the bottom of her heart.

Betsy's story, especially one part, incessantly flapped around her like bat wings. If Betsy's ma died, why didn't her pa put her and Faith in an orphan asylum? The riddle of why some fathers keep their children splintered into shards as sharp as broken glass. She covered her head with her arms, recoiling at the cutting thoughts.

Finally, exhausted, Sarah Emily fell asleep to the moans of the howling storm.

A tug at her apron roused Sarah Emily from sleep. She bolted upright. Horrified, she saw a gray rat backing out of her pocket, a slug of her bread hanging in its sharp teeth. She watched wide-eyed as it ran to a far corner with its prize. Another rat, just off to the side of the pile of rags, chewed on yet another hunk of her bread. "You stole that out of my pocket," she screeched. Remembering the powerful feeling talking out loud gave her, she added, "You're not only ugly, you're thieves."

Leaping off the rags, she struggled to recall the words Betsy had taught her. "I'm in the shadow of death; are you with me, God?" she shouted so loud another rat darted out from under the rags and hid behind a broken shovel.

Sarah Emily looked around the wretched place. The rats were eating her bread. The boxes of records were ruined. Pain ripped her heart again. Questions, questions and more questions kept bending her dejected spirit. *How am I ever going to know who I am? Why do I have to live in an orphan asylum? If I can't find my past, and my present is awful, how can I have a future?*

In a flash, determination trampled the dejection. She jerked her chin up. "I may be just an orphan, but that doesn't mean I'm always going to be," she spoke to the rats, to the boxes, but mostly to herself. "I'm going to find out who I look like, and someday someone is going to love me. I'm going to be a lady, a real lady with fine dresses...and long hair." She tore off the hat and threw it onto the rags. It landed with a muted plop, flinging up dust and the rancid smell. She fingered the jagged edges of her hair where Miss Percy had cruelly whacked it off in chunks—no style, just whacked.

The opened boxes and ruined records seemed to mock her dreams. In a feverish frenzy, she replaced the lids and threw the nasty rags over them until not one part of one box could be seen. She stood straight and shook her finger. "Now, you're buried. But somewhere I'll find out who Sarah Emily Butler really is!"

Thunder hammered and roared across the sky, causing the wobbly shed to creak and groan with each flog of the wind. She ran to the hole in the wall and watched the trees lean and sway. "Every gust of wind sounds like it's wrestling with the last," she said, feeling alarm swell and tighten in her stomach. Wrapping her arms around her middle, she looked at the ceiling. Soon, there wouldn't be a dry inch anywhere in the shed the way the wind was blowing the rain through the holes.

Out of the shrieking gale came the faint whimpering she had heard earlier. Only this time, a scratching went with the whimpering.

She looked out her peephole until she found the source of the noise leaning against the door. "Oh, you poor thing. Look at you. What a drenched dog you are." She ran to the door and pushed—and pushed. Finally, in frustration, Sarah Emily slid to the floor and strained to see out a split in the warped boards. "I'm sorry, but that rock is so big, I can't get the door open, not even a smidgen, to let you sneak in."

The shivering dog cuddled closer, panting hard.

"You should go find someplace dry." Sarah Emily stroked the little wisps of wet fur poking through the cracks, but the soaked dog wasn't budging. An excited tickle fluttered in Sarah Emily. "I'm going to keep you," she boldly announced to the dog. "I don't know how, but I am going to keep you. I just know it." She flattened her cheek against the door. "And I'm going to call you Mine. Yes. That'll be your name. Mine. I don't have much that I can call mine, even knowing who I am." Sarah Emily looked back at the heap of rags and thought about what was under them. She thought about the dog on the other side of the door, and the darkness in her heart brightened. She found a crevasse just big enough to worm her little finger through, and with the tip, she rubbed tiny circles of love on the dog's matted fur.

"Sarah Emily Girl, are you all right?" The muffled words echoed through the noisy storm.

She jumped up to look out the hole in the wall but couldn't see anyone between the blowing sheets of rain. "Mr. Wilbur, is that you?"

"Sarah Emily, are you all right?"

"Yes, I'm okay." Her shouts stretched the cords of her throat. If she squinted, she could make out his tall form bundled in an over-sized old brown coat, clamping his work hat down on his head with one hand.

"If you aren't one wet critter," he said to the scraggily, dripping dog when he got to the shed. "And where in this storm did you come from?" He pushed and grunted, moving aside the heavy rock and then flung open the door.

Sarah Emily lunged for Mr. Wilbur, clinging like a barnacle to him, not caring that she was getting even wetter. "I'm so glad to see you. The rats and the storm . . ." She dissolved into sobs, so relieved to see him, but thoroughly aggravated with herself for acting like a child.

"You're going to be fine, just fine," he calmly told her. "It's over."

The drenched dog came bounding in, back half dancing and slapping Sarah Emily's legs with each happy to and fro.

"I've named the dog Mine—because it came to me," Sarah Emily blurted out in a single breath. Then she dropped to her knees and hugged the wet fur to her.

Mr. Wilbur squatted beside her. The dog happily licked his face, first one side and then the other. "Certainly is friendly." He laughed as he tried to push away the lively animal. "Mine is a fine name for a boy or girl, and it looks like this is a girl."

"A girl! That's perfect." Until that moment, what the dog was hadn't occurred or mattered to her.

"This is an awful nice dog, but you know Miss Percy won't take kindly to her." Mr. Wilbur laid one callused hand on her shoulder and his other on the dog's head.

Mine let out a low cry, plopped down and stared at the two of them. Her tail made broad, slow sweeps through the years of dirt that had become the floor.

Sarah Emily edged closer to the dog and put her arm around its wet neck. "I named her Mine because I don't have much that is mine. I'm going to keep this dog," she said with all the force she could gather. "Will you help me?"

He appeared to waver for a moment.

"Please?"

She could almost see his mind trying to fit around this unusual request. But it didn't take long before a twinkle flittered from his eyes, then a big smile, and finally an outright laugh that filled the shed. "Ah, well then, all right. I'll see what I can do—no promises, but I'll see," he said, rubbing the dog. "I guess it would be kind 'a nice to have a dog around."

Mine jumped up, noisily licked his cheeks and then whirled around, wet fur flapping, and did the same to Sarah Emily's giggling face.

"We'd better get back before this storm gets stirred up any more." He took off his hat and rubbed his hand across the top of his hair. He replaced the hat and rose to his feet. "I saw the storm doing nothing but getting worse and knew you couldn't stay out here any longer." He wriggled out of his brown coat. Under it was a smaller black one. "Here, I wore an extra for you." He shucked the second coat and she slipped into it. Then he pulled a large square of canvas from his overalls' front pocket. "Drape this over your head, and let's get inside. Miss Percy doesn't know I've come for you."

Sarah Emily stopped buttoning. "Miss Percy doesn't know?" Her fingers squeezed the round, cold, dented metal.

"No. I didn't tell her. I'll take care of Miss Percy. Now, here's what I want you to do. When we get inside, go straight to the dormitory and dry off," he said, working back into his brown coat. "And as soon as you do that, I'm sure Cook will see to it that you have something to eat. You must be starved."

"Starved? I could eat a rocking chair!"

"Sorry, Cook is fresh out of rocking chairs. Said so, just this afternoon," he told her, reaching out to scratch the dog's head. "And Mine, I'll find something for you to eat too."

"And what about a dry place to hide her 'til we decide how to introduce her to Miss Percy?"

"Okay," he said, shaking his head. "Okay. And can I get you a million dollars or maybe a trip to Europe while I'm at it?"

"No, thank you. That isn't necessary," she said, mimicking a pompous tone. "Something for the dog to eat and a place to sleep will be quite enough for today." She was going to tell him everything that had happened in the shed...about Betsy and Timothy coming...about the rats getting the bread...about the boxes of records.

But he held the door open. "Ready to go? We need to get moving."

Yes, she was ready, but frightened at the thought of Miss Percy's anger. "You know, if Miss Percy finds out you brought me in, we'll both be in trouble," she told him.

"Now, don't you worry. I said I'll take care of Miss Percy."

Just then lightning slashed the sky and Mine snuggled tighter to Sarah Emily.

"Come on," he said. "We've got to get out of here."

"Hurry, Mine. Let's go." Sarah Emily took the canvas, swung it over her head, and pushed against the wind with Mine close beside her. The rain had the trees stuttering and bouncing. Sarah Emily wasn't sure if she was more tired or hungry. "Was it only this morning, Mr. Wilbur, I was sitting on the bench with you, and the sky looked so promising before it turned gray and mad?" she raised her weary voice to be heard over the storm.

"You've had a mighty long day, haven't you?"

"The longest." She sighed as her hunger, weariness and hopelessness from the boxes of destroyed records seemed to, without warning, harden into lead bricks and pile on her back.

Mr. Wilbur must have seen how tired she was because he took her arm and tried to encourage her with, "Come on, the worst is over." His voice wavered in the wind as he kicked a spiny tree limb out of the way.

She wasn't sure the worst was over, but she did have a dog, and something warm to eat was not far off.

The wet trio stopped at Mr. Wilbur's tool barn. Amongst his rakes and shovels, he found an old blanket that would be a perfect bed for Mine.

"Now you behave yourself out here." Sarah Emily knelt beside the dog and kissed the top of her head, feeling a tad better. "Mr. Wilbur will be back with something good for you to eat. I already love you, and you're going to love me. I just know it," she whispered into a soggy ear.

"Oh, I almost forgot to give you a message from Timothy," Mr. Wilson said while he moved some tools back to give the dog plenty of room. "He wanted you to know that Miss Percy sent him to work at the mercantile. In fact, he still wasn't back when I came out here. But that's why he couldn't come to check on you this afternoon. Now, it's inside for you, Sarah Emily Girl."

But she didn't move. Her mind took a loop thinking about Timothy and his concern for her.

"Hey, I thought you were hungry. Let's go." Mr. Wilbur jiggled the door.

"Yeah. I'm hungry and I'm sure Mine is too," she said, looping her mind back.

"But I'm afraid there are no rocking chairs on the menu tonight for either of you."

"One of these days I'm going to bake one so you can see how tasty they are," she said, chuckling with him. Alongside Mr. Wilbur, she made a dash from the tool barn to the back door, barely able to keep her balance as she sloshed in the gushy mud.

When Sarah Emily stepped into the kitchen, the familiar sight of Cook, the warmth of the room and the smell of the vegetable stew made the events of the day melt away.

Cook's stirring in a huge pot came to an abrupt halt, and her eyes grew as big as the biscuits she baked. "Law, child, what are you doing out of that shed? And you, Mr. Wilbur ... " she shook her head at the soaked man. "You've gone and got yourself in trouble again. I don't envy the both of you when Miss Percy finds out what you done." She gave another shake of her head as if there were no words for their foolishness.

"Seems like you and Sarah Emily share the same worries about Miss Percy." Mr. Wilbur took off his wet coat and slung it on the hook beside the door.

"And rightly so," Cook told him, pouring coffee beans into the grinder. "I'll get a pot of good, strong coffee going. Just the way you like it." She turned the dull silver crank, and the rich, unmistakable scent of coffee washed over the room.

"Thanks. That's what I need." Mr. Wilbur hung Sarah Emily's coat.

"I'm off to get out of these wet clothes," Sarah Emily told them as she started toward the stairs.

"There will be a bowl of stew waiting for you," Cook whispered, never looking up from the coffee mill. "Now, not a word to Miss Percy, you hear?"

"Not a word," Sarah Emily whispered back and smiled. She sprang up the steps two at a time, certain that Cook and Mr. Wilbur had the biggest hearts in the whole round world.

At the top of the stairs, she paused as thoughts of Miss Percy barged across her mind. Sarah Emily's stomach clumped. She pressed her hand against the clump, and all at once the string that lashed her thoughts one to another snapped. Questions spilled and rolled in every direction. What will Miss Percy do? Take the leather strap to her, or maybe even send her back to the shed? How was she going to learn who she looked like? And—she pressed her stomach harder—how will Miss Percy take to having a dog?

From the kitchen below, Sarah Emily heard the spoon scraping the sides of the pot and Cook mumbling, "Law, there's going to be trouble tonight. And I don't be knowing nothin'."

Chapter 6

hrough the frosted glass on the office door, Mr. Wilbur could see the silhouetted sharp angles of Miss Percy's bony frame hunched over her desk. He took a second to remind himself to appear casual about bringing Sarah Emily in from the shed. After sucking in a deep, fortifying breath, he knocked.

"Who is it?" Miss Percy snapped.

He heard the bite in her voice and rolled his eyes. He reached up to smooth down his hair, knowing she would go into a snit about it being combed by the whims of the wind or some such nonsense. It would be good to have hair tonic again, if for nothing more than to hush her up.

"It's just me, Jenkins," he said, opening the door, determined to answer her back cheerfully. "I see you're working." There, that sounded cheerful enough.

She looked up, her eyes like knives. "Yes. I'm working. What do you want?"

"I thought that might be the case—you being busy. So with the storm getting bad, I got Sarah Emily out of the shed for you." Pleased at the breezy, off-handed manner he heard from himself, he eased into the crimson wingback chair facing her desk and brushed some imaginary fuzz from his knees.

"What do you mean, you got her out of the shed for me?"

"Is this hot tea, Mildred?" He touched the teapot beside a stack of papers, acting too distracted to have heard her question.

"What *else* would I have in a teapot?" Her voice was pinched, eyes narrowed, while she woodpecker-tapped her pen on the desk. "Now, about Sarah Emily—"

"Wonderful! Hot tea." He cut her off as he stood, wishing for Cook's good coffee. "My cold, wet bones will appreciate that. I'll get myself a cup," he said over his shoulder, walking through the arched doorway to the adjoining parlor.

"Jenkins, I'm talking to you. I asked you a question."

Her fury followed him. "Oh, did you?" He glanced back. "Sorry. What did you ask?" And he kept walking, feeling a bit anxious, hoping he wasn't pushing this nonchalant act too far.

At her exquisite china cabinet, he hooked his finger through the filigreed pull and opened the glass door. From Miss Percy's impressive collection of china cups and saucers, he chose the most masculine one he could find, a cream-colored one wreathed in a simple, dignified gold band. Commanding himself to walk in the manner of a leisurely stroll, he returned to her desk and reached for the teapot. He poured the hot liquid into his cup, intently focusing on each drop.

Mr. Wilbur could hear Miss Percy quickening her pen tapping, while taking in deep, angry breaths. He was careful not to let on he was aware of her huffing with each aggravated heave of her chest. It was a shame she wasn't half as sweet as that rosewater she always wore.

After taking a slow drink of tea, he leaned back into his chair, wiggled about and adjusted the cushion behind him. He hoped now he hadn't gone too far since he was exerting much more commotion than necessary to get settled in a chair. It was beyond his forthright nature to be able to gauge how much was too much. "Powerful storm, isn't it?" He nodded toward the window and lifted the cup to his lips again.

Miss Percy shot up like a sprung spring and leaned over the desk. Since she was not much more than a skeleton in a dress, he was sure he heard her bones rattle. "Jenkins Wilbur," she said, "what *have* you done with Sarah Emily?" Two thin slits of gray eyes fiercely stared at him.

"Why, Mildred, I just brought her in and sent her to the dormitory. It's raining like it's trying to fill an empty ocean out there." He smiled over the gold band on his cup. "I certainly didn't want *you* to have to go out in this sort of weather."

She wilted back in her chair.

Bending forward, he picked up the teapot. "Here, let me pour you some more."

Her cheeks colored to the shade of fresh raspberries. "Why, thank you, Jenkins," she almost purred, fiddling with the collar of her dress.

He loathed it when the only way he could get her to calm down was with bogus charm. Sometimes, a little of that was the only thing that would work with this merciless woman. She usually got over her silly, coquettish responses to it quickly, for which he was thankful. They seemed about as natural on her as a rattlesnake wanting to snuggle.

While he refilled her cup, Mr. Wilbur noticed that, as usual, Miss Percy was drinking from her favorite one—the one sprinkled with tiny yellow flowers inside and out. It always puzzled him why that particular one remained her favorite since it had a sizeable chunk missing from the edge, and she had so many perfect ones to choose from.

Awkwardly holding the cup with her left hand to avoid being cut, she drank with a touch of coy playfulness in her eyes as she gazed at him.

Then, quick as turning a page, something flickered behind her eyes, and she plunked her cup down. A slosh of tea swirled in the matching saucer. A few drops splashed onto her papers, widening into brown ragged spots. "Are you trying to distract me, Jenkins? Because it won't work."

Well, that bout of feminine demureness was gone faster than

usual. He tightened his grip on the cup handle.

"From now on, I'm going to watch that girl like a skinny cat watches a cornered fat mouse. No more pranks or stunts from her. Next time, I'll put her in the shed for—" The clanging of the dinner bell brought Miss Percy's spewing to a curt halt. She picked up her papers, rapped the edges on the desktop, opened a drawer, and dropped the stack into a file folder.

Closing the drawer with a firm shove, she stood. "This business with Sarah Emily is not over! Now I've got to go to the dining room." She secured a stray strand of black hair into its tight coil. "Those orphan brats have been inside all afternoon because of the storm and, I'm sure, will need to be settled down."

Mr. Wilbur cringed, and a burning stung the back of his eyes when she said "orphan brats." He started to tell her how much he hated it when she called them that, like he had done countless other times. He wanted to shout to her that if she would take a minute and notice, she would see how wonderful they were, each of them. But what he really wanted to say was that what she was doing to them was unforgivable. Instead, he bit his tongue for Sarah Emily's sake. Now was not the smart time to say any of that.

So he said, "I'll just finish my tea and be along in a minute." The door slammed behind her. Quickly, he put his cup down. *Whew, I'm glad I don't have to drink another drop. Why doesn't that woman ever have coffee?* But his dislike of tea was soon forgotten as he hurried down the back stairs to the kitchen, the comforting aroma of coffee coming to meet him.

In the kitchen, Cook was moving about with efficiency, pouring cold milk into pitchers. Near the back door Mr. Wilbur saw crates stacked head high.

"Looks like this month's rations got here," he said, pouring himself a cup of coffee, eager to run the tea taste out of his mouth.

"Came right after you and Sarah Emily went upstairs. I had to stop and clean up the mud the delivery boys tracked all over my clean floor."

"Number right this time?" he asked, blowing steamy spirals off his coffee.

"What do you think? Look for yourself," she told him.

He opened the beige envelope laying on the top crate. He pulled out a thin sheet of paper that crackled like crickets as he unfolded it. In large swooping letters it read: rations for thirty-seven orphans and staff. It was signed in the same swooping hand: State of Illinois. It always made him snigger that the State of Illinois had such nice handwriting or could even hold a pen, for that matter.

"Right now, there are thirty-four orphans, and you, me, Miss Percy and Miss Dickens to feed," Cook said. "Don't that make thirty-eight by your ciphering?"

"Certainly does. Thirty-eight right on the nose." He smiled.

"It's not funny, Jenkins. It doesn't matter if one person leaves or four leave or ten come, the state is always one short with the rations they send. It beats everything the way they can always be one short like that," she said, stirring the pot too hard.

"No wonder the allotment the state office gives me for the other things I have to buy at the mercantile don't go far. Of course, it's not enough to begin with, but I'm always having to stretch because the rations are always one short. One short." She huffed and seemed to run out of steam.

They went through this every month. He suspected that sometimes Cook used some of her meager salary to buy extra food, just like if he knew things were running low, when he could, he would slip some money into the account at the mercantile, though neither of them ever talked about it.

"Did Sarah Emily get dried off? She hasn't come down to eat," Cook said.

"I don't know what's taking her so long. I've been with Miss Percy."

"Don't tell me nothin'." She filled the last pitcher with milk.

"You know I won't." He patted her shoulder as he shuffled sideways past her. On the cast-iron stove, true to her word, there sat a big bowl of vegetable stew off to one side. Gratitude and admiration for Cook surged in him for how hard she worked to fix good meals, and for the tender hugs and kisses and pats she gave, touching each orphan like every child deserved to be touched. It was those motherly, loving gestures she sneaked in that kept their spirits from starving. All was done without fanfare, and certainly without Miss Percy knowing. Yes, Cook was far more valuable than just for her cooking.

"So, you were gone again this afternoon." He drank, savoring the strong coffee.

Cook pulled a large ladle out of a crock full of upended cooking utensils. "I was?" She arched an eyebrow.

"Still not going to tell me where you've been spending your afternoons, huh?"

She sunk the ladle into the kettle. "Make yourself useful and tote this stew to the dining room."

"I guess you're not," he mumbled, chuckling to himself. Then he swallowed the last swig of coffee before setting his cup down and picking up the kettle. When he returned to the kitchen, he leaned against the pantry doorframe and watched Cook slice bread. He decided now was as good a time as any to bring up the dog. "Did I mention Sarah Emily found a dog today?" He made it sound like an everyday occurrence. "I've got it hidden in the tool barn, and I was wondering what the four-legged critter could eat tonight."

Cook plunked the knife down. "Law, a dog! Miss Percy isn't going to be liking this. No, not liking this one little bit. Does that girl go looking for the wagonloads of mischief she gets herself tangled up in? Wasn't a day in that shed enough?" All the while she fussed, she gathered several soup bones and dropped them into a black pail. They clunked against the metal bottom. Then she took three thick slices of bread she had just cut, dunked them in the pot of vegetable stew until they were saturated to the point of dripping and dropped them into the pail. They hit with a soft slush. She turned to Mr. Wilbur. "I don't be knowing nothin'."

"I know." He nodded at Cook's favorite expression when she didn't want Miss Percy to know what she was doing.

Cook set the pail by the back door and went to the sink. "Get some bread out for Sarah Emily before I take the rest of those baskets to the dining room," she said, pumping water to wash her hands.

Mr. Wilbur pushed himself off the doorframe. At the oak worktable in the middle of the kitchen, he took three slices of bread, laid them on a small plate and put it beside the stew. "Cook," he said.

She finished drying her hands and rehung the towel, looking over her shoulder. "What?"

"You really are a dear. I don't know what any of us would do without you."

A slight, bashful smile played at the corners of her mouth. "You'd have somebody else doing the cooking, that's what you'd do. And you'd be doing just fine." Then her whole face became a smile, causing her caramel-colored cheeks to rise into plump balls. "Now you stop that silly talk. And just remember—"

"That you don't be knowing nothin'." He finished her familiar sentence. "I know you don't want it talked about so Miss Percy finds out what you do for Sarah Emily and the others. And goodness knows, I'm not going to tell her. But it really does make a difference around here, all the kindness and, well, just the loving things you do. I am curious, though, about what you've been up to these past months, nearly every afternoon." He held up his hands in mock surrender. "But I'm not going to push."

"It wouldn't do you no good if you did push." She tilted her head to one side. "You'll know soon enough. I learned a long time ago there are some things in this life we can't do nothin' about. And to my way of seeing things, Miss Percy is one of them." A sharp glint shot from her eyes and she spoke firmly. "So I'm spending my afternoons working on something I can do. I think life would be better for folks, no matter who they be, if they'd follow that rule."

"You're right about that." He nodded and buttered a thick heel chunk of bread to his taste, the best part.

"Of course, I'm right." Cook smiled, and the pleasant expression she usually wore came back.

"Okay. No more questions about what you're doing." He bit off a corner of bread.

"Good. But I do want to say something about what *you're* doing."

"What *I'm* doing?" he said, nearly choking on the mouthful of bread.

"Yes, this morning in the dining room when you told Miss Percy you'd buy that lace for Cora in front of everyone. You need to be more careful about being so—I don't know—so bold. We can do a lot more quietly, around the edges, not intruding on her show of authority. That seems important to her for who knows what kind of crazy reason."

"Aha! You can scold me, but whatever you're doing is a big, well-kept secret." He feigned irritation, but she was right. "You've warned me about this before. It's just that when she takes off on a rampage like she did this morning over that scrap of rag Cora had, it makes me so angry. There's just no call for her to act like that."

"You don't think I don't want to snatch that scrawny woman up and smack her across this worktable when I hear her carrying on like that? But I know it'd just get me fired and then what good would I be to these dear orphans?" Cook's voice softened. "I understand what makes you do what you do; all's I'm saying is, be careful. You know, as well as I do, that you'd be one miserable old man if you had to look for work someplace else." Then she headed for the dining room with her arms full of bread baskets, and at the same time, Sarah Emily bounded in.

"I put on dry clothes, but I'm still freezing." She tugged the coal-colored shawl tighter around her arms.

"Cook and I were beginning to wonder what was taking you so long. Thought after your day of adventure, you might've gone to sleep." He put Cook's reprimand aside for now, but he wasn't dismissing it. He'd learned long ago, Cook had a way of being wise that shouldn't be ignored.

"Too cold. And remember, I'm starving," Sarah Emily said, reaching for the bowl of stew.

Cook hurried back into the kitchen. "Law, child, don't eat standing up." Grabbing the back of a straight chair, she moved it to the corner, out of view of anyone entering from the dining room. "There, now sit down and enjoy your supper. If Miss Percy comes in, she won't see you."

"Thanks." Sarah Emily sat down.

Mr. Wilbur moved the plate of bread to the cabinet next to her.

"Rations come in right this month?" Sarah Emily asked, eyeing the crates.

"If one short is right," Cook said.

"I've seen a few of the lists from the state office with all our names, and mine isn't ever on it," Sarah Emily said. "Don't you think that's strange since I've been here twelve years?"

"Who knows who's keeping those records. But I do know, they can't count," Cook answered.

"Since we can't do anything about that, have either of you seen Betsy?" Sarah Emily asked between bites of stew.

"Not since Miss Percy called her out of class this afternoon," Mr. Wilbur said, pouring himself another cup of coffee.

Cook stopped wiping crumbs off the worktable. "I just saw Betsy come in the dining room. Why?"

Sarah Emily took another bite and lowered the bowl to her lap. "While I changed clothes, she was in the dormitory. And I thought she seemed more than upset about getting her hair cut, closer to sad. I can understand, though, with the gorgeous hair she has. The color is like a canary with a shimmer of gold dust sprinkled on its feathers, don't you think?"

"That it is," Cook said as she plunged the dishcloth into soapy water.

Sarah Emily reached for a piece of bread, laid it back down, looked at Cook and then at Mr. Wilbur. "Why does Miss Percy whack our hair off anyway?"

Cook wrung out the cloth and began wiping the stovetop. "You know Miss Percy says it's easier to keep your hair clean that way, and it makes it harder for lice to take hold. But if I had my suspicions, I'd say there's more to it than that."

"What do you mean?" Sarah Emily picked up the bread and this time took a good-sized bite.

"To be honest, I don't rightly know." Cook stopped in mid-swipe.

"But it seems to me her reasons push her stronger to cut it than just wanting you all to have clean heads."

Mr. Wilbur refilled his coffee cup, waiting to set the pot down while Cook continued her swabbing. "I do have to admit that's true enough about it being more than just easier to keep clean. But why Miss Percy does most of what she does is a mystery to all of us."

"Yeah. Like making us hold onto the rope 'til we're sixteen. That is just plain ridiculous. Past about seven years old, we shouldn't have to do that," Sarah Emily said, clearly disgusted.

Cook nodded in agreement, then turned to Mr. Wilbur. "And while we're talking about hair, why's yours sticking up like a ghost tapped you on the shoulder and said, 'Boo?'"

He nearly dropped the coffeepot back onto the stove. His hand went to his hair. "I'm out of hair tonic. Can't a man run out of hair tonic without everyone making it a public debate?" He wished he hadn't sounded so gruff or appeared so rattled.

"No need to hiss like a wet cat." Cook tossed the dishcloth into the sink, dried her hands on her apron, picked up two milk pitchers and started toward the dining room. "It's just not like you to have your hair in such a mess. Besides, you were in River Bend yesterday." She looked back. "Isn't it the mercantile there that carries the kind of tonic you like?"

"Yes," he said firmly, making sure he had sanded the rough edge from his tone. "I just forgot to pick up some. Now, what was it you were about to do in the dining room?"

"Take this milk and see how Nettie's coming with the serving." Cook left the kitchen without another word about his unruly hair.

Sarah Emily ran her hand up the back of her own neck. "Miss Percy makes us look like boys, the way she keeps our hair so short. Except I've got this right in front." She rolled her eyes up toward her fast-growing bangs. "It grows faster than the rest and hangs in my eyes. At least this Christmas I'll get one of the hair clasps the Ladies' Aid Society gives us when we've turned sixteen."

At the mention of the hair clasps, Mr. Wilbur's mind swerved to his encounter in town two weeks ago when he'd overheard some of

the women from that group talking. They were buying drapery material for their meeting hall, saying their old drapes were in tatters, and
they couldn't stand them one minute longer. Of course, that meant
they'd have to cut corners in their budget someplace, one of them
had said. They hated it, but the only place they could find that all
agreed on was the hair clasps at Christmas for the older girls at the
orphan asylum. *Ladies' Aid Society,* his mind growled. Aid? Who?

After Sarah Emily spent the day in the shed, he wasn't about to
tell her they weren't giving the hair clasps this year. He hoped, if he
had figured right, she wouldn't have to be disappointed anyway.
He was squeezing his pennies a little tighter and not buying hair
tonic for himself. And then, maybe, he could get the girls their hair
clasps for Christmas. He wasn't going to say anything, even to
Cook, in case he couldn't save enough money.

He realized he was clenching his teeth so hard his jaw ached, and
Sarah Emily was still talking. He raked his fingers through his hair
and centered his attention on her as if he had not missed a word.

"Until Christmas," she was saying, "as bad as I hate having my
hair cut, I'd cut this worrisome chunk if I could get a hold of Miss
Percy's scissors. Now, what about the dog? Did you get her something to eat?" Positioning the stew bowl under her chin, she
finished off the last bites, peering up at Mr. Wilbur.

"Whoa, girl." He reared back and laughed, glad to be off the
subject of hair clasps and, in general, hair, hers and his. "When you
get going, there's no stopping you. You go from subject to subject
quicker than a frog jumping lily pads."

"Sorry. I guess I've got too many things on my mind right now."
Sarah Emily put the empty bowl on the counter. "I don't care what
Miss Percy says. That dog is going to live right here with me. She's
an orphan. I just know it." Sarah Emily lowered her voice. "And
Mr. Wilbur, I've got to find out about my folks. I want to know
who I look like." Her shoulders visibly drooped, and she stared at
the floor. After a long pause, she said, "Being an orphan leaves you
with so many unanswered questions that you have a hole in your
heart so big you can hear the wind howling right through."

"I know, but Sarah Emily Girl—" He paused for a ragged sigh

to escape. "You won't always be living here. One day you'll have a family and home of your own. You can't just think of yourself as an orphan. Your future is fresh snow, just waiting for your footprints to make a path in it."

How he wished he could make life better for her and for the others. But the state agency only cared that Miss Percy didn't cause any fuss, operated on a strict budget and took in as many orphans as they sent. As long as she did those things, he knew, nothing would change—which was another reason to heed Cook's advice that he not challenge Miss Percy publicly. There were other jobs with much better conditions, but where could he work where he felt needed as much as here?

Cook bustled back in.

"You can't count on life always being fair." Mr. Wilbur gripped the edge of the cabinet. "Because it's not."

"Law, if that's not the truth. Life's not always fair." Cook's smile was as broad as a melon slice. "But you do have some say in how you handle it."

"This is a day to mark on the calendar, for sure." Mr. Wilbur chuckled, scratching his weather-worn nose. "Cook's been telling us how she feels about things."

"Shush. You don't need to be marking anything."

His gaze left Cook and touched Sarah Emily. "Cook's right, you know. It's more important what we *do* with the hard things that come to us."

"I suppose you're both right. But yesterday, at the corner of Lilac Lane—"

"Here. Eat this, quick." Cook handed Sarah Emily a hot biscuit, sliced through the middle, spread with blackberry preserves and put back together sandwich-style.

"This is one of Miss Percy's biscuits! We never get these."

"With the day you've had, I figure you deserve it," Cook said.

"And with preserves." Sarah Emily lifted the warm treat to her nose. "This smells almost too good to eat."

"You best be eating it, or I will," Mr. Wilbur teased, graying eyebrows shooting up.

Lifting the top of the biscuit, Sarah Emily licked off a tongue-width path of preserves, closed her eyes and smacked her lips. "It tastes like a bowl of fresh blackberries sprinkled with sugar."

"You love preserves better than anyone I ever be knowin'," Cook said, piling Miss Percy's biscuits on her pink plate.

"You're right. I do love them." Sarah Emily put the biscuit to her mouth, cupping her hand underneath to catch the crumbs. She had downed the last of it and was wiping her sticky hands on a towel when Miss Percy barged through the door.

"Where are my biscuits?"

Sarah Emily sat still as a stick.

"Right here," Cook said as she handed Miss Percy a tray. "And a bowl of your blackberry preserves too. No need to get so excited."

"Bring me a pot of tea." The strike of Miss Percy's heels marching out stamped an angry rhythm on the wooden floor, each footfall setting with precision.

Cook pressed her hands into her round hips. "It's about as impossible for that woman to be civil as it is for an empty flour sack to stand upright."

"Yep. Just about as impossible." Mr. Wilbur poured himself a half-cup of coffee.

"That was too close for me," Sarah Emily said, setting her dishes in the sink. "I'd better get upstairs. Besides, Betsy was going to eat fast and meet me in the dormitory so we could talk. But I want you to know I appreciate the supper."

"Cook's got a fine meal all prepared for the dog too." Mr. Wilbur gulped down the coffee, laid his cup in the sink and grabbed the pail's handle. "I'll go on out with this and make sure she's okay for the night."

"You two are the best," Sarah Emily said, her tone and smile sincerely grateful.

It was easy for him to see she felt that way. She depended on them, but there was only so much they could do. Ah, well, he swung the pail and made his way to the tool barn. He, like Cook, would do what he could. And just what *is* she doing? He smiled to himself.

Chapter 7

Once in the dormitory, Sarah Emily quickly shimmied into her long-sleeved flannel nightgown and climbed into bed. Tucking the covers under her chin, she held the blanket against her as tight and snug as a vine climbing a wall. The stew had helped to warm her, but she was still chilled from a draft that blew in from a gap around the window frame. She would tell Mr. Wilbur about it tomorrow. "Mr. Wilbur!" *I got so caught up in the biscuit from Cook that I forgot to tell him about the mothers and baby I saw on the corner.*

At that moment, Betsy hurried in, saying, "I ate as fast as I could."

Sarah Emily sat up, willing her gaze away from Betsy's hair—jagged, yellow spikes that had been hacked with angry scissors. At least Sarah Emily had something happier to talk about that might help Betsy to get her mind off what had happened to her hair. As soon as Betsy closed the door behind her, Sarah Emily said, "I'm glad you beat the others back here. I've got something to tell you."

"About your day in the shed? I know it must have been awful." Betsy walked across the room, but she looked like either she wasn't quite sure how to hold her head anymore, or her head didn't fit right on her body.

Then again, Sarah Emily thought, it might be sadness, the kind that comes down so hard it throws you off balance. Sarah Emily reached for Betsy's hands. "Yes, being in the shed was awful. But something good happened."

"Something good?" Betsy lowered herself to the edge of the bed, her hands still in Sarah Emily's.

"You'll never guess what came to me today while I was in that terrible place. A dog! A dog came to me."

"A dog? Can we have a dog?"

"Well, actually, no one has." Sarah Emily let Betsy's hands slide out as she leaned back on her pillow, nibbling the side of her bottom lip. "It must be that Miss Percy doesn't like dogs. That must be it. And that's probably why we never had one. So, that means we've got to make certain, sure and certain, that she likes *this* one."

"Tell me all about the dog." Betsy's interest was apparent in her grin.

Sarah Emily had been so intrigued by Betsy's exuberant golden hair with its flowing curls that this was the first time she had noticed that when Betsy truly smiled, deep dimples appeared. "Oh, Betsy, the dog's adorable. She's light brown—near about the color of a newborn fawn. And her ears, they are the cutest or maybe the silliest, I haven't decided yet—one flops down and the other shoots straight up." Giggling, Sarah Emily flung both hands in opposite directions. "Like this." Then she gathered her knees up to her chin, wrapping her arms around her lanky legs. "So I named her the best name I could think of—Mine. She found me when I was locked up in that awful old shed, and she waited outside, even though she was wet as a fish. Betsy, you'll see real soon, that in an orphan asylum there isn't a lot a person can really and truly call *mine.*"

"I know." Betsy touched her hair and then snatched her fingers away as quickly as if they had touched a cold, dead body. "How *are* you going to get Miss Percy to let you keep a dog?"

Sarah Emily dismissed the question with a wave. "I've just had the best idea." Clapping once, she pressed her folded hands against her chest. "So let's not worry about Miss Percy right now. Here's my idea. What if I name the dog Ours? That way you, Timothy and I can share her. We'll all have something. You're going to love her. I just know it."

"I've never had a dog before. It sounds wonderful! But what about Miss Percy?"

"That is a problem." This time, Sarah Emily considered the question. "There's got to be a way to make Miss Percy think she *needs* Ours to live here. We *are* going to keep this dog! I just know it."

"You've said that about a hundred times since I came yesterday."

"Said what?"

"'I just know it.' You keep saying, 'I just know it.' How do you know?"

"Oh, that. It's just that, well—life—it doesn't always seem to fit right. There's little I have any control over. And so saying 'I just know it,' silly as it sounds, gives me some power, inside my own head anyway. It's not much, but it makes me feel better."

"Just the little I've seen of Miss Percy, I don't see how this can be one of those times that you know." Betsy leaned in, her dimples showing, and put a hand on each of Sarah Emily's poking-up knees. "But I'd love to be wrong."

"I know. Having a dog would be about the best thing to happen here. I'll think of something," Sarah Emily said, glad that talk of the dog pleased Betsy. "But, now, tell me, how was your first day here?"

Betsy's reaction was immediate. "I miss being home. I really miss it. I've never been with so many other folks before."

Sarah Emily's heart stammered. "I know, you'll never like it here. None of us do. But I told you last night, you'll get used to it." Maybe if she said that often enough, Betsy would start to believe it. Sarah Emily let her gaze roam the dormitory. The gray wall where their nightgowns drooped like withered scarecrows. The beds lined up in the center of the dormitory floor so Miss Percy could march up, down and around each one, brandishing her strap. The tattered gray blankets that covered the beds. The shabby pieces of old sheets at the windows that were supposed to be curtains. No, how ridiculous—Betsy wouldn't believe the lie no matter how often it was said.

So she may as well lay out the truth of their situation. "We really don't have any choice except running away—and where would we go? Some of the girls have run away and gotten married. I think they'd marry anybody to get out of here. Marjorie's run away a couple of times, not to get married, although she does have a boyfriend. But the sheriff always brings her back. If you ask me, it'd suit me if he didn't. She's a loner, and trouble is never far behind her."

"Really? A boyfriend?"

"Yeah. I don't know who he is, but she slips out at night a lot, she told me, to see him."

"Speaking of boyfriends," Betsy perked her eyes and lips upward, "is Timothy your boyfriend?"

"Boyfriend? Gracious sakes, no. Where ever did you get that idea?" Sarah Emily was more flustered by the question than she would have expected.

"I guess I got that idea seeing how much he cares about you."

"It was Timothy who rescued me the day my pa left me here, and ever since we've been best friends."

"That's wonderful," Betsy said. "Pa never let us go nowhere or have friends. But Faith and I were best friends." Gloom masked Betsy's face.

If Sarah Emily could get Betsy to talk about her home, it might help her. And, too, Sarah Emily wanted the conversation about Timothy being a boyfriend to end. "So!" Sarah Emily said, leaning against her pillow. "Tell me about your home."

"Sure." Betsy's expression brightened and she drew her legs up on the bed. "It's small—on a couple of acres that Pa farmed. Ma had the house fixed nice and homey. I know because Faith tried to keep it that way."

Excitement and yearning tumbled together in Sarah Emily's heart at hearing about a real home. "What was your favorite thing?"

"Oh, that's easy! I had three favorite things: the little room that Faith and I shared, Ma's pink and white china in a pine cupboard in the dining room, and her flower garden that she'd planted with all the colors of tulip bulbs when she found out she was going to have another baby. She and Pa were so excited because they'd begun to think Faith was going to be their only child."

"And those tulips kept blooming year after year. I half expected Pa to pull them up, seeing as they were in celebration of my being born." Tears plumped in Betsy's eyes. "But I hoped he wouldn't because whenever I saw them, I felt they were Ma's way of saying she was glad about me. Of course, she didn't know my coming would cause her to die." The plop, plop, plop sounds of Betsy's tears echoed through the room as they hit the bed. She pressed her fingers into both closed eyes, covering her face.

Sarah Emily tipped forward and laid her hand on Betsy's arm. If she thought she was cheering Betsy up, clearly she wasn't. "Maybe you can get your ma's china since you don't have any other family," Sarah Emily said softly, hoping that would help.

"I'd like that." Betsy sniffed, roughly drying her cheeks with her sleeve. "But there's not much chance of that. I heard Mrs. Clay tell Miss Percy, when she brought me here yesterday, that everything is being sold to pay Pa's debts."

"And that's probably true. He was drinking so bad the last couple of years, he didn't farm much. He owed everybody money. And if I know anything, I know Mrs. Clay will take Ma's china, because she's admired it as long as I can remember." Her voice fell flat. "Probably already packed it up, took it to her house and eaten a meal off it."

"I'm sorry, Betsy. Life for orphans just isn't right. It just isn't right." They sat silent. What else could she say? It wasn't right. That was the long and short of it. Just one more thing to cram to the bottom of her heart. After several silent drawn-out minutes, Sarah Emily asked, "How did you spend this afternoon, you know, after Miss Percy cut your hair?"

Betsy's fingers immediately slid across the bottom of her unevenly chopped-off hair. She dropped her hands to her lap and took a deep breath. "It was hard for me to concentrate after, you know…" She touched her head again, "but Miss Percy told me to look around so I'd figure out where things were. I think I've gotten a feel, though I got a might turned around coming back from supper. Thankfully, Nettie saw me and pointed me in the right direction. Of course, I couldn't go outside today, because of the storm, but I've been wondering about those beautiful houses we passed as we came down Lilac Lane yesterday."

"Yeah. Aren't they the biggest, grandest houses you ever did see?"

"I never knew houses could be so big."

"Rich folks live in them. And there's more big houses on the streets behind us on the other side of the woods," Sarah Emily said. "This used to be the schoolhouse for those rich folk's children. They were the only ones in the state to have a three-story schoolhouse. Anyway, a fire gutted it, didn't burn it down, but pretty much ruined the insides. Somehow the parents got the state to build them another building, even fancier, a few streets over. It has a bigger play yard, and last year they put in an indoor necessary room."

"Indoors?" Betsy's eyes widened and didn't blink for several seconds.

"Of course, I've never seen it, but I've heard it's indoors."

"Imagine!" Betsy shook her head. "So how did this become an orphan asylum?"

"The old orphan asylum was across town, but that building was falling down and wasn't big enough. Since the state owned this building, they fixed the insides from the fire." She sat up and spread out her arms. "So here we are. They moved here just before I came. But the neighbors have never been one bit happy about having us down here, even after all these years. I heard they thought this building would be torn down and a beautiful park put here or another fancy house. They call us, 'That end of Lilac Lane.' And you can be sure, they say 'that' even meaner than I just did." She folded her hands and laid them in her lap. "They don't even like us walking down the street."

They talked on, and then she told Betsy all about the boxes of musty, mangled records she had discovered in the shed.

"Just how did it come to be that you're an orphan?" Betsy's finger burrowed into her hair, searching frantically for a piece long enough to twist.

Since there wasn't any, Sarah Emily watched Betsy settle for twirling her finger round and round, pushing the hair down flat in a little circle, showing a dot of pink scalp in the center. It angered Sarah Emily to see the pain in Betsy's eyes. *Where does Miss Percy come up with these ideas?*

Somehow Sarah Emily managed to skirt around her anger and steer her thoughts back onto the right road. *About how I came to be an orphan.* She stretched out her long legs. "Before I came here, I don't remember much. And Miss Percy won't tell us anything about our families. But I'm almost certain Ma died, and I kind of remember living with my grandparents. Then when I was four-years-old, Pa brought me here."

"How old are you now?"

"I'll be sixteen next month, October 26. How old are you?"

"We're almost the same age," Betsy said, seeming to like that. "I'll be sixteen January 13. You were saying about living with your grandparents—what happened to them?"

"Like I said, I don't remember much, but I think they died, too."

"But your pa, he's alive?"

"I guess so. Although I don't know that for a fact because he never has come to see me." For a second, she closed her eyes against that painful rejection, but she wouldn't allow herself to stay there. "Would you like to see my parents photograph?" she asked. "It was taken right before they got married. I think that's when because Ma isn't wearing a wedding ring."

"You got a photograph?" Again, Betsy's dimples showed themselves.

"Yeah. Right here." Sarah Emily bent over the side of her bed, pulled out the cardboard carton and carefully lifted out her precious mahogany box.

At once, Betsy touched the polished wood. "Where did you get this?"

"The box belonged to my ma. Pa said she loved it, and he gave it to me the day he left me here. This photograph of the two of them was inside."

Betsy held the sepia-toned picture up to the oil lamp, studying it for a long time. "How come you keep it under your bed instead of on your shelf in the wardrobe?" she asked, turning the picture more toward the light.

"I like the feeling of having my parents close at night."

"I can understand that. They surely are a handsome couple." Betsy handed the photograph back.

"Yes, they are." Sarah Emily examined the faces. "Wouldn't it be something if you could order the people on a picture to come to life, or could shake it so the people tumbled off, stretched to full size and took off with life right where the photograph captured them?" Sarah Emily traced the faces of her parents with a light finger. "I'd love to know who I look like. But I can't tell that I look like either of them."

"I know you can't tell from the picture, but don't you know if your ma or pa had green eyes like you do? Or your light brown hair?"

"No, but I need to find out." Sarah Emily put the photograph away and slid the box under her bed, wondering just how she would go about that. Without knowing who she looked like, she was standing on the stringy, loose fringe of life.

"I wish I had a photograph of my folks," Betsy said. "Since Ma died when I was born, and we don't have any photographs, I don't know what she looked like." Then she sat up straight and proud. "But Faith used to say my hair was the same color as hers."

"You look like your ma?" Sarah Emily could hardly get the question out fast enough. She scooted closer to Betsy and said it again, "You look like your ma?"

Betsy looked startled. "I don't know if I favor her. I only know her hair was yellow like mine, and she wore it long. Is that what you mean?"

"I guess so. I'm not sure. What else do you know about your ma?" Sarah Emily kept her eyes buckled on Betsy.

"Pa loved to tell about how after she washed her hair, it smelled as fresh as a spring rain, and how pretty it looked when she'd tie it back with a pink, satin ribbon.

"The hairbrush, that was hers. Pa kept it on the dresser in their room, but Faith and I used to sneak in there and use it. As soon as Mrs. Clay told me to get my things together, I knew right then, I'd never see that house again or anything in it. I couldn't bring ma's dishes, but I could bring her brush. I guess now it *really* is all I have left of her."

Betsy's shoulders curled anxiously forward. "Today, while Miss Percy was chopping my hair off, it pained me—not on my head, but inside." Betsy pressed her palm into her stomach. "Right here." Her expression sagged as if her face were made of dough. "It was like she was yanking my ma away from me—again."

"Miss Percy doesn't give much thought as to how we feel about anything," Sarah Emily said somberly. The events in the dining room that morning rushed to Sarah Emily's mind, and she remembered Betsy's humming. "What was that song you hummed while you were rubbing my head?"

"That was 'Skip to My Lou,'" Betsy said, livening up.

At last, Sarah Emily relaxed. She had landed on a subject that didn't seem to inflict pain on Betsy.

"One time Pa sent me to the next county to get eggs and a couple of laying hens 'cause ours all died of a sickness that plagued the chickens in our area. Anyway, on my way home, I passed this church, and they must've been having a party. It was so beautiful." Betsy stared out the window and seemed to drift away from the dormitory to watch the party again. "They were on the front lawn with oil lamps lighting up the night, and the moon was round and fat, hanging right above the steeple. A man was playing the fiddle while the rest were singing and skipping around in a big circle. I'd never seen folks enjoying so much merriment."

Betsy bounced from the bed. "Do you want me to show you how it goes, with the words and the skipping?"

"Can you?" Sarah Emily, caught in Betsy's excitement, sat up straight and hugged her knees to her chest.

"I sure can! Each boy joins hands with a girl, and they all form a circle with one boy standing alone in the center. Then, while the group skips around him, he picks a girl, and her partner has to go into the center." Betsy held her hand out to an imaginary boy and began to skip and sing around the iron beds, "Lost my partner, what'll I do? Lost my partner, what'll I do? Lost my partner, what'll I do? Skip to my Lou, my darling."

Sarah Emily was mesmerized by the sweet clarity of Betsy's voice as she sang and danced around the grim dormitory.

With bliss beaming from her face, Betsy skipped by Sarah Emily's bed, grabbed her hand and pulled her up. Never missing a beat of the song, she sang, "Little red wagon, painted blue, little red wagon, painted blue," while Sarah Emily gleefully skipped beside her.

By the time Betsy got to the last verse, "Skipping faster, that won't do, Skipping faster, that won't do," the two collapsed onto Sarah Emily's bed, lost in a giant bubble of laughter.

After she caught her breath, Sarah Emily rolled over to look at Betsy. "That was fun and the loveliest singing I ever heard."

"I love to sing. Music comes real natural to me. Pa wouldn't let me sing a note when I was around him. He said Ma sang while she did her chores." Her voice began to shake like brittle leaves as she said, "He told me he couldn't stand to hear no more singing after she was gone. Faith said it was because I sounded exactly like her. I guess he couldn't do much about my hair looking like hers, but my singing…"

Sarah Emily sat up, alert. "Your hair is the same color as your ma's, *and* you sing like her?" She must have been more forceful than she meant because Betsy drew back slightly.

"I don't know what you're getting at."

"It's special for you to know who you look like."

"Well, then I guess I look a little like my ma, but I wish I could have sung with her—even if only once. Ever since I heard this song and saw what great fun it was bringing, I've had a longing in my spirit to have a party and have everyone smiling and skipping to my Lou!"

"That would be wonderful!"

They lay back flat across the bed, legs dangling off the side, with Betsy humming her tune.

"Betsy," Sarah Emily whispered, several minutes later, "Did you cry when Miss Percy cut your hair off?"

"No!"

Sarah Emily was stunned at the abruptness of Betsy's answer, but before she could say anything, the clock in the hall announced it was time to get ready for bed. The other girls rushed in, and a torrent of activity began as nightclothes replaced dresses and stockings.

Soon Miss Percy would appear with her black leather strap.

When the clock gave off eight mournful dongs, Miss Percy arrived in a cloud of sweet rosewater. Miss Percy went directly to Sarah Emily's bed, and towering over her, snapped the leather strap. "You will help Cook for the next week with breakfast. And that starts tomorrow morning. You are to be up an hour before everyone else. If you are late, it will be two more weeks. Do you understand me?" Miss Percy's sharp words echoed in the tense silence of the room.

"Yes," Sarah Emily answered so small she could scarcely hear herself.

Miss Percy's glare swept around the beds. "Get to sleep, you orphan brats." She lowered the wick, and the light from the oil lamp went out of the dormitory. So did Miss Percy.

Sarah Emily lay thinking about Ours, her day in the shed, Betsy's yellow hair and beautiful singing.

"Sarah Emily, are you awake?" Betsy whispered.

"Yes."

Betsy climbed out of her bed and knelt beside Sarah Emily's. She put her arm on the edge of the bed and rested her chin on it. "I'm sorry about you getting another punishment because of me."

"Don't worry, it was only Miss Percy's strap I was scared of, and she didn't hit me. Being with Cook isn't punishment at all."

"That's good." Betsy didn't move for a minute, then she lifted her head. "I wanted to tell you how come I didn't cry while Miss Percy was cutting off my hair."

Sarah Emily rolled over to face her and saw the puddle of moonlight framing ragged, pointed shadows from Betsy's hair onto her face.

"Faith used to say that courage is like a kite. You don't know if it's any good 'til you get it in a fierce northwest wind. That's when it really flies its highest and best. I had to know I was going to have courage to live here without my sister. Miss Percy cutting my hair was like my fierce northwest wind."

"Did you want to cry?"

"I wanted to cry. I wanted to scream. I wanted to hit her, but I knew none of that would do any good. Faith thought courage was important. She said our ma was a woman of courage."

"You've got courage too, Betsy. And someday we'll have long hair. I just know it."

Betsy started to get up, but hesitated. "Sarah Emily," came her halting whisper, "can I tell you something else?"

"Sure."

"After Miss Percy was through cutting my hair off, and she left me alone, I cried."

Chapter 8

he next morning while Sarah Emily dressed without making a sound, she saw all the girls were still fast asleep—all except Marjorie, who was in bed with her dress on and had snatched the covers over herself when Sarah Emily got up. But, this morning she couldn't be bothered with Marjorie and her boyfriend's escapades. Besides, most of the time it was best not to know what Marjorie was up to anyway.

Sarah Emily grabbed her coat and made her way toward the door. That early-morning, glorious, rich scent of cinnamon rose to her nose.

"I'll come help you."

Startled by Betsy's loud whisper, Sarah Emily turned and saw Betsy sitting up, pushing back her blanket. Instead of lush curls tumbling around her face, spikes of hair shot every which way.

"Go on down so you won't be late." Betsy waved toward the door. "I'll get dressed and be there in half a minute."

"No, you don't have to," Sarah Emily mouthed, as she tiptoed toward Betsy's bed. "But thanks for offering to help."

"I was the one who should have been in the shed, not you."

"That's not your fault. But, I mean it, thanks for offering to help." Sarah Emily smiled. It was hard to believe Betsy had been at the orphan asylum only two days because Sarah Emily already felt like they had been friends forever. She bent down closer to Betsy, afraid their talking would wake the others. "Before reporting to Cook, I'm going to make a quick check on Ours to see how she fared last night."

"Tell her to be looking for me too," Betsy whispered back. "I'll come meet her today." Betsy got out of bed, shivering and rubbing her arms. "Any ideas yet on how to get Miss Percy to accept her?"

"Not yet. I'm still working on it. Now, listen, you can't help me this morning. Miss Percy would be even madder, and then we'd both be in trouble. No need for that." Sarah Emily pulled on her coat. "It's cold. Get back under the covers and try to get a little more sleep. I'll be fine."

When Betsy acted reluctant, Sarah Emily urged her again. "Really, it'll be better if you don't come with me."

"Okay." Betsy edged into bed, covering up. "I sure don't want to get you in any more trouble."

"Don't worry. See you at breakfast." Sarah Emily quietly closed the door behind her, thrilled with the wonder of having a true girl-friend. There were other girls she enjoyed, like Nettie, the last girl to come before Betsy. Nettie was sweet, and who wouldn't love her endearing unguarded eagerness to be kind? But Nettie was much younger, only eleven years old.

Timothy had always been her best friend. He'd been the one to help her see the folly of running away the time she had been so mad when Miss Percy forced Cora to go all day without eating because she'd dropped her breakfast tray. He'd been the one who had spent hours with her pouring over the books in the bookcase at the back of the schoolroom encouraging her to learn everything she possibly could. When Miss Dickens came and didn't care if they learned or not, some of the others thought that was great, but not Timothy; it meant he saw to it that he and Sarah Emily studied harder. He'd been the one who had shared her longing for a family. They talked endless hours pondering over such things as what a family did at bedtime or how a family would act if one of them was sick. Of course, there was this matter now of Timothy not believing her about who you look like regulating who you will be. But, all in all, Timothy was, and had been, a true friend.

But to have a girl friend too—it was almost more than she could take in.

Once outside, the air felt sharp with autumn. Sarah Emily tried to warm her hands in her pockets, but instead, her fingers tangled in the patches that freckled the coat. "Up before the sun," she huffed, aggravated with Miss Percy as she felt her way by the slim light from a sliver of moon.

She opened the door to the tool barn and was immediately greeted with such lavish wet kisses, her irritation with the early morning hour couldn't possibly hang on. After all, she had a girl friend *and* a dog.

"Hey, how are you doing this morning?" She hugged the furry head and lowered herself to the blanket bed Mr. Wilbur had made. The dog plopped down beside her.

"I need to talk to you about something." She held the dog's head with both hands, rubbed the top with her thumbs and spoke directly into eager eyes. "I know I named you Mine yesterday, but after talking to Betsy last night, I'd like to call you Ours. That way you'll belong to Timothy and Betsy too. You don't know either of them yet, but you will soon." For a moment, she snuggled the warm shaggy head next to her cheek. "What do you think of that, girl?"

Brown eyes locked with Sarah Emily's, then a wet tongue slashed across her face and a tail wagged.

"I'll take that to mean the name change meets with your approval. Okay then, Ours it is!" She leaned against the wall and the dog nestled her head in Sarah Emily's lap. "Girl, if there's any way you can win Miss Percy's heart, you need to be at it first thing this morning. I know that's a tall order." She tilted down to speak secretly into Ours's stand-up ear. "It's only fair I warn you, though, there's a huge debate if she even has a heart." Sarah Emily laughed out loud and the dog's tail wagged faster.

"Now, I'd best get to the kitchen, but I'll be back with some breakfast for you as soon as I can. First, I'll bet you'd like to go outside."

Ours lumbered up, and Sarah Emily scrambled to her feet. The instant the door opened, Ours dashed out. In no time, she was back beside Sarah Emily with a pleased look in her brown eyes. "Your eyes are the very same color as Timothy's. You'll love him and Betsy too. I just know it." She scratched the dog's head and then pointed to the blanket. "Now try to be quiet 'til we figure out what we're going to do with Miss Percy." Ours trotted to her bed and lay down. "Good girl. Remember, be quiet, but mostly remember, I love you."

Sarah Emily closed the door and, under a whitening sky, ran to the kitchen, side-stepping a puddle from yesterday's storm. If only they really could figure out something to do with Miss Percy! Even a smile from her every now and then would be an improvement.

Once inside, she saw that Cook already had the wood stove ablaze, and the warm kitchen smelled of cinnamon and coffee. Lined up on the worktable were six loaves of hot bread. Huge bowls on the floor, beside the stove's warmth, held great mounds of creamy white dough just waiting for the buried yeast in them to swell. Loaves of bread, rising dough and Cook—they gave the kitchen a steady rhythm that Sarah Emily found to be medicine for her soul. She removed and hung her coat, not dreading this hour alone with Cook at all.

Cook was at the bison-sized cast iron stove just lifting the lid of a heavy pot and tipping her head back to escape the great billows of runaway steam. She set the lid down; the hollow clink-clunk of metal against metal rang through the kitchen. Then without wasting a movement, Cook hoisted up a massive blue crock.

Sarah Emily watched the dry oatmeal splash into the boiling water, and she felt a wellspring of love for Cook. Cook tried so hard to fix meals as good as she possibly could with the short supplies from the state and the meager allowance she had at the mercantile.

Cook turned to set the crock back on its shelf and saw Sarah Emily. Her round eyes elongated into ovals as her eyebrows peaked up. "Law, child, how long have you been standing there? I didn't see you come in."

"I've only been here a second."

"Am I going blind? I didn't see you come down those stairs." Cook glanced toward the back stairs that led into the kitchen.

Sarah Emily grinned. "I came from outside. I went to see the dog first."

"The dog?" Cook pressed her lips together and shook her head, but her eyes were merry. "I should've guessed. Now tell me, having to get up early and help me—is this your punishment for yesterday? As if being in that shed isn't punishment enough! I know that place with its cobwebs and creepiness makes one shiver chase another down my spine." Cook stirred the oatmeal. "Although I thought your little show in the dining room yesterday morning was funny enough to have won you a prize instead of punishment."

"Thanks." Sarah Emily pulled the top of her ill-fitting dress to rest properly on her shoulders. "I didn't have much time to think about it first."

"From what I see, you don't need much. One of these days, though, one of your stunts might make you wish you weren't so hasty."

Sarah Emily grinned and gave a conceding flap of her arms. "You're probably right. I should think these things through better. But when there isn't time to prepare, one has to do whatever it takes. At least, that's been my experience." She walked toward Cook. "How long do you think a person should contemplate before launching a plan?"

"How long? Uhmm. I don't rightly know for sure." Cook studied a far corner of the room for a moment. "I'd think, the minimum time should be as long as it takes a pot of water to boil," she announced with conviction.

"A pot of water to boil," Sarah Emily said, thoughtfully. "Certainly, I should be able to do that. Next time, I promise to try. In answer to your question about if this is my punishment, I'm to help with breakfast all week since I came in before Miss Percy said I could."

"Well, here." Cook held the spoon out to Sarah Emily. "Come and stir this oatmeal while I slice the breakfast bread."

"Sure." Sarah Emily moved to the stove. "But, you know, I don't really consider this punishment since I get to be with you."

A smile nudged itself into a corner of Cook's mouth and pushed across her lips. "I don't mind your company myself. And it makes the work go faster. I'm thinking about getting some things underway for supper this morning."

"That's right. You've been leaving every day after lunch and not coming back 'til nearly supper time."

"Well, have I now?"

Sarah Emily knew by Cook's expression, a kind of squished smile, bottom lip tucked under the top, that was the end of the subject. Closed. Finished. Sarah Emily would have liked to thank her again for last night's biscuit, but knew better than to do that too. Cook would want it forgotten. Instead, Sarah Emily took the huge spoon in both hands and began stirring the oatmeal.

Cook wiped her fingers with the corner of her apron then reached for the bread knife. Sarah Emily watched the big knife in Cooks' capable hands make even strokes in and out of the crusty loaves, cutting thick uniform slices. As Sarah Emily stirred, her mind drifted to the day Cook had come to the orphan asylum nearly four years ago.

There were stories that Cook's husband and seven children had all been killed in a fire that burned their home to ashes. But Cook never, ever spoke one word about it. She didn't say so, but Sarah Emily always thought there was something in Cook's eyes that said her family had been ripped away from her too.

Once all the loaves were reduced to slices and piled in baskets, Cook came over to check the oatmeal's progress. After pronouncing it good, she said, "You keep stirring while I get Miss Percy's cinnamon buns ready."

Sarah Emily did her assigned task, but observed Cook arranging fresh buns on Miss Percy's pretty, pink plate. *The pink color is delicious enough, and then to get those buns too . . . and preserves anytime she wants.* Sarah Emily could almost taste the preserves from last night and stirred the boiling oatmeal harder as a rise of resentment boiled in her. Every summer Miss Percy bought just enough fresh raspberries, blackberries and strawberries, solely for herself, so Cook could make preserves to last until the next summer. Miss Percy cut their hair off. Miss Percy tossed their records into the shed to be ruined. Miss Percy ate off a dish the delicate color of rose petals, while they ate off dishes the murky color of mud.

Suddenly, she remembered Betsy talking about her ma's pink and white china, and her resentment swelled even more. How can things that ought to belong to one person go to someone else? And how can it be that you could end up in an orphan asylum like this?

"Law, will you look here?" Cook never looked up from the worktable but smoothed the front of her apron. "Only three buns fit on this tiny plate. Whatever am I going to do with these extra two? I'll just leave them right here and put them away later when I get the chance. I've got to get some things in the pantry now. I might be in there a minute or more."

Sarah Emily smiled, understanding exactly Cook's ways. Those extra buns were meant for Sarah Emily.

As soon as Cook disappeared into the pantry, Sarah Emily put down the spoon and grabbed a bun, delighting in its fragrance. She took a big bite. "Mmmm," rumbled at the back of her throat, her knees flexing as her eyes closed in complete ecstasy. It was sweeter, softer and more delicious than she had even imagined. The gooey richness made her tempted to stuff the whole thing in her mouth.

But she stopped before another crumb passed her lips. This would be a grand treat to share with Betsy and Timothy. She put the bun with the missing chunk in the center of a napkin, laid the whole one beside it and folded the cloth snugly around the precious delicacies. Then into her apron pocket she stuffed the parcel for safekeeping.

She was contentedly licking the sweet residue off her fingers when Miss Percy barged through the swinging door, her right hand clutching the top of her dress.

"Sarah Emily?" Miss Percy's face looked as curdled as last

week's milk. "Sarah Emily, I want to talk to you."

Cook dashed out of the pantry, jerked the bubbling kettle to the cool part of the stove top and studied first the spot where she had left the extra cinnamon buns on the worktable, and then Sarah Emily.

Sarah Emily ever so slightly shook her head at Cook and lifted her shoulders in a bewildered expression trying to convey, *Miss Percy didn't catch me with the buns, and I have no idea what she wants.*

Cook closed her eyes, swallowed hard and then turned to Miss Percy. "Law, Miss Percy, whatever are you doing in here? Your breakfast isn't ready yet."

"I'm not here for breakfast! I'm here for my brooch!" She dropped her hand, exposing the empty place where the brooch was usually attached.

Sarah Emily had never seen Miss Percy so frantic. Nor had she realized, until now, how strange she would look without that brooch. Her black leather strap and jeweled brooch were as much a part of Miss Percy's daily dress as insignia on a soldier's uniform. Now, here she stood with neither.

"Your brooch isn't in the kitchen. What are you talking about?" Cook asked.

Miss Percy's hand went back to the top left of her blue frock. "I got undressed in the dark last night and didn't notice my brooch was missing. Just a minute ago, when I was going to take it from yesterday's dress..." Her voice trailed off while she glared at Sarah Emily.

She backed up from the push of Miss Percy's eyes.

"Is this your idea of how to get at me for putting you in the shed? Because if it is, I'll get you... You have *no* claim to that brooch!"

Sarah Emily backed up several more steps, nearly tripping over a bowl of rising bread dough.

Cook hurriedly walked to the stove. "Miss Percy, now you misplaced it, that's all. It'll turn up. Look here, I have your tea all ready." Cook poured the steaming brew into Miss Percy's favorite chipped cup and handed it to her. "You'll feel better once you drink this."

While Sarah Emily struggled to figure out what Miss Percy meant by saying she had no claim to that brooch, Ophelia burst into the kitchen through the back door. "Miss Percy, Miss Percy, get the shotgun. There's a beast in the tool barn! It's wild. I'm sure of it."

"What next?" Miss Percy replaced the cup on its saucer just short of slamming.

Sarah Emily closed her eyes in disbelief. *Of all things, I should have remembered it was Ophelia's week to bring up fresh water for the wash bowls. When she was outside, she must have heard the dog.*

Sarah Emily opened her mouth, ready to try to squelch Ophelia's fervor to shoot, but Ophelia sucked in a noisy breath, eyes as big as dinner plates, wringing her apron, and began wailing in her highest register, "I heard this ferocious sound coming from the tool barn, and when I opened the door, the beast came barreling out. Nearly knocked me out of my socks! It's running loose around back." Her usual hysteria multiplied, her arms outstretched, Ophelia flung herself toward Miss Percy.

"Law, I don't be knowing nothin'." Cook took several steps backwards.

Miss Percy jumped out of Ophelia's path, sloshing tea.

The door banged open, and a brisk breeze whooshed through the kitchen. Ours loped in, tail wagging, tongue flapping, paws dancing and mud flying. She skidded to a stop at Miss Percy's feet and began a most thorough and intimate sniffing.

"My stars! Get this beast away from me!"

"That's the varmint!" Ophelia shrieked. "Where's the shotgun? Oh, Miss Percy, I can't watch. It's going to rip the flesh right off your bones." Ophelia covered her eyes with a trembling hand.

Mr. Wilbur raced into the kitchen, suspenders dangling, clutching his britches. "I could hear the commotion all the way in my room. And just who is going to shoot who?" he shouted into the frenzy.

Sarah Emily dashed across the kitchen to grab Ours, but the dog was out the door faster than a chased rabbit. And then she was back inside before anyone could catch their breath or make sense of the whole mad scene.

Again, Ours skidded to a halt in front of Miss Percy, dropped something at her feet, sat down and looked up proudly as if expecting a grand reward.

Mr. Wilbur bent to retrieve the thing that Ours seemed to think would please Miss Percy. "Why, Mildred, it's your brooch."

"Give me that!" She snatched it from him and set her cup on the worktable.

Following a close examination, she finally admitted that all the stones were present, and it really had suffered no damage.

"It must have fallen off your dress when you were taking Sarah Emily to the shed yesterday," Mr. Wilbur said, who by now had his britches properly hitched and was drinking a cup of coffee. "That was the last time you were outside before the big storm, wasn't it, Mildred?"

"Yes."

"It only makes sense then, when Ophelia let her out this morning, the dog must have found it. When she sniffed you, your scent matched."

"I beg your pardon." Miss Percy straightened her back as if that could retrieve her dignity.

"That's not a bad thing. It just means the dog could tell you were the owner of the brooch—probably connected you by your rosewater. I dare say there is some hunting hound somewhere in this dog's family tree. Mystery solved. Now, on to breakfast."

"Not so fast." Miss Percy pumped the toe of her shiny black shoe on the wooden floor while Ours waited patiently for, it seemed, at the very least, a pat on the head. "That doesn't explain why *this* dog was in the tool barn in the first place." She pushed each word out through clenched teeth.

Ophelia uncovered her eyes. "Does this mean we don't need the gun?"

"Good heavens, girl." Mr. Wilbur laid a hand on her shoulder. "No one is doing any shooting. Calm yourself."

Miss Percy folded her arms across her chest. "My question has not been answered yet."

Sarah Emily's head buzzed with the unexpected appearance of Ours. She hadn't worked out a plan yet, but something had to be done, so she quickly stepped forward and urged Ours to stand up. With a great display, though her courage was spongy, she swept her hand through the air just above the dog, and said, "Miss Percy, I'd like to introduce you to my new dog, Ours."

"Your new dog?" Miss Percy's face turned bright red as she pinched her lips together, in her bitter-pill fashion.

"Yes." Sarah Emily struggled to sound matter-of-fact. "She came yesterday. And as her first act, she found and brought to you your missing brooch. I'm sure she's going to be valuable to all of us. Don't you think so?"

"Yes, Mildred." Mr. Wilbur stepped forward. "This dog will be good to have around." Then he added with a great deal of sincerity, "I think she looks like a fine animal."

Everyone studied the dog. Ours's hairy head was cocked to one side, making her strange ears appear even stranger. Her enormous paws were the size of pancakes. Her long, skinny tail looked as if it were attached to a pole one could hang the wash on, while her fur had the texture of something a bear might wear.

"Fine dog, my foot." Miss Percy dropped her arms to her sides. "This animal is not staying here!"

In one quick movement, Ours jumped up and placed her front paws squarely on Miss Percy's shoulders. In unison, everyone gasped, with Cook adding, "Law, oh Law!"

Miss Percy blinked her eyes once and, it seemed, didn't breathe for several seconds. Then her cold expression slid off her face as smoothly as a chunk of ice slides off a window in the noon sun. Miss Percy slowly reached out and cradled Ours's face in her hands. "Why, you are a fine dog, aren't you? And because you are, you may stay."

Ours licked her cheek and jumped down, paws landing on the floor with a satisfied thud.

While the onlookers stood in stunned silence at the mysterious thing that had just happened, Miss Percy regained her stern tone and commanded breakfast be underway. She picked up her teacup and stomped out in her usual stomping fashion, but with a smile like Sarah Emily had never seen on Miss Percy before. It looked like a remembering smile.

"Law," Cook broke the resulting silence, "I wouldn't have thought this mishap would have that sort of ending." Having said that, she went to the stove and moved the boiling coffee to the back.

Mr. Wilbur ushered Ours and Ophelia outside. And Sarah Emily stirred oatmeal, all the while thinking, *There is just no explaining some things.*

A little later at breakfast, Sarah Emily delighted in telling every detail—with just the right embellishments—to Betsy, Timothy and everyone else since word of the dog was out. She wouldn't have thought it could have been any other way since Ophelia's tongue was known for flapping like a hanky on the clothesline in the wind.

Breakfast was finished in record time, and Sarah Emily led the excited parade outside to meet Ours before school began. And just as Sarah Emily had been certain, Timothy and Betsy fell immediately in love with the dog.

On their way to the school building, they opened the kitchen door looking for Cook, but before Sarah Emily could say a word, Cook said, "Law, now I've got another hungry soul to feed on the meager food I have to work with." Then, the tiniest smile darted across her face. "There'll be a pail by the back door everyday. Now, off to school with you."

Sarah Emily's eyes met Cook's, and a silent thank you was said.

Ours happily sauntered alongside to the school building. "Getting by Miss Percy was miracle enough. Miss Dickens was yet another story," Sarah Emily explained to the eager dog why she couldn't come in the classroom.

The morning crawled along. The assignment was writing lists of nouns while Miss Dickens silently read her book. Sarah Emily kept looking at Betsy, Timothy and the clock until, finally, ten o'clock came. "Recess at last! I thought it would never get here," she said as they met by the back door and found Ours waiting just outside.

Betsy pulled her thin coat tighter, rubbed her hands together and peered up. "I hope the sun is warming things a bit."

For a while, some of the others patted and played with Ours. Then amidst much protest, Sarah Emily called Ours away. Along with Timothy and Betsy, they found a place under a clump of maple trees just off to the side of the school building. Since the trees had given up their leaves for autumn, the sun shone through the empty branches and warmed the bed of leaves on the ground to make the perfect spot for visiting. As the three sat down, Ours was right there. While they discussed their favorable unexpected turn of events with Miss Percy, Ours began to sniff and paw at Sarah Emily's pocket.

"I nearly forgot! Wait 'til you see what I have!"

Timothy and Betsy leaned forward expectantly.

When Sarah Emily saw their intense interest, she lazily leaned back against the tree, put her hands behind her head and playfully yawned. "Maybe I'll take a little nap. I was up awfully early this morning, you know."

In a flash, Timothy and Betsy were digging in her pocket as she giggled and pushed them away.

"Sarah Em, there is such a streak of mischief in that head of yours," Timothy good-naturedly teased.

"Hmm. You think so?" She grinned and lifted the parcel out of her pocket.

Making a great display, she folded back the corners of the napkin to reveal the two buns, one missing a large bite and one intact.

"Where did you get those delicious looking things?" Betsy inched closer.

"From Cook. She slips us treats, or like she did with these, she purposely left them on the counter for me and then went into the pantry, but she doesn't want us to say anything to her. It's almost like if we don't talk about it, it isn't happening and she doesn't have to worry about Miss Percy finding out. Cook has such a soft heart." Sarah Emily handed the napkin and contents to Timothy. "Here, you divide them three ways. You're better at such things."

Betsy held onto Ours while the division was made. Then the three settled back against the gnarly tree trunk to savor every morsel. "Let's eat it slowly, like we are at a fancy tea party," Sarah Emily suggested.

"Tea party? Not me." Timothy grunted and popped his entire portion into his mouth and leaped to his feet. "Ours, come on, how'd you like to learn how to fetch?" And as he walked away, they heard him mumbling, "Tea was first used for only medicinal purposes."

"What was that medicinal tea business?" Betsy looked suspiciously at Timothy.

"He is always learning facts, and every chance he gets, he tries to recall them. He's convinced that learning everything he can will help him when he leaves here. Don't pay any attention when he starts spouting off something he's learned. He really doesn't expect a response. He's just trying to see if he can remember something about the subject—like the tea. He amazes me at how much he knows, and all the things he can do." Sarah Emily watched Timothy throwing sticks for the dog. After a moment, she said to Betsy, "Come on, let's eat our cinnamon buns."

Betsy and Sarah Emily nibbled theirs in dainty little bites and talked about the pure bliss and ecstasy that certainly would accompany an invitation to a tea party.

"Sarah Emily," Betsy said, "do you reckon it's proper to do 'Skip to My Lou' at a tea party?"

"I would reckon—if you did it in fancy clothes." She nibbled her bottom lip, considering the possibility. "Someday we'll have a 'Skip to My Lou' tea party and fancy clothes. I just know it!"

At that moment, Miss Dickens came out and rang the bell for class to begin again.

They got up from the crunchy maple leaves and started across the yard while Ours crisscrossed among them, loudly licking the sweet, sticky remains from all their fingers.

Sarah Emily's mind became spinning clock hands wildly winding backwards from a "Skip to My Lou" party to another party she'd seen last summer. Memories zoomed past the lemony sunshine, lively music and feminine decorations of the party— right to the mothers and daughters enjoying each other. She forced her memory to a screeching halt. She wouldn't let that clock rewind one more second—not today. She only wanted to revel in the good fortune of having a girl friend, a dog and cinnamon buns—nothing sad today.

"You know what?" Sarah Emily said just as Timothy flung a stick for Ours to fetch. "Sometimes, don't you want to grab Cook and give her the biggest hug for the special things she does?"

"Yeah." Timothy nodded. "She'd let you hug her. But, like you said, you'd better not say anything about her secret presents." Ours returned with the stick.

Miss Dickens rang the bell for the second time.

"We'd better get inside." Sarah Emily clapped her hands. "Ours, come with me." She led the dog around to the side of the school building and, leaning over, left a big kiss on top of her furry head. "You have to stay out here 'til school is through." Sarah Emily watched Ours obediently stretch out in a sunny spot. "That's good. You spend the time taking a nap."

When Sarah Emily straightened up, she saw Miss Percy and a man on the front walk. They were standing under the black iron ORPHAN ASYLUM OF LANDER letters. His back was to the school. Miss Percy was clutching her brooch with one hand and flailing the other in wild gestures "…money…done it all these years…it's mine…"

Bits of sentences blew across the yard like ashes from a paper thrown on a fire. Only fragments could be caught, but not enough to piece together the whole thing.

The man turned. Sarah Emily saw his face and gasped, tightly stuffing all the air inside her body.

"You all right?" Betsy asked, coming around to where Sarah Emily was. "It sounded like you were choking or something."

"That's him!"

Ours stood up and barked.

"Him who?" Timothy asked, as he also rounded the building.

Sarah Emily started running. "Pa," she screamed. "Pa."

The man's face went still.

"Pa, it's me—Sarah Emily." She ran faster, her arms stretched out, reaching for him.

Without a word, he reeled away from her. Taking long quick

steps, he made his way toward the street and a waiting wagon.

Sarah Emily saw him leap up on the seat and snap the reins. That caused her to groan and stumble on the uneven ground. She righted herself and, with the backs of her hands, swiped at the tears gushing from her eyes. "Pa," she called again, but this time the word was lost in her sobs.

"Stop that blubbering and get to class!" Miss Percy commanded, heading for Sarah Emily.

"That was my pa." Like a rag, Sarah Emily collapsed onto the ground and buried her rasping moans in her hands. "That was my pa. My pa."

"Don't be silly. Do as I say, and get back to school."

It didn't matter what Miss Percy was saying. She could have threatened to throw her back in the shed right then and there, Sarah Emily's insides were too raw to care. She rolled on her side and drew her knees up to her chest. This was the very spot, under the orphan asylum sign, where he had turned his back and left her the first time.

Remembering when she was four, the way he wouldn't look at her, the way he had marched off even when she screamed after him, "Pa don't leave me here. Please Pa," all became a sharp shovel, digging, stabbing, unearthing hurt places and images, ones that were supposed to be deeply buried and sealed in the farthest depths of her heart.

She was too stunned and shattered to cram them back down. They oozed out, slime from under a rock. Her pa had left her before. Now, he'd left her again.

"I'll not have a spectacle out here for the whole town to see. If you aren't on your feet this instant, I'm going to get my strap."

"Miss Percy," Betsy pleaded, "please don't get the strap. Can't you see her heart is cracking with pain?"

"You don't tell me what to do. And believe me, she will not die of a broken heart. I'm quite certain of that."

"Sarah Em, you've got to get up." She felt Timothy's hand on her arm. "It's going to be okay. Maybe you were mistaken. That probably wasn't the man in your photograph."

Timothy's touch and words brought her eyes up to his. For a second, she was lost in his caring and reached for his arm, clutching it, desperate to stop the clawing in her heart. Somehow, Timothy was always there when she needed him.

"Come on," Timothy said, bracing her elbow in his hand. "I'll help you up." But Ours bounded to Sarah Emily and licked her face with such vigor she couldn't move.

A group had gathered, gawking in the stunned, open-mouthed way one would at the aftermath of a tornado—staring at leveled buildings, uprooted trees and crushed bodies.

"Get to class," Miss Percy demanded, giving her official double-clap. "All of you. This foolishness has gone on long enough."

The gawkers fled.

Sarah Emily gently pushed Ours away and stood up between Timothy and Betsy. Swabbing her eyes, she took in a deep breath, hoping it might push out some of the grief inside her before saying, "Miss Percy, I'm going to find out about my pa and why he left me here." She meant it and didn't care what Miss Percy thought or did. She smoothed down her damp apron and linked arms with Betsy and Timothy.

Miss Percy said nothing, only covered the brooch with her hand, and set her jaw as rigid as iron.

Sarah Emily marched with Betsy and Timothy to the school building. She tilted her head up several notches, in spite of her knees wobbling like a newborn kitten's.

***

The mood in the dormitory that night while they got ready for bed was somber. All the girls had witnessed Sarah Emily's breakdown and most were sympathetic.

Betsy changed into her nightgown and reached into the wardrobe for her hair brush. She brushed her hair every morning and night, though it was so short she could have merely flattened it down with her hands, but it wasn't to fix her hair, Sarah Emily understood, but to hold her mother's brush.

Betsy's face distorted.

"What's wrong?" Sarah Emily asked, getting out of bed.

Betsy didn't answer. She began scrambling through all her belongings on her shelf. She swept them out onto the floor. She pulled her satchel down, stirring through its contents. Finally, she dumped it out on the floor. She spread the lot into a thin layer, patting everything. "It's gone. My hair brush. Ma's hairbrush." Her voice cracked in the center of each word. "It's gone."

Betsy's announcement was so shocking, Sarah Emily felt it depleting her of the ability to move or think.

Cora, however, immediately started searching. Under beds, in the wardrobes, behind the washbowl table, her little face poked about like some sort of rodent.

Nettie helped, along with several of the other girls. Sarah Emily made herself move to Betsy, holding her while she sobbed.

The brush was gone. Every inch of the dormitory was searched, and the brush simply was gone. The clock bonged eight times, and Miss Percy would be coming in for her nightly check. Sarah Emily eased Betsy into bed. "As soon as Miss Percy leaves, I'll get in bed with you."

"Betsy's brush is missing," Cora said when Miss Percy arrived.

"What? What brush?" Without waiting for an answer, Miss Percy said, "Doesn't matter. I've got too much on my mind tonight to be worried about some silly brush." Leaving the room, she said, "Just get to sleep."

Sarah Emily crawled into bed with Betsy. She let Betsy's convulsing sobs come against her shoulder and heard her say in wavering, uneven breaths, "The only thing I had left was that brush." Sarah Emily's heart cramped with pain for Betsy, terrified at how she would feel if she didn't have her ma's mahogany box anymore.

Fitful sleep pulled Sarah Emily into short dozings, but she was awake again when Marjorie came in. Betsy let out a little moaning cry in her sleep, and Sarah Emily hugged her tighter.

In the shaft of moonlight, she saw Marjorie close the door, take off her coat, peel off her dress and apron and squirm into her nightgown. Marjorie slipped into bed.

Thoughts of Marjorie and her mysterious boyfriend were swept away from Sarah Emily with the image of her pa running to the wagon, leaving her again. It flooded her mind, and she felt as if she were fighting for breath, drowning in waves of the mental picture.

But another image insisted on rising to the crest, and when she got a good look at it, the angry sea inside her calmed. It was Timothy kneeling beside her—Timothy speaking gently to her—Timothy looking at her with kindness.

Kindness? Was that what it was? Yes, it was. But it was more than that, although, at the moment, she couldn't put a name to it.

Chapter 9

The blue and gold days of autumn gave way to the frosty grays of winter. Sarah Emily never quit pondering about the man who, under the ORPHAN ASYLUM OF LANDER sign, not just once but twice now, had turned his back on her.

Sarah Emily, Ours, Timothy and Betsy's lives and spirits were intertwining like happy squash vines. They spent every available moment together. That was, every available moment that Miss Percy didn't have Timothy hired out. More and more, she was seeing to it that the boys were scheduled to work as often as possible, and the mercantile always seemed to need help. And meanwhile, the girls were kept busy taking on the boy's chores as well as their own.

And then, at last, it looked like Christmas. Sarah Emily loved the look and smell of the garlands of greenery and bunches of holly berries that Cook placed here and there about the orphan asylum.

Hair clasps weren't far off now.

With her arms full of milk pails, Sarah Emily slung her head to the side to swoop the long, unruly rope of hair out of her eyes.

"Are these the ones you want?" she asked Cook, setting the

pails in the center of the worktable, and looping the hair behind her ear.

"Exactly right." Cook heaped an armload of pine branches in one. "Fill the other," she told Sarah Emily.

Sarah Emily picked up a large bunch and dropped them in. Instantly, the old, battered-metal milk pail took on a charm. Sarah Emily had been given the chore of helping Cook get everything ready for Mrs. Hancock's visit. When that was finished, they turned to fixing the pails to decorate either side of the front door with Christmas. The smell of pine seeped into every corner of the room like welcome sunrays on a cold day. Being with Cook on a Saturday afternoon, laughing and talking, was no chore.

"Even though it's a little more than two weeks yet 'til Christmas, these will keep right on smelling good even into the new year," Cook said, putting the finishing fluff on the red bow she had tied around the branches in the first pail.

Just as Sarah Emily and Cook stepped back to admire their work, Miss Percy showed up in the doorway, chipped teacup in her hand.

"Did you brew my chamomile tea? I have a dreadful headache." She stopped in mid-step, her eyes narrowing, scanning the decorations scattered on the worktable. "We don't need all this. The tree in my office is quite enough."

Cook never hesitated, reaching for the other red ribbon and looping it around the back of the branches in the second pail. Pulling the two ends even at the front, she proceeded to tie another bow.

"Did you hear me?" Miss Percy set her teacup down and splayed her hands on the worktable, leaning forward into Cook, nearly nose to nose.

"Certainly." Cook let her eyes stare into Miss Percy's for a moment. "You ever know me to be hard of hearing?" Then she turned away and moved toward the sink. "Your tea is on the stove." She picked up a large pitcher and pumped water into it. Returning to the worktable, she poured it into one of the pails. Cook dabbed a cloth at water dribbles while Miss Percy lifted the corners of the tea towel covering a platter.

"I see the sugar and butter got here." Miss Percy began filling her teacup, keeping her eyes on it longer than necessary like someone not wanting too much importance put on their words.

"Yes, Mr. Mitchell's delivery boy brought them first thing this morning." Cook's voice was tinged with suspicion.

Over the past weeks, it had been obvious to everyone that the oatmeal was getting thinner, Miss Percy's tea was getting weaker, and hard as it was to believe, there were mornings the scent of cinnamon didn't drift upstairs. Rations were definitely dwindling.

Timothy had been sent to River Bend every day the past week to work on a section of the railroad that had buckled in the freezing snow. Part of his wages would have gone toward room and board had he stayed overnight. Since Miss Percy wouldn't hear of that and the orphan asylum only had one wagon, every day Mr. Wilbur took him and then had to go get him. Sarah Emily waited for Timothy by the front door each evening. He came in dragging, exhausted and starving.

But butter and sugar for Cook to bake the cakes for that afternoon arrived just in time.

"Everything needs to be perfect for Mrs. Hancock's visit," Miss Percy said and took a small sip of tea. She closed her eyes and slowly kneaded her forehead with the tips of her skinny fingers. "First, though, I'm going to lie down and see if I can get rid of this piercing headache. Mrs. Hancock will be here promptly at two-thirty." She opened her eyes. "You know, she's a very important woman."

Sarah Emily couldn't work up any sympathy for Miss Percy's headache, but resentment easily showed up. To keep it in check, she spotted some stray twigs and pine needles on the floor and knelt down to scoop them up. Without the slightest hint of imagination necessary, it was plain to see that something was happening to the rations. But, in spite of that, a new dress for Miss Percy and two new china cups and saucers were delivered two days ago. Sarah Emily gathered the last of the pine debris and dropped it into the trash basket. She brushed her hands off, watching Miss Percy irritably putting her teapot and teacup on the tray and leave.

"Seems like the Christmas spirit passed her right on by," Cook said as she picked up a pail brimming with Christmas greenery. "Bring that other one, and let's get these by the front door before her Royal Highness Hancock arrives."

✦─❦─✦

"I think this will be the best tree ever," Sarah Emily said to Timothy and Betsy. For the next few minutes, she wanted to forget about her frustration earlier in the kitchen. And more than that, she wanted to enjoy being with Timothy since she had seen so little of him last week.

Her excitement started to swell and bubble. She was sure it must be as visible on her face as the ornaments hanging on the Christmas tree she was sneaking in to see, but she couldn't help feeling this way. It was nearly Christmas. And maybe, hopefully, surely, Mrs. Hancock was bringing their gifts, specifically, hair clasps.

With one hand on the doorknob of Miss Percy's parlor, she raised the other to punctuate her words. "Now remember, look at it real hard so you burn a likeness of it into your brain. I want us to be able to tell the others exactly what it looks like. And we've got to keep an eye on the time. It's one-thirty now. Mrs. Hancock is due here at two-thirty."

"Who is Mrs. Hancock?" Betsy asked.

"We'll tell you later. Let's get in Miss Percy's office before we get caught out here in the hall."

"Yeah. But you've got to open the door or we'll never get in." In a flash Timothy wrapped his hand around Sarah Emily's and turned the brass knob. "Need some help?" He grinned as he flung the door open.

"Timothy Marshall—" Her protest hung in her wide-open mouth at the sight of the tree.

"What a beaut!" Timothy halted with his first step into the room, causing Betsy to bump into him.

"Ouch," Betsy said, darting around him. Then, she stopped abruptly. "Ohhh," she whispered, cupping her face in her hands.

The tree stood before them, majestic and magical, even if

slightly leaning to one side. Sarah Emily breathed so hard and quick of the sweet, rich scent, a twinge of light-headedness made her teeter for a second. On the branches hung the paper snowflakes and stars she and the others had so carefully designed and cut out. Their paper chains wound around the tree and happily hid the many bare places with their red and green loops. Crowning the tree was a huge metal star, pocked with years of dings.

"Why don't Miss Percy let us come in here and enjoy the tree?" Betsy's question broke the awe-struck silence. "It only seems right since we made most of the decorations."

"That doesn't make any difference." Sarah Emily cut her gaze from the tree to Betsy. "She doesn't want us to wear out her parlor. Says it's too nice for orphans." Sarah Emily looked again at the tree. "Have you ever seen anything so beautiful?"

"You're right, Sarah Emily." Timothy twirled one of the snowflakes. "This might be our best tree."

"Don't Christmas trees have the most wonderful smell ever?" Sarah Emily filled her lungs. "I'm going to tell the others it looks and smells like a fancy lady, bathed in her best bath salts and all gussied up for a party by wearing her finest jewelry."

"That's a perfect way to describe it," Betsy said in hushed breaths. "I had no idea Christmas trees smelled this good or were so beautiful."

The wonder in Betsy's voice caused Sarah Emily to clasp her friend's hand. "Is this the first Christmas tree you've ever seen?"

"Yes. I'd never thought about how it makes the whole room smell so wonderful, even though, every year, Faith would tell me what Christmas was like when Ma was alive. But somehow the part of how it smelled got left out. Maybe she just took for granted I'd know that."

"Really?" Timothy moved closer to Betsy, looking like he had just unearthed a buried treasure. "She told you about Christmas with your ma?"

"Tell us, please. Timothy and I've speculated about such—you know, how a family does."

Betsy wriggled her hand free from Sarah Emily's. "I guess I can tell you what Faith told me. I just ain't never told nobody. I've always thought if I kept it tucked inside and didn't let it out, it was a way of keeping what little bit of my ma and Christmas that I had. Now with her brush gone too . . . " She looked first at Sarah Emily, then at Timothy. "But that's plain silly. If you really want to know, I'll tell you."

"You bet we want to know." Timothy rushed around to the other side of Betsy and sat down.

Glancing at Timothy, Sarah Emily saw he was ready. One leg was out straight, the other bent up at the knee with his elbow propped on it. The spark in his eyes told her he was every bit as excited as she was.

Sarah Emily sat down Indian-style beside the crimson chair. *Family. I'm going to hear about a family.* Sarah Emily was eager to peek into a window of life that had always had the blinds snapped tightly shut to her.

Betsy, between them, fastened her gaze on the tree.

Sarah Emily and Timothy fastened their gaze on Betsy.

"Go ahead. We're ready." Sarah Emily leaned forward, closer to Betsy, and waited while Betsy breathed in until her chest and shoulders rose then sank slowly as she let the air out.

"Every Christmas Eve," Betsy finally began, "Faith would snuggle down in bed with me, and in the dark, in no more than a whisper so Pa didn't hear, she'd tell me how, near to Christmas day, she and Pa would bundle up in warm clothes, and they'd go to the woods behind the house to search for the perfect tree. When Faith got old enough, Pa would let her pick which one she liked. Then Pa would chop it down, thunk it on the ground a couple of times to shake off the snow, and they'd drag it home. Faith said they'd laugh and talk all the way back, and Pa would tell her Christmas stories."

Betsy turned to Sarah Emily. "I don't ever remember hearing Pa laugh or tell a story." As though she had cast her mind back to search every cranny, she said, "No, I never heard a laugh or a story." Then shaking herself like a dog slinging off water, she went on. "When Faith and Pa brought the tree home, Ma would have hot cider waiting for them. They'd sit around drinking the cider and warming by the fire. After they thawed out, he would set the tree up and get it ready for Ma and Faith to decorate. Faith said he'd always say, 'Okay, time for the women folk to get the tree all fancied up.'"

Betsy kept staring at Sarah Emily, but Sarah Emily knew Betsy was seeing right through her to somewhere else. "Drinking cider with your ma and pa," Betsy said, her voice as soft and delicate as feathers. "Doesn't that sound wonderful?"

Sarah Emily didn't answer. Betsy wouldn't have heard her anyway. But yes, it did sound wonderful—more wonderful than she could even imagine. There, in Miss Percy's parlor, with the drifting fragrance of the tall spruce tree and the early afternoon sun filtering through the lace curtains and warming the room, those stolen moments were taking on more importance to her than just seeing the tree. Family—she was hearing about family. Squeezing her folded hands together, she eagerly waited for Betsy to begin again.

Timothy didn't move or speak

Betsy got up from the floor and twisted one of the paper snowflakes swinging from the tree. "Faith said Ma could crochet better than any woman in the county." Holding onto the snowflake, Betsy turned to the two sitting on the floor. "Ma won all kinds of blue ribbons for her crocheting." Betsy tapped the paper ornament; it made a crisp *ping* and spun round and round. "Every year Ma crocheted a new ornament—a snowflake, a star, or a snowman. Faith said her white handiwork covered the tree like fresh-fallen snow. It was when Faith turned six that Ma taught her how to crochet. And from then on every year 'til Ma died, they'd each make a new ornament."

"Did Faith teach you how to crochet?" Sarah Emily asked just above a whisper, careful not to break the fragile feeling in the room.

"Yeah. Faith tried." Betsy's smile was sweet, her chin dipping downward. "But I just ended up with a string of knots."

Timothy stood, walked to the other side of the tree and leaned against the wall, facing Sarah Emily and Betsy.

He's trying to act like this is just girl talk, Sarah Emily thought while she watched him jam his hands into his pockets. But she knew how many hours they'd spent sitting under the maple trees imagining what a family would be like. She knew him so well, better than anyone else knew him. She understood how much he longed for a family—just like she did.

"Whatever happened to your ma and Faith's hand-done ornaments?" It gushed out of Timothy like the bottom ripping out of a filled bucket.

Betsy's smile disappeared and her expression froze. "Faith said after Ma died, Pa burned all the tree ornaments along with Ma's blue ribbons. He vowed there'd never be another Christmas tree in that house. And when Pa made a vow, he meant to keep it." Betsy walked to the other side of the tree, took off a crumpled paper snowflake and sat down beside Sarah Emily. Holding it in her hands, she looked at it hard, so hard as if staring might make it turn into one of her ma's handmade ones.

"I've never said this out loud to anyone." Betsy closed her fingers around the snowflake. "Pa blamed me for Ma dying. It was my fault, no one else. It was me, she died while birthing me." Betsy sounded angry—angry with herself.

Instantly, Timothy was at her side, on his knees. "Your ma wouldn't want you saying that."

Sarah Emily lifted Betsy's apron and wiped the tears that fell from Betsy's eyes as she said, "Timothy's right. I don't know a lot about your ma or any ma, for that matter, but I do know there isn't one anywhere who would want you blaming yourself."

Betsy leaped to her feet, and the snowflake plunked to the floor squashing one of its paper tips. "Maybe Ma wouldn't, but that's why Pa took to drinking after I was born." Her words came quick and hard, banging like an axe. "And that's why he looked at me two ways—sometimes he'd start to look at me with a gentleness that put a craving in me to run to him for a hug. Then just as quick, his eyes would turn stone hard and cold."

She crossed her arms and rubbed them briskly as if a chill circled her. She slowly nodded her head. "That's it." Now her words dripped out, thick and slow like molasses being coaxed from its jug. "Pa blamed me for Ma dying. That's what made Pa look at me two different ways."

For a moment, Betsy's mouth grimaced. Then, as if willing herself to go on, she tilted her head back and unclasped her arms. "In the evening, after the tree was all decorated with Ma and Faith's ornaments, they'd sit around and sing Christmas songs. Pa also vowed after Ma died there'd never be singing in the house again."

"Betsy," Sarah Emily stood, "at least you got to hear about your Ma and know something about her. And...and you know you've got the same color hair and you can sing like her." Folding her hands tightly in front of her, she drew them to her chest. "Oh, Betsy, don't you see how grand it is for you—you know what kind of person you're going to be!"

"For Pete's sake, Sarah Em." Timothy raised up on his knees with his back stiff and slapped his thighs. "I've told you before, you don't know if that's the true test of who a person is or not!"

"Yes, I do." She stamped her foot so firmly it fanned her skirt. That was a childish response, and she knew it. But his constant insisting that she was wrong was, well—it was just as childish. "And I'm going to find out who I look like, just like Betsy knows." She reached over and put her arm around Betsy's shoulders.

"You're hopeless." Timothy shook his head and listed back on his heels. "Do you know that?"

Sarah Emily let his question dissolve into the air as though it were of no consequence to her—a trifling, ludicrous thing to say—while Betsy rehung the paper snowflake. Timothy was not going to talk her out of this. She would know who she looked like. For all his reading, he hadn't come up with any better way to know yourself.

"Okay, you two," Timothy said, standing, apparently sticking with his "you're hopeless" proclamation. "We'd better high-tail it out of here before we get caught."

"Oh, you're right." Sarah Emily glanced at the clock on the mantle. "We've been in here longer than I thought we would. It's nearly two-thirty, and Mrs. Hancock is never late. Let me make sure old you-know-who isn't in the hall." She opened the door a crack.

A loud racket in the front yard startled Sarah Emily. Then the sharp, swift clicking on the wooden floor of Miss Percy's heels headed for the front door. Sarah Emily quickly closed the parlor door. With Betsy and Timothy close behind, she raced to the window in time to see Mrs. Hancock stumbling up the front walk, balancing in her ample arms a stack of brightly colored tins, and Cora racing toward her.

"Get out of my way!"

Even through the closed window, Sarah Emily could hear the brusqueness in the woman's irritated voice. "It's Mrs. Hancock. She's here." Sarah Emily motioned Betsy and Timothy to come see.

They crowded in behind Miss Percy's crimson brocade chair while Sarah Emily held the lacy curtain to one side. Timothy opened the window just enough so they could better hear what was being said. Icy air whipped into Miss Percy's parlor.

"What a hat!" Betsy pushed closer to the window. "I ain't never seen one like that."

"Shhh." Timothy pressed a finger to his lips. "Don't talk so loud or she'll hear you. But you're right," he whispered back, "that's some hat. It looks like she's got a whole flock of birds on her head." He snickered. "This might be her daffiest hat yet."

They all stared at the black thing with three feathered and flocked in red velvet birds, each perched on its own burlap-covered stick of varying heights. Every step Mrs. Hancock took caused each bird to swirl in its own dizzying circle.

"Who *is* Mrs. Hancock?" Betsy edged in closer. "You never did tell me."

"She's the President of the Ladies' Aid Society. It's a group of church ladies who think it's their duty to help orphans," Timothy explained. "She always brings us cookies at Christmas."

"And hair clasps," Sarah Emily said, her eyes searching for something other than cookie tins.

"That hat, it'd make a corpse smile." Timothy shook his head. "But then I've never seen one on her that couldn't."

"Cookies," Betsy said, a wistful longing trailing the word. "What a nice lady."

"I guess, maybe she's nice." Timothy was thoughtful for a moment. "She never has a word to say to us, and she acts like we have a disease or will give her lice." Timothy dangled his hands over the girls. "I'm going to drop orphan lice on you," he said, wiggling his long fingers.

Sarah Emily and Betsy giggled and swatted at his hands as he ruffled the top of their hair.

After a minute of horseplay, Sarah Emily caught her breath. "Now, stop being silly and help me think how we're going to get out of here. You know, Miss Percy will be bringing in Mrs. Hancock for tea right away." She tried to sound stern, but giggles kept slipping out until Mrs. Hancock let out a shrill howl. Sarah Emily's attention was yanked back outside.

"It's Ours!" Sarah Emily groaned from her window view as the big dog came bounding around the corner. "Ple-e-ase stay away from Mrs. Hancock."

"Oh no!" Betsy clapped a hand over her mouth.

Ours skidded through the snow and came to a blunt stop, splattering little snow flurries all over the bottom of Mrs. Hancock's finely tailored black coat.

The red velvet birds began to sway this way and that, and Mrs. Hancock began to sway that way and this. With a final lurch, the top two tins rolled off the stack in her arms and onto the ground while she valiantly clutched the others.

"Get that mongrel away from me!" Mrs. Hancock wobbled desperately, straining to regain the balance of the load she was carrying. Ours turned to greet Cora, and in so doing, flung more snow onto Mrs. Hancock, causing her and her load to teeter and wobble again.

Cora scooped up one of the fallen tins and held it up to the fuming Mrs. Hancock. "Are there cookies in here? The older ones said so." Sarah Emily could hear the hope of a six-year-old in Cora's voice.

"Get away from Mrs. Hancock!" Miss Percy marched out onto the front steps, the door slamming behind her. She bellowed, flailed and shooed, but neither Cora nor Ours moved an inch.

"Run for your life, Ours!" Timothy pleaded in a frantic whisper from the parlor window.

Miss Percy rushed toward Cora, snatched the tin from her hands and picked up the one still on the ground.

Cora puffed out her bottom lip.

Mrs. Hancock swiftly sidestepped her to get to Miss Percy. "This orphan of yours got under my feet. And where in the name of all that is sane did that mongrel come from? I'm certain the cookies are all broken. Honestly Mildred, it gets harder and harder to try to do God's work."

"I know just what you mean." Miss Percy followed the admission with a knowing sigh.

"Are those cookies for us?" Cora asked louder and more insistent this time.

Balancing both cookie tins in one hand, Miss Percy turned toward Cora and patted her head. "But they are God's children, and, you know, Lydia, I've been chosen to care for them." Her voice oozed concern while her pious expression rested on little Cora, but ignored her question.

"There she goes again with that cooing," Sarah Emily told Betsy. "She only does that when someone else is around—someone she wants to impress." Then with her head framed in the window, Sarah Emily watched and listened to the two women outside.

"Cora, take the dog around back," Miss Percy said, and with her free hand let her fingers trail Ours's back.

"All I wanted to know is are those cookies?" Cora said, loud enough for the women to hear as she herded Ours away.

"Here, let me help you, Lydia." Miss Percy reached for some of the tins still heaped in Mrs. Hancock's substantial arms. "Come in, and we'll have a nice cup of hot tea. That will make you feel better."

"Yes, that should put some dignity and civilization back in my spirit. Mildred, I don't know how you do it, living *at this end* of Lilac Lane. All these orphans, and now—this dog."

Miss Percy lowered her head. "It is my calling, you know, to care for these poor dear orphans. And, as for the dog, well, I do try to give them what pleasures I can."

Sarah Emily clenched her teeth and balled her fists.

"Yes, your calling. You've told me that *more* than once, Mildred," Mrs. Hancock said icily.

As soon as they had their bundles adjusted and situated, the two started up the worn brick steps.

Timothy closed the window. "I thought those birds were going to fly right off her hat." He bobbed his head around, mimicking Mrs. Hancock.

"Hey, Bird Man. We need to get out of here and fast." Sarah Emily couldn't help but laugh at Timothy's antics as she squeezed out from behind the chair. He could be such fun, in spite of that serious side of his, she thought with tenderness, and her right toes twitched.

That odd thing again. She had finally made the connection that it only happened when she was thinking about Timothy, and that embarrassed her. She put her other foot on top to try to stop them, but it didn't work. She tried stretching her toes, but she still couldn't get them under control. How ridiculous! She didn't have time for this. "Come on you two," she said, stomping her right foot much too hard as she walked.

"Yeah, we'd better go." Timothy sobered and followed her.

"Betsy!" Sarah Emily saw she hadn't moved. "Come on."

"Cookies." Betsy left the window. "Faith and I used to make cookies."

Leaving the parlor, Timothy closed the door behind them just as Miss Percy and Mrs. Hancock rounded the corner.

"What are you three doing?" Miss Percy asked.

"Us? Oh, nothing. Just walking down the hall." Sarah Emily kept her face blank and a tight hold on Betsy as they hurried past. *Please, Betsy, don't ask about the cookies,* she silently pleaded.

As soon as Sarah Emily heard the parlor door firmly close behind the two women, she let go of Betsy's arm. Sarah Emily looked at Timothy. He cocked his head to the left. Sarah Emily nodded, understanding the signal.

"Betsy, follow us," Timothy said.

Chapter 10

$\mathcal{S}$arah Emily led the way. Veering off into the skinny passageway, she heard Timothy and Betsy's tiptoeing footsteps following close behind. While all three moved in unity, without saying a word, Sarah Emily ached to know if there were hair clasps in addition to the tins of cookies—good as they would be if Miss Percy let them have any—waiting to be brought in from Mrs. Hancock's carriage.

Since last Christmas, each time she saw one of the girls wearing a shiny silver one, she had wished for her own. Of course, everyone agreed they would look better in long hair, but she would love one anyway. Sarah Emily touched her short hair and felt the place beside her left ear that outgrew the rest where she would put her new clasp. She imagined how it would look smartly holding the unruly lock out of her eyes.

Since Betsy wouldn't be sixteen until January, and sixteen was the age the Ladies' Aid Society had set, Sarah Emily wished she could think of a way for Betsy to get one. It would, she was sure, make Betsy feel better about her hair, especially with her hairbrush still not being found. She glanced back to make sure Betsy saw where they turned to climb the steep, narrow stairs.

There didn't seem to be any clues as to what had happened to the brush except that the sheriff said there had been a lot of mysterious robberies lately. But how anyone knew about Betsy's brush was what stumped everyone. It was evident to Sarah Emily that loosing the brush had taken a sizeable chunk out of Betsy's spirit. In the absence of her brush, she quickly raked her fingers through her hair each morning and night, never saying a word about it. Outwardly, though, she'd been brave and staunch—far more than Sarah Emily thought she would be if something happened to her mahogany box.

"Don't say a word in here," Timothy instructed Betsy when they reached the top and stopped at a wide door latched shut with a heavy black slide lock.

Sarah Emily scrunched her nose and held her breath while she slid the bolt, knowing its scratching sound would grate into the silence. She always wondered, when she was sneaking into this seldom-used storage room, if it would be better to slide the bolt back in one quick movement. But she was afraid that would be even louder. And what if she accidentally slammed the bolt into the metal stop at the other end? The bang of that would surely bring Miss Percy running, and access to this listening spot would be lost.

She opened the door. It gave a short rusty whine. They filed in behind her. Nimbly stepping past the creaks in the floor she had mentally mapped from other visits, she kept a watch on Betsy. Although Betsy's eyes were full of questions, she remained silent.

The dark musty room was still filled with stacks of crates and trunks, just as it had been the last time she and Timothy were in there. She deftly wound around the first two stacks to the third row, going precisely to an opening in the middle where there were several large knotholes in the floor.

Timothy touched Betsy on the shoulder. When she looked at him, he mouthed, "Watch me," while tapping his chest. He lay face down, centering an eye over one of the holes.

Sarah Emily pointed to another hollowed-out knothole in the floor, and Betsy lay down, just as Timothy did, then Sarah Emily.

Below in Miss Percy's parlor, the colorful column of cookie tins stood in the corner, and the women were arranging themselves for tea.

Along with Sarah Emily, Timothy and Betsy could see and hear everything from their undetected catbird seats.

"Select a cup from the china cabinet, Lydia," Miss Percy instructed her guest as she checked the tray Cook had filled with an assortment of tiny cakes and a lovely pink teapot. Then she picked up her chipped cup from the desk.

"Mildred, you do have the most exquisite collection of teacups I've ever seen." Mrs. Hancock poked as much of her head, hat and all, as would fit in the china cabinet.

Poingggg! The birds sprang up and vibrated when she came out saying, "Is this new? I don't remember seeing it before." Turning around and seeing Miss Percy with her cup, Mrs. Hancock said, "And I have never understood why you insist on always drinking out of that one with the chips. It seems to me it should simply be thrown away."

Miss Percy said nothing, only stiffened, hugging her cup close to her chest.

"Oh, Mildred, now don't get upset. You know me. I firmly believe in saying what's on my mind. And what's on my mind right now is, I simply don't understand why you must drink out of that broken old thing. You have so many lovely ones." To make her point, she held out the cup and saucer with a delicate rose pattern and perfectly scalloped edges. The china cup clinked against its saucer like a tinkling chime. "I'll say it again. I don't understand why you keep that chipped one."

"Must you understand everything about everyone?" Miss Percy mumbled as she sat down to pick up the teapot and pour their tea.

"What did you say?" Mrs. Hancock said, settling into the crimson chair across from Miss Percy.

"Just asking if you want cream or lemon in your tea, my dear." Miss Percy smiled and handed her a plate. "And do have one of Cook's sumptuous cakes."

"Thank you. And I'll have cream," Mrs. Hancock said as she

took the largest cake from the tray, reminding Sarah Emily of a swooping hawk plucking up a baby mouse. "You must have Cook submit one of her recipes to our Ladies' Aid Society Pie and Cake Cookbook. She really bakes the most remarkable creations. All these little individual cakes are just adorable."

A kink began to throb in Sarah Emily's neck. She rubbed it and turned her head to use the other eye. She knew with cake and tea served, the ladies were ready for a long session of conversation.

"The lilacs were the most breathtaking I've seen in many a year. Don't you think so?" Mrs. Hancock took a liberal bite of cake. "Of course, as you are aware, I'm sure, most of the spectacular ones were at the *other* end of Lilac Lane."

"Yes." Miss Percy held the chipped cup in her left hand and sipped tea. "They certainly were beautiful, and the fragrance was just heavenly."

"Whatever do you think, Mildred, about the cavorting between Mr. Edwin and Mrs. Smothers?" Mrs. Hancock and her birds leaned forward as if this very conversation must be kept hushed.

"Oh, my, it's scandalous, just scandalous!"

"Why, gracious sakes," Mrs. Hancock said, all a flutter. "Mr. Smothers—God rest his soul—has only been gone a little over two years."

Sarah Emily silently chuckled at the thought of meek Mrs. Smothers and old bachelor Edwin who hobbled everywhere on his ornately carved cane, cavorting—in any manner.

"Do tell me, what's been going on with them?" Miss Percy centered her cup on its saucer.

"Mildred, you'll be horrified. Simply horrified." Mrs. Hancock leaned forward again, hat-birds doing likewise. "Sadie Miller saw them kissing!"

"Oh my!" Miss Percy patted her chest with little spanking sounds, as if to keep herself breathing in the face of such shocking news.

Sarah Emily wasn't surprised at Miss Percy's reaction since she had probably never had a beau. It was doubtful, Sarah Emily thought, that Miss Percy ever wanted one.

"Have another cake, Lydia," Miss Percy urged.

"Well, I really shouldn't," Mrs. Hancock said sadly, her gaze lingering on the cake tray.

"Oh, but I insist."

Mrs. Hancock cheered up. "Very well, then, thank you. I will." She studied the selections and chose a generous one with white fluffy frosting.

Sarah Emily looked at Timothy and Betsy, their attention still below. She sighed softly, impatience wiggling in her for the talk below to turn to what the Ladies' Aid Society was giving for Christmas. She repositioned herself over the peephole.

The women discussed Mrs. Jensen's mysterious illness—which they both were *certain* was just a good case of hypochondria, no matter the raging fever she was reported to be suffering. Mrs. Hancock couldn't get over the huge amount of fabric Polly Fletcher bought on sale at Mitchell's Mercantile. "I know Polly needs the work, and I certainly don't begrudge her that," she said with great oozing compassion. "But what kind of a dressmaking job could she have possibly secured that would call for that much fabric?" And then the crooked path of their conversation led them to wondering about the new family who just moved into the lovely, immaculate white and green house at the far end of Lilac Lane.

Those two women could keep up this pointless nattering for hours. And while they're at it, Sarah Emily thought she wouldn't mind having one of those cakes herself.

Mrs. Hancock tapped her fork against her plate, gathering up the last crumbs from her second cake. "And isn't it a shame the way Mrs. Parker has put on so much weight this past year? Poor dear—some ladies just can't seem to control their appetite."

"Yes, some seem to have no self-control. Would you care for another piece of cake, Lydia, dear?"

"Oh, no. I couldn't." Mrs. Hancock set her plate aside and blotted the corners of her mouth with a pale pink linen napkin. "But I might wrap up that chocolate one for Mr. Hancock, if you please. He does so love chocolate."

"Of course, Lydia. And why don't I just wrap two? Then you can join him in tea and cake after dinner should you feel the need for a tiny bite of something to tide you over before bed."

Sarah Emily's stomach grumbled just thinking about the times she would have liked a tiny bite of something to tide her over before bed.

"What a lovely thing for you to do." Mrs. Hancock and her birds leaned back. "I do sometimes think I will faint with hunger in the evening hours. Oh, about Christmas gifts." She smoothed her skirts over her spacious girth.

Finally, they're getting somewhere, Sarah Emily thought with relief.

"I nearly forgot—" Mrs. Hancock's words halted at a clatter coming from above her. Her head jerked back, ogling the ceiling, straining to identify the commotion.

The storage room door had been pushed open and Sarah Emily heard Ours leaping and lunging around the trunks. Sarah Emily went rigid, not daring to breathe. It dawned on her that in her effort to be quiet and avoid another rusty squawk from the door, she hadn't closed it tightly. The dog was making such a clamor, the two women below were now standing and studying the ceiling. Miss Percy with her mouth open, squinting her eyes as if trying to see between the boards, and Mrs. Hancock's birds dangling and dancing at her back in a near upside down position.

Timothy bolted to grab Ours the same moment Sarah Emily did. Betsy watched silently, alarm plastered on her face. Sarah Emily could hear Miss Percy below.

"There were cardinals that tried to live in there last year. Found a hole in the side of the building and were making nests, pretty as you please. Jenkins had to get them out. Maybe they've returned."

"Well, if it's birds, then my guess, from the racket they're making, they would be ostriches," Mrs. Hancock huffed.

At last, Sarah Emily and Timothy had the large dog happily and quietly lying down.

"Whew! That was close," he mouthed to the girls.

Betsy nodded.

Sarah Emily patted Ours and cautiously peeped down through her knothole.

"That's odd," Mrs. Hancock said as the ladies, their eyes still scrutinizing the ceiling, lowered themselves half-inch by half-inch back into the brocade chairs. "Truly peculiar the way the noise stopped so suddenly."

"Yes, I'll have Jenkins check up there and see if the birds are back."

Sarah Emily lifted her head and signaled to Betsy and Timothy that it was safe to resume their spy positions. She spread one arm over Ours who licked her face and laid her shaggy head on her shaggy front paws. Sarah Emily sighed, patted Ours and went back to the goings-on below.

Mrs. Hancock adjusted her birds. Miss Percy poured more hot tea.

"As I was about to tell you, Mildred," Mrs. Hancock leaned back, taking a quick sip of tea, and then resting the saucer atop her shelf of a bosom, "there are several large tins of olives in the carriage for the orphans for Christmas."

Ugh. Sarah Emily scrunched her face, and her hopes withered. How had olives replaced hair clasps?

"I believe it's those big, black olives," Mrs. Hancock continued. "Since I despise olives of every sort, can't even stand to look at them, or worse yet, smell them, I didn't check to see what kind they were. Mr. Mitchell donated them. Said they were slow movers. He just couldn't sell them at the mercantile." She stopped to look at the cake tray again and waggled her hand at a fat yellow cake. "Maybe I'll have just a half of that slice of pound cake to go with my tea. Anyway, about the olives. Of course, I told him they should be just fine for orphans. Don't you agree, Mildred?"

"My, my, yes. They will eat anything." Miss Percy neatly set the whole slice of cake on Mrs. Hancock's waiting plate. "And you know, Lydia, it just gets harder and harder to feed them on the meager rations and allotments the state gives me each month."

When Sarah Emily heard that, she scrambled up. The others looked at her and she motioned for them to follow her out. "Quietly!" she mouthed. She was angry and sick of stuffing those thoughts away. It was time to do something—now—and there wasn't time to plan or think, not even the time it takes water to boil.

The four met in the hall. Ours scratched behind her down-ear.

"That was it!" Sarah Emily closed the storage room door behind them. "I'm fed up with her saying she can't feed us on what she gets from the state. When she sends Timothy or any of the others out to work, she gets all their pay. Do you get any of it?" She stared at Timothy, knowing perfectly well the answer.

He didn't say anything, only gave a slight shake of his head.

"She can't feed us on what she gets, because she's doing something else with the allotment. I'm sure of it! Where else would she get the money for her fine clothes and china teacups? It has to be from that and your working all last week on the railroad job that she got the butter and sugar to have all those cakes to feed to that mountain of suet, Mrs. Hancock." Sarah Emily nibbled her lower lip, and an idea began to take form. "We're going to throw Miss Percy and her Ladies' Aid Society friends a party!"

Timothy and Betsy shot identical gawks at Sarah Emily.

Then after a brief moment, Timothy appeared to have recovered, and he laid his hand on Betsy's shoulder. "Sarah Emily's ideas don't always make sense at first, not to a normal person anyway." He flashed a broad smile at Sarah Emily, then looked back at Betsy. "I guess you haven't been here long enough to see her like this, but she can come up with schemes as easy as snow makes flakes."

Betsy's eyes danced, alight with shared mischief. "You mean like when I first got here, and she pretended to be having a fit in the dining room?"

"Oh, hush, you two." Sarah Emily slapped at the air. "We don't have a second to waste while you talk nonsense. Now listen, and listen good." As if she understood, Ours sat down and looked at Sarah Emily with great concentration.

"We're going downstairs to tell Miss Percy we want to have a Christmas party for her friends."

"Sarah Emily," Timothy shook his head, "I'd think that as you get older, your ideas would make more sense. But this one's going to take the prize for being the wildest you've ever hatched up."

"She ain't going to let us have a party," Betsy countered as if good sense had been snatched out of the other two.

"Oh yes she will." Sarah Emily tingled with the budding plan. She propped each heel of a hand on a hip. "We're going to tell her in front of Mrs. Hancock.Then what can she say? Come on, that lady and her birds will be leaving soon."

She latched onto their arms and pulled them forward and down the stairs, while Betsy anxiously was saying, "With rations so low, what will we serve?"

"Shhh. They're coming. Don't worry, I've got it figured out," Sarah Emily said just as the parlor door opened.

Ours's lavish tail-wagging stopped the moment she saw Mrs. Hancock.

"Mildred!" Mrs. Hancock took several steps back, positioning her plump body behind Miss Percy's stringy frame. "There's the beast that got under my feet and caused me to drop the cookie tins."

"Lydia, she won't hurt you." Miss Percy leaned down and patted the dog's head. "Just a little rambunctious at times, aren't you, girl?" she cooed, and Ours gave a little lick to Miss Percy's cheek.

That dog certainly has a way with Miss Percy, Sarah Emily thought. *Wish I knew how she does it.*

By now, Mrs. Hancock was moving toward the door, keeping a watchful eye on Ours. "Mildred, you must come to my house for tea very soon," she said, twisting into her thick black coat, being careful not to crush the cakes she was taking home.

"Yes, I'd love to," Miss Percy said, helping Mrs. Hancock get her arms stuffed in.

"Mrs. Hancock?" Sarah Emily blurted out.

Both women turned to look at her. "Whatever do you want?" Miss Percy said.

"I...we," Sarah Emily waved her hand in front of Timothy and Betsy who smiled and nodded, "want to have a party for Mrs. Hancock and her Ladies' Aid Society. They always bring us gifts at Christmas. Then, for effect, she let her voice drip with gratitude. "And we want to show them how much it means to us."

"I don't think—"

Mrs. Hancock laid an interrupting hand on Miss Percy's

shoulder and stepped toward Sarah Emily. "What a lovely idea. I'm sure, Mildred, the other ladies would love the opportunity to get to know your poor unfortunate orphans better."

"Yes, of course," Miss Percy said. Lifting her knobby shoulders, stretching her scrawny neck, she turned her back slightly to Mrs. Hancock and glared bullets into Sarah Emily.

"What about Friday afternoon?" Sarah Emily spoke up, looking past Miss Percy and directly at Mrs. Hancock. She could only hope she sounded confident because inside she wasn't. "Three o'clock?" she asked, pushing forward with her plan, never taking her eyes from the beaming Mrs. Hancock.

"Three o'clock, Friday, it is." Mrs. Hancock handed her cakes to Miss Percy. "Hold these, please, while I get my gloves on." After buttoning her coat and pulling on her gloves, Mrs. Hancock took possession of her take-home pastries. "I had a lovely visit with you today, Mildred, and I'll look forward to Friday." She studied Ours, who was sitting contentedly between Betsy and Timothy. "Nice dog." It sounded more like a question than an endearment as she lightly brushed the furry head with her gloved hand.

Ours didn't move.

Please, don't growl, Sarah Emily sent out a silent request.

Thankfully, Ours stayed still and quiet.

Mrs. Hancock pulled her hand back and shook it slightly as if she had just touched a dusty table. She opened the front door and stepped outside.

"Good Girl," Sarah Emily leaned down and whispered into Ours's up-ear.

"Good bye, Lydia. You be careful on that snowy ground," Miss Percy trilled. "See you Friday." She closed the heavy door harder than necessary and whirled around.

Sarah Emily and friends were tiptoeing off in the other direction.

"Come back here. Right now."

Her commanding tone swung them around. Ours slid her front paws straight out on the wooden floor, plopped the back half of herself down with a thump and stretched her mouth around a cavernous yawn.

Miss Percy clenched her fists so tight, the knuckles looked like they might burst through. "Now, just what do you orphan brats think you're doing by suggesting a party?"

"We thought...we knew you'd like it if we threw a nice party for your friends," Timothy spoke up.

Again, Timothy had come alongside to help her with one of her plans. Sarah Emily's toes started to twitch.

"Nice party." Miss Percy released an exasperated laugh.

Sarah Emily's toes quieted instantly.

"I know you're up to something, but since Mrs. Hancock thinks it's such a good idea, there's not much I can do now." Her right fist unlocked a bony finger to jab at them. "Maybe there's not much I can do—now. However, if you pull any of your shenanigans, there will be plenty I can do later." She turned on her heel and left the four alone in the hall.

"Shenanigans? You, Sarah Emily?" Betsy said with a smile so big her dimples appeared as soon as Miss Percy was out of sight and hearing.

"Betsy, you know, if we help on this, we'll be numbered in the shenanigan-making." A grin slid across Timothy's lips. "Are you game?"

"I can do this myself," Sarah Emily spoke before Betsy could answer. "I don't want the two of you getting into trouble because of me."

"Are you kidding? Count me in. I may live to regret it, but there's sure to be some fun first," Betsy said.

Timothy nodded. "You couldn't pay me enough to miss this."

"You two are the greatest friends anybody could have." Sarah Emily squeezed in between them and looped her arms over their shoulders. "It just gets me so riled when that Mrs. Hancock and her group act like they're doing so much good work, but they don't even try to know what we really need—or anything about us. And Miss Percy makes others think she's doing what she's supposed to with what the state gives her—like taking care of us." Sarah Emily lowered her gaze and looked at Ours. Her voice got whisper thin. "And she won't tell us anything about our families."

"Sarah Em," Timothy steered himself around to face her. "You're thinking about that man who was out front with Miss Percy a while back, aren't you?"

"*That* man is my pa."

"You don't know that for certain, do you?" Betsy reached up and laced her fingers in Sarah Emily's hand, still draped over her shoulder. "He did leave without saying anything to you."

"He's the man in my picture. He has to be my pa." She squirmed her fingers out of Betsy's and put two full feet of space between them. "Just because after your ma died, your pa kept you and mine didn't, doesn't mean that man isn't my pa."

A pang shot across Betsy's face.

At once, Sarah Emily wished she hadn't said that, at least not so harshly.

"Sarah Em, think about it. Why would your pa leave you here?" Timothy touched her arm.

"I don't know," she said softly to the floor. "I don't know why he left me here." She looked up. "But if that isn't who he is, why is he in the picture with my ma? And why is he the one who brought me here?" She jerked her arm out from under Timothy's hand. "I'm going to find the answers to my questions."

"Sometimes it's better not to know all the answers," Betsy said.

"Not for me." Sarah Emily exhaled and tried to steady herself. "I aim to know everything about who I am, who I look like and where I came from. Don't you understand, Betsy? That's the only way I'm ever going to know what kind of person I'm supposed to be." Sarah Emily didn't give Betsy a chance to speak. "Come on." And when Timothy tried to say something else, she raised her hand to stop him. "We've got a party to plan."

"You mean, shenanigans to plan." Timothy rubbed his hands together and looked eager to get at it.

Chapter 11

Two-thirty, Friday afternoon, the town of Lander was hooded with a pewter sky and splattered with snow. *Will the ladies come out in this weather?* Sarah Emily stood in the dining room pressing down the pleats of her clean apron with nervous hands. Her fretful gaze flitted between the window and the door. From the window, not one carriage of ladies could be seen. Through the door, orphans were rushing in.

Had she done the right thing to suggest this party? She was only doing it because this Christmas it looked like there weren't going to be any hair clasps—just olives and cookies. Mrs. Hancock didn't care as long as she felt important and looked good to the Ladies' Aid Society, and Miss Percy didn't care as long as she could serve cake and tea and look good to Mrs. Hancock.

And Sarah Emily meant for neither of them to look good—at least not today.

She knew her reason for having the party was wrong, but somehow there had to be some right in it to give those two a taste of their own medicine, wasn't there? Her stomach took on a wrestling match with the right and wrong of the whole idea. Oh well, it was too late to call it off now even if she thought she should. *Exactly how long does it take for water to boil?* She must find out.

"I washed up," Ben growled at her. "You happy now?" He had a scrubbed face; even his pointy chin had a shine to it, though he had missed a ring of dirt circling his neck.

"There had better be some good eating for this!" James said, jabbing a thumb toward his slicked down hair.

"Are we really going to have cookies?" Cora called as she ran in, as excited if she were getting a pony. "Oops, I forgot something." She threw up her hands and was back out the door.

Ours sprawled in the corner, pretending to doze, but she opened one eye, flapping and swishing her tail across the wooden floor anytime someone stooped to give her a pat. She was brushed to a silky sheen and festooned with a red ribbon that Cora had retrieved from a cookie tin and insisted Ours wear around her neck—an act of great generosity and unselfishness on Cora's part.

"Everything looks beautiful," Nettie purred when she found Sarah Emily in the growing group. "Yes, beautiful." Nettie folded her arms, pride glowing from her smile. "We did a pretty good job of fixing this place up, didn't we?"

In spite of her jitters, Sarah Emily took stock of the dining room. Most of the tables were stacked out of the way against a wall. The benches were lined up like garden rows, straight and evenly apart, waiting for guests. Two tables were pushed together end-to-end to hold refreshments. From somewhere, Cook had found long pieces of red cloth to cover them.

A couple of the boys had swept and washed the floor clean, leaving the dining room with a sweet fragrance instead of its usual vinegary smell. When she asked the boys why it smelled so good, they shrugged and told her Cook had poured something in the rinse water.

The girls certainly had done a great job of looping red and green paper chains around the walls and tying sprigs of holly berries in the window frames.

Most certainly, the words "party" and "cookies" had worked wonders to gain cooperation from nearly everyone. "Yes! It looks

like we're about to have a party—and a good one! I just know it."
Sarah Emily felt her fears dissolving and an explosion of confidence in her carefully laid plans.

Timothy rushed into the dining room, holding Cora's hand. He wore his best shirt, but a good three inches of his arms stuck out beneath cuffs of the outgrown sleeves. The left elbow was held together with a pink rosebud print patch from one of Miss Percy's old dresses, which he loathed. "Rather have the hole," he had said after the patch had been applied. It was another sign of solidarity with Sarah Emily's plan that he showed up in it. His hair was combed and precisely parted. "Hope I'm not late. I wanted to help you with the last minute details." He tugged at his shirtsleeves.

"Look at my hair." Cora beamed up at Sarah Emily. "I found this bit of string when I was gathering the trash, and I thought it would look pretty. This is what I forgot." She touched the twine at the top of her head that was cinched in a crude bow around a short chunk of hair. "Timothy tied it for me." She looked at him with adoring eyes.

He dropped his gaze to his shoes and slid his hands into his back pockets. "Aw, I didn't do anything. I just tied it for her when I saw her struggling to get it in her hair. That's why I'm a little late."

Sarah Emily smiled at him. Unlike some of the other older boys, he always had time to help the little ones. She liked that about Timothy. That was just one thing in a long and growing list of things. Suddenly her toes twitched. Funny how they had been best friends for so long, and she could talk to him about almost anything. Her toes twitched again. Everything, that is, except this silly sensation she really didn't understand herself—and would feel feather-headed to mention.

Her toes kept up their bewildering behavior. She plunked her other foot on top to try and stop it.

Timothy stared at her feet. "With one foot perched on the other like that you look like some kind of strange bird. Why have you recently taken to standing like that?"

"Oh, I don't know." She quickly put both feet squarely on the floor. Cora was squirming in front of her. "Say something!" She molded her mouth into a tiny pout. "Don't you like my hair?"

"You look beautiful." Sarah Emily looked at the little girl, welcoming an interruption in the subject about her feet. She casually tried to mash the chunk of hair down that sprouted from the center of Cora's head. *Sproing.* It had a mind of its own. Sarah Emily tried to mash it again. *Sproing,* for the second time. Leaving well enough alone, she placed both hands on Cora's shoulders. "You do have a way of fixing yourself up!"

Again, Cora beamed.

"Careful now, this apple cider is hot," Cook was saying.

When Sarah Emily turned to see Cook, excited children were gathering around her. That was no surprise, but Sarah Emily was surprised at her dress. Of course, her hair was combed just so, and she wore a spotless white apron. But it was tied over her old dark brown dress—her special dress that was reserved for funerals and weddings. It was faded and frayed, and Sarah Emily assumed her new dress would have been ready by now.

Setting the steaming kettle on the table, Cook reached to fix the collar on one of the younger boy's shirt, playfully scolding, "Caleb, you little wiggle worm, hold yourself still."

"Where's the new dress?" Sarah Emily asked after Cora wandered away to show her hair off to the others.

"Did I say I was going to wear a new dress today?"

"I just thought by now you'd have your new one—the one made from that beautiful green swatch of fabric you showed me."

"Not quite yet—but soon, very soon. Betsy's going to be bringing in the cups from the kitchen. Why don't you put your mind to helping her get them on the table instead of my dress?" Cook grinned her end-of-conversation grin.

Sarah Emily smiled back, and then the thought rose out of nowhere that Cook hadn't been gone in the afternoons lately.

The door flung open, banging against the wall, and Marjorie rushed in. "Are the Ladies' Aid Society ladies still coming?" She was winded and already pointed to race back out the door.

"I'm surprised you're interested at all," Sarah Emily said. "To tell you the truth, I didn't think you'd come."

"Just answer my question."

"Yes, they're coming."

Marjorie nearly catapulted herself out the door.

Betsy came across the dining room with a tray of Miss Percy's cups and saucers—not her very best ones, but nice ones just the same—that she'd given permission to use since it was the Ladies' Aid Society coming. Miss Percy had been nervous about them being used, but relented when she couldn't figure out a way, without looking bad to Mrs. Hancock, not to let them.

"Anything else you need me to do in the kitchen?" Betsy asked when the last cup was neatly arranged on the table.

"Not a thing right now." Cook finished straightening Caleb's collar, leaned down and pulled him into a quick hug. "But I appreciate all your help," she said to Betsy as he scampered away.

Sarah Emily lifted the kettle lid. "Smells like you've got cinnamon and other good things in here."

"Cinnamon arrived this morning."

"Just like the butter and sugar earlier in the week." Sarah Emily knew Miss Percy had been without her cinnamon buns for . . . how long had it been? Well, however long, it couldn't have gone on much longer. Sarah Emily closed her eyes and breathed deeply, filling herself with the tantalizing aroma of the spice and crisp apples. She allowed herself one more wonderful whiff of the steaming drink and then replaced the heavy cover. She couldn't just stand there smelling the cider and wondering where the money for the cinnamon came from; she had a party to organize. "What about the food?" Sarah Emily said, looking at Cook.

"Food? I don't be knowing nothin'." Her voice was playful, and she nodded toward Betsy.

"The food's ready." Betsy's eyes gleamed with satisfaction, and her dimples deepened. "It's *all* ready."

"Great!" Sarah Emily said. Betsy's reaction told her that part of the plan was in place. Now they needed the ladies to arrive.

"Sarah Emily? Where are you?" The irritation in Miss Percy's voice was as evident as shoeprints in deep mud as she stormed into the dining room. She wore her good dress, not a bit frayed, and the color hadn't faded a drop from its rich deep blue. It was a beautiful dress, and Sarah Emily thought it especially showed off the exquisite jeweled brooch.

At hearing Miss Percy's voice, Ours leaped up and trotted toward her.

Miss Percy started rubbing Ours's up-ear and then her down-ear, seeming to forget her search for Sarah Emily. "Well, look at you," she said in a soft warble. "Aren't you the pretty one with a shiny red bow around your neck?"

As if an invisible string attached to the top of Miss Percy's head had been yanked, she stood erect, scrunched her pointed nose and loudly sniffed—making rows of wrinkles between her eyes. "What *is* that I smell in here?" Like a rat's nose twitching up and down, she sniffed several more times. "Why, if I didn't know better, I'd swear it smells just like my rose water."

Sarah Emily whirled around to Cook.

Cook breathed deeply. "Why, so it does. Nice, isn't it? But, Law, I don't be knowing nothin'."

Just then, the whinnying of horses sent Sarah Emily to the window. Two stately carriages had arrived, and Mr. Wilbur was helping the ladies out.

"Okay, everybody," Sarah Emily called. "Ladies are beginning to arrive. Line up. We want to give them a proper greeting."

The boys stopped their game, scooped up marbles and hid them in their pockets. The girls jumped up from the benches where they had been talking.

"Does everyone remember what they're to do?"

"I'm to serve the cider," Nettie said, moving toward the table.

"I'm to help them off with their coats." Timothy held out his elbow in exaggerated readiness. "And escort them to their seats."

Then Sarah Emily saw Cora forming silent words and said, "Are you all right?"

"Yeah. I think so." The color drained from Cora's face, her eyes glazed and fixed on the door. "I was just saying the words to my poem once more before those ladies come in." She blinked several times, pulled her gaze from the door and looked at Sarah Emily.

"I surely do hope I don't mix up my words."

"You won't. You did it perfectly the last few times we've practiced." Sarah Emily knelt down at eye level with Cora. "And if you do, just go on like it was meant to be that way." She brushed a light kiss on Cora's cheek, and the little girl ran off to get in line with the others.

Everyone was whispering and giggling while running to their places. Ours yelped and wagged her tail. The air crackled with anticipation.

Miss Percy latched on to Sarah Emily's apron strings and jerked her back. She bent down so her lips were pressed tight against Sarah Emily's ear. "You remember what I told you about shenanigans?" She let go, and Sarah Emily lurched forward, then righted herself, while swiping her hand across her buzzing ear.

Drawing in a full breath, Sarah Emily rubbed her nervous damp hands on her apron, turned and mustered as much confidence as she could in a split second, "Miss Percy, why don't you come with me to welcome our guests?"

The door opened, and tiny snow flurries preceded Mrs. Hancock as she entered the dining room, brushing snow off the brim of her new red Christmas hat. The hat sat at a jaunty angle and sprouted gold poinsettias. Tucked beneath some of the foliage in the front, a stuffed, stiff, white rabbit peeked out. Sarah Emily looked closer. No, it was a squirrel. It's long furry tail was wrapped around a pine cone.

Miss Percy held out her arms and they briefly hugged, their backs rigid.

Mrs. Hancock stomped the snow from her shoes, after which, she straightened herself so much that her head bowed backwards just a bit. In this arrogant position, she surveyed the room. She began to pull off her gloves, pinching the end of each finger and giving a snap of her wrist. The squirrel nodded his head with each tug. "Well, well, how about this?" She opened her handbag and slipped in her gloves. "The orphans giving the Ladies' Aid Society a party!" With a sharp click, she closed the golden clasp on her beaded bag.

"Mrs. Hancock, may I help you with your coat?" Timothy said

to her with a surprising amount of dignity.

Sarah Emily attempted a little curtsey. She had seen a picture of that in a book. "I'm honored to have you as our guest." She had read that. All the reading and learning with Timothy was paying off. Sarah Emily continued to receive the guests as if she had been trained by the Queen of England herself.

"Timothy will show you where to sit, and Nettie will get you some hot apple cider." She loved the way her words sounded—mature, efficient and in control. And even more than that, she was elated by the way they shocked Miss Percy. *Just wait 'til she hears Cora and Betsy today.*

Miss Percy continued to stare, her dead-animal stare, her mouth hanging open until another lady said hello to her.

"Yes. Do come in and have some cider." Instantly, Miss Percy had a smile on her face, and her tone was ever so friendly and merry.

It was an amazing thing she could do. She could open some internal drawer and pull out a mask for whatever character she needed to be at that moment. They were so thin, though, Sarah Emily would have thought everyone could see through them to her perpetual discontent.

"Hot cider!" the lady said. "That would be wonderful." Her three chins jiggled as she reached up—Sarah Emily was a good four inches taller—and patted Sarah Emily on the head. "Mildred, how sweet your orphans are." Then she swabbed her hanky across her hand and allowed Timothy to show her to her seat, holding her hand slightly curved, offering him only the tips of her fingers.

Sarah Emily's proud mood slipped. She grabbed Betsy's arm. "Did you see that?" she whispered, leaning in close. "Did you see her wipe off her hand after she touched me? It's just like the other day when Mrs. Hancock shook her hand off after touching Ours."

"Yes, but never mind that now." Betsy pulled her away from the door and held up the sleeve of one of the ladies' coats, rubbing the edge of it between her fingers as tenderly as if the coat were a new-born baby's delicate hand. "Feel how warm and soft."

Sarah Emily touched the coat, at first just barely, almost afraid to feel something so choice. But the fineness compelled her to flatten her hand, letting it sink into the luxurious, brown fur and imagine the comfort such a coat would bring on a bitterly cold day. "This is a grand coat, isn't it?" she said, kneading her fingers into the plushness.

"Do you think we'll ever have a new coat?" Betsy asked.

"For this winter, I'd settle for a less old one, but not for always, Betsy. Someday, we'll have new coats. I just know it. You know how Mr. Wilbur keeps reminding us we won't be orphans forever."

A splash of cold air brought in more partygoers, prompting Sarah Emily to the front of the room. When the guests were seated, she counted fourteen ladies. All in all, things were going well, and it was time for the festivities to begin.

Chapter 12

*S*arah Emily cleared her throat. The rattling of cups and saucers, along with chattering, stopped. The silence blasted her ears. Everyone stared, waiting—waiting for her to speak. She inhaled and slid her gaze across each row of ladies. *All I have to do is talk. Just talk. Open mouth and talk. Surely, I can do that. Yes! I can do that.*

And then she exhaled, ready to begin. "We wanted to invite you here today to show you how much we appreciate the things you send us at Christmas. Living in an orphan asylum, there aren't many treats and surprises." Gathering resolve, she went further, "Most of us don't even know who we look like." She was certain they all knew who they looked like, but wanted them to be reminded of how wonderful that knowledge is.

With her cup of cider perched at chest level, a lady looked at her neighbor. "Whatever does she mean?"

"I have no idea what the girl's talking about," came the reply.

For a second, their reaction confused and flustered Sarah Emily, but she wasn't about to be stopped. "Now, we'd like to introduce ourselves to you," she said, trying to appear as calm as a duck on water, knowing that underneath she was paddling for all she was worth. She lightly touched the top of her dress, hoping the shaking of her hand couldn't be seen. "I'm Sarah Emily." And then she nodded to Marjorie, the first in the lineup of orphans against the wall.

Marjorie had her head turned to the window, peering intently at something outside. James elbowed her, and she flinched, spraying her mouthful of cider. "Huh? Oh, my name's Marjorie." She frowned a serves-you-right frown at James as he slapped at the mist of cider on his shirt.

On down the line it went. Ben was the last, and as soon as he told who he was, Sarah Emily turned her attention back to the ladies. "We have some entertainment planned for you that we hope you'll enjoy." She nodded at Cora. "Come on," she said, motioning her forward.

Cora tipped her cup and sucked in a loud slurp, draining the last drop of cider. She swiped a hand across her lips and handed her empty cup to Nettie.

Miss Percy shuffled her feet and twined and untwined her fingers, a jittery little smile squeezing her lips when any of the ladies looked her way.

With the extravagance of youthful zest, Cora came to stand beside Sarah Emily. She fidgeted back and forth, skirt twirling around her ankles, the chunk of tied hair zooming out the top of her head, bobbing like a single antenna on a bug.

Sarah Emily slipped her arm around the girl's shoulder. "Cora is six years old, and she would like to recite a poem for you." Sarah Emily patted Cora, stepped back and watched Cora's topknot of tied hair waggling from side to side. Sarah Emily remembered how Cora pinned maple leaves all over her apron last fall. "For decoration," Cora had said. She did love to fix herself up—and any one else who would let her. Sarah Emily slid her eyes over to Ours who was sporting the red ribbon.

Cora was suddenly self-conscious and dipped her chin, drawing halting loops down the side of her dress with a tiny forefinger. Then taking a deep breath and another, she stood straight as a sword and commenced reciting.

> Old Meg was brave as
> Margaret Queen
> And tall as Amazon.
> An old red blanket
> Cloak she wore
> A chip-hat had she on.

Then without missing a beat of the poem, she crossed her tiny hands over her heart, looked heavenward and continued, deep sorrow dripping from every word.

> God rest her aged bones somewhere.
> She died full-long agone!

With the last word, she loudly exhaled and dropped her head to her chest, as if to truly mourn the unknown Old Meg. After a brief pause, Cora uncrossed her hands, lifted her head and smiled broadly at her audience, glowing with innocent exuberance.

"That's not a Christmas poem," one lady said.

"More importantly, what kind of poetry is that for a child to recite?" another said as horrified as if Cora had just pulled out Old Meg's aged bones from her pocket.

Condemning gasps came from several, while others puckered their lips, casting sideways looks at one another.

Sarah Emily stepped forward, applauding. The other orphans were wildly clapping and whistling.

Flinging her arms out wide, Cora said with every bit as much conviction as pride, "I'm going to be an actress someday."

"An actress," a horrified woman snapped. "How vulgar."

Others nodded in agreement and huffed under their breath.

"Mildred," an over-fed woman said, rising slightly and craning forward to see Miss Percy at the end of the row. "I'd think you'd know that an actress is not a proper pursuit for any young woman—even for an orphan!" Then she heaved her girth back onto the bench.

Embarrassment and anger bulged Miss Percy's eyes and reddened her face. Her face became so red, in fact, Sarah Emily was happily certain that if she parted her tense lips, even her teeth would be red.

Ladies held their china cups primly and showed only disdain for Cora's fine dramatic acting and choice of future profession. But Cora skipped back toward her place in line obviously pleased with herself and completely unaffected by the appalled response they had shown.

"Would anyone like more hot cider before we have the next entertainment?" Sarah Emily asked the ladies, hoping to divert their attention.

"I want more cider!" nearly all the orphans yelled in unison.

Miss Percy looked like a caged animal desperate to run, but with no place of escape anywhere in sight.

Although Cook had the excited Cora pressed against her in a tight hug, "I'll get more cider for everyone," she said. "There's plenty."

"I'll help." Mr. Wilbur ruffled Cora's topknot, gave her an approving smile and then followed Cook to the kitchen, his own hair as matted as a bird's nest.

When Cook brought in another batch of the fragrant beverage, she seemed alive with delight at the whole scene.

Several ladies slightly nodded, indicating they wanted more.

While Nettie helped Mr. Wilson and Cook serve the cider, Timothy edged up beside Sarah Emily. "Where did Cora learn all those emotional gestures?"

"I have no idea. She didn't do any of that when we practiced. But you heard her, she wants to be an actress."

"She's got the flair for it! That's for certain."

"Yeah, and it sure caused quite a stir," Sarah Emily raised her nose haughtily in the air, "with the Ladies' Aid Society." She drew her lips into a tight ring and said each word with overly precise enunciation. They laughed hard and loud until she felt the burn of Miss Percy's glare. "We've got to stop. Old-you-know-who isn't pleased we're enjoying ourselves," she said between bursts of giggles.

Timothy pushed his hands into his front pockets and tilted his head toward the fireplace. "I can't remember the last time we had a fire in here. It can be thirty below, and we don't even get to burn a twig. But I suppose we couldn't let the Ladies' Aid Society catch a chill," he said rolling his eyes.

"Yeah, as I recollect, the last time that fireplace was used was when the man from the state came to check on us. And that was, what, about four years ago?"

Timothy nodded and started to walk away, then slowed.

"You want to say something else, don't you?" Sarah Emily put her hands on her hips. "I can see right through you, Timothy Marshall, as clearly as a freshly washed window pane."

He pulled his hands out of his pockets and hooked his thumbs in his overalls' bib, his elbow straining the rosebud patch. "Well, since you think you're so smart, why'd you go saying all that about who we look like?"

"Because, I thought it was important for the ladies to remember that all of us don't know that yet. We're still figuring it out." She closed her mouth, jiggled her head and said firmly, "Timothy, you should know that by now."

"Well, I don't know that. It's like you're seeing something that looks solid, right and believable—the answer to some longing you have. But when you get further into it, I think you're going to see it's nothing but fog, hollow fog." He looked directly at her, that pair of familiar creases forming between his eyes. "Sarah Em, when are you going to get this crazy notion out of your head?"

She said nothing, only returning his stare. After a few seconds of this visual stand off, he walked away. He stopped by the gas lamp on the edge of the mantle, and she heard him mumble, "In some large cities people cook with gas." She had seen it over and over, in any situation a fact could surface. She was just glad he hadn't pursued their disagreement any further because she was a little shaken by what he had said. Hollow fog? But right now, she couldn't show her unease, she had a party to tend to.

Everyone had his cup refilled with cider, so Sarah Emily called Betsy to the front and announced, "Since this is a Christmas party, we thought some singing would be nice. We have our own singer, Betsy, who has the voice of a spring songbird."

Betsy walked forward licking her lips and swallowing in noisy gulps.

"Betsy sings like her ma. Mind you now, she doesn't know what her ma looked like, though." Sarah Emily paused just long enough to throw a smug look at Timothy. What she really wanted to do was stick her tongue out at him. Then she stepped back so all attention would be on Betsy, but for a moment her mind wandered. Surely, the ladies understood what it means to know who you look like. Why Timothy couldn't get it straight, she couldn't imagine. She sighed and sent her attention to Betsy whose sweet sounds began to fill the room.

"Skip, skip, skip to my Lou—"

"Why, that's not a Christmas song." The same lady who pointed out Cora's non-Christmas poem spoke up again.

Betsy choked back her song and looked at the annoyed guest. "I don't know any Christmas songs." She poked a finger into her hair and twisted at a short chunk. "This is the only song I know all the way through."

"Mildred, your orphans don't know any Christmas carols?" the lady sitting next to Miss Percy asked.

"Well... I... " Miss Percy sputtered, and her face tightened as she jerked her head to the side. "I do the best I can." Her tone was offended; her words were tart. "We can't afford a music teacher. Miss Dickens is away visiting family, but when she returns, I'll speak to her about this. I shouldn't be expected to do everything."

"You needn't get so huffy, Mildred." The lady cleared her throat to mark her annoyance, and she thrust her chin forward. "Not knowing any Christmas carols—well, go ahead then, dear... Betsy, is it? Sing on." She waved her hand.

Sarah Emily was pleased. She soon realized that Mr. Wilbur was looking her way. *Was he ever going to use his pine-scented hair tonic again?* she wondered. He winked. She was sure he was remembering last Christmas when he tried to teach them a Christmas song, but Miss Percy had told him to go back to work, saying orphans didn't need to know such things. It was unmistakable; the party couldn't have been going any better.

Betsy dropped her hand from her hair and readjusted her shoulders. "Skip, skip, skip to my Lou... " Her beautiful voice floated around them. By the time she was at the fourth verse, "Fly in the sugar bowl, shoo, shoo, shoo... " all the ladies were smiling, and Mrs. Hancock seemed unaware of it, but her toes were tapping.

The ladies occasionally would nod at one another as they listened. "And without any musical accompaniment," one lady from the second row exclaimed.

Behind the ladies, Mr. Wilbur and Cook stood at the kitchen door wearing huge smiles while rocking back and forth. The fifth verse, "Cows in the cornfield, two by two..." had them clapping their hands in time to Betsy's perfect rhythm.

On the seventh and last verse, "Skip a little faster, that won't do..." more of the ladies' toes were tapping, and a few of them even had swaying shoulders.

Everyone seemed to be enjoying Betsy's easy, natural singing— everyone except Miss Percy. Her back looked positively unbendable, and her hands sat woodenly on her lap, wrapped around each other in a tight knot.

Yes, this is all going very well. Sarah Emily watched the smiling faces of the Ladies' Aid Society members and the sour face of Miss Percy. Sarah Emily was joyous.

At the end of Betsy's song, a simultaneous intake of breath from the onlookers absorbed the room. The ladies leaned over to put down their cups and saucers for an eruption of rousing applause.

"Oh, Betsy," a lady spoke up, her vivid purple dress exactly matching the large clusters of grapes that grew from the edge of her hat, "you must, you just must come and sing at our church."

"Do you mean it? Do you really mean it?" Betsy covered her mouth and nose with both hands to contain her excitement.

"What a wonderful idea," another lady said. "But, of course, we'll have to teach her a hymn, something proper for church."

Betsy moved back to her place in line beside Nettie, who hugged Betsy profusely, and Sarah Emily called out, "Ladies. Ladies." They stopped their prattling and looked her way. "It's time for refreshments. Ophelia, would you please get the tray?"

"Of course, I'm looking forward to serving our guests." Ophelia's prissy tone matched her prissy expression. With a flip of her skirt, she spun toward the kitchen.

In a moment, Ophelia was back holding a tray with a crisp white linen tea towel draped over it. She advanced directly to Mrs.

Hancock. "Since you're the President of the Ladies' Aid Society, I'd like to serve you first." Her tone was exaggerated, as only Ophelia could do.

Sarah Emily stole a glance at Betsy. Their eyes met and exchanged looks of satisfaction. Sarah Emily thought, maybe, she should feel bad about involving Ophelia without telling her everything, but it didn't take too much soul-searching for her to admit, she didn't feel one bit sorry. And who could be better for this part of the plan than Ophelia anyway?

"Why, thank you, dear," Mrs. Hancock was responding, puffing out her chest.

Balancing the tray on one hand, Ophelia pinched the center of the linen towel and whipped it off. Olives—black, mushy olives—started rolling around, sloshing juice onto the broken cookie pieces beside them. Mrs. Hancock covered her mouth, cheeks bulging, as she lurched forward. The squirrel that was perched on the side of her hat began to lose its balance, one paw dangling precariously over the edge.

Miss Percy's mouth formed an, "Oh my," but no sound made it past her lips.

"I didn't know what was on the tray," Ophelia started to whine. "Honest I didn't. It was all her doing." She flapped the white towel toward Sarah Emily while inadvertently thrusting the tray closer to Mrs. Hancock's face.

"I am...I am just this side of fainting," Mrs. Hancock moaned in wispy syllables. With closed eyes, she dug in her sleeve, retrieved a lace hanky and dabbed at her mouth. "Olives...I can't stand olives."

Ophelia's feet were planted, and it seemed impossible for her to move—her or the tray. "I didn't know what was on the tray." She repeatedly sniveled, "It's all Sarah Emily's fault." She threw a pitiful, but self-righteous look at Sarah Emily. "How, just tell me how, could you do this to me?" she whimpered.

"Give me that!" Miss Percy yanked the tray from Ophelia and set it on the table.

The lady who had earlier wiped her hands after touching Sarah Emily went directly to inspect. "Why are all these cookies broken?"

"Broken?" another said, hurrying over to see for herself. "Why, I baked dozens of these cookies, and they weren't broken when we packed the tins."

Mrs. Hancock moaned again, and they quickly rushed to her side.

Miss Percy hunched over Mrs. Hancock. The ladies fanned her with their hankies. Ophelia paced the floor with "Ohhh me," escaping from her in wailing, drawn-out cries. The orphans were devouring the broken cookies and helping themselves to more cider. Ours propped her forepaws on the table and loudly lapped up cookies and dribbles of cider. Mr. Wilbur and Cook stood with their arms crossed, a satisfied look on their faces as they viewed the chaos with Miss Percy being swallowed up in the bedlam.

"Some of the cookies got broken..." Miss Percy stammered. "I'm so sorry...I was going to give the children the whole ones...I'm sorry...Would anyone like more cider? I'm really sorry...I didn't know they were going to serve the olives..."

"Olives!" Mrs. Hancock lurched forward again, her hanky muffling tiny mewling sounds.

"There, there, dear," Miss Percy crooned. "You'll be fine." She rubbed Mrs. Hancock's forehead, pushing the hair away from her face.

"Don't rub so hard. Are you trying to push those hairs back in her head, root first?" one lady snapped.

"Surely someone has their smelling salts with them?" the lady in the purple dress with the matching purple grapes begged.

"I do," someone answered and produced a sharp-scented vial of crystals, which she promptly wagged under Mrs. Hancock's nose.

Sarah Emily couldn't have been more pleased. At the sight of the olives, Mrs. Hancock turned even greener than expected, and Miss Percy was more flustered than Sarah Emily had ever seen her.

Then, from outside, she heard an agitated whinny from the horses. Out of the corner of her eye, she thought she saw a man looking in the window, but when she turned to get a better view, no one was there.

The horses whinnied again. Ours hurled herself off the table, standing alert and expectant, her up-ear cocked as if trying to catch a certain sound. Mr. Wilbur whispered something to Cook and then bolted toward the door calling the dog. He and Ours hurried out the back door.

All the while, the ladies fanned and clucked over Mrs. Hancock.

Without any warning, a man blasted into the dining room, shoved Sarah Emily to the wall and pointed a gun at her head.

Chapter 13

The moment, the instant, the gunman laid a hand on Sarah Emily, Timothy lunged forward, a guttural groan sliding out of him as though being pushed up from the deepest part of him. Shrieking from the ladies ricocheted around the room. Cook exhaled a loud, "Law," and the younger children crushed into her open arms.

"Don't move," the man shouted. "Shut up, and do what I tell you." He cocked the gun and the sound of the metal click had them all, ladies and orphans, frozen like fish in the winter pond. "That's better," he said, letting a sinister grin play at one side of his mouth while his exasperatingly calm gaze meandered from one trembling person to another.

The smelling salts bottle crashed to the floor, flashing the acrid scent into the air.

"What was that?" he yelled.

Barks of coughing rose into the silence as the sharp odor infused the room.

"What *is* that smell? Answer me." He swiped at his eyes with the back of his free hand.

More coughing was the only answer he got.

"Answer me. Now!"

"My smelling salts," came a quivering voice that disintegrated into a coughing fit to rival a cat with a fur ball.

"Smelling salts?" For a half-second, that unexpected answer seemed to confuse him, but he quickly seized control again. "Well, good, then none of you fancy, rich broads will be doing any fainting." Water dripped from his eyes; he blinked and swiped again. "You," he waggled a hand at Marjorie, "open a window."

A slap of cold air entered the room, and he sucked in a lung full. Then he grabbed Sarah Emily from where he had slammed her against the wall and whirled her in front of himself, facing the ladies. "Now, all you fine women are going to give me your jewelry and money, and then this pretty girl won't get hurt."

"Oh no." The lady in purple clutched her purse.

"I told you to shut up," the gunman yelled. "And no one is going to move until I say so."

Again, everyone went rigid.

Except Timothy. He stepped closer, then stood with his legs slightly apart, fixing a piercing stare on the gunman.

"You too, boy, or I'll hurt this girl."

"Timothy, please, do as he says." Sarah Emily's heartbeat could be measured in gallops. The whole invasion had happened so fast, and she was so scared, she couldn't make anything fit together. Reality thinned out. This wasn't what she had planned for the party. Where did he come from? The only thing she did know, for sure, was that she was terrified.

Timothy made another move toward the intruder.

The man yanked Sarah Emily's arm, and when she howled in pain, he yanked again. "I'm not kidding."

"Timothy," Sarah Emily pleaded. "Please don't..." Her mouth was too dry to finish.

Timothy stepped back. "Okay, I've backed off. Now stop hurting her."

The gunman's mocking laugh penetrated Sarah Emily and landed like lead in her pounding chest.

He spun her around to look at him. "I knew this was going to be easy, soooo easy. I can do this job with one hand tied behind my back." Flinging one hand to his back and waving the gun in the air with the other, he repeated, "Sooo easy."

Seizing the opportunity to get away, Sarah Emily sprang backward.

He grabbed her arm. Then, as though proud of his smooth maneuver, he grinned.

His grin disoriented Sarah Emily for a second. Here she was terrified, and he was grinning. Maybe she had it all wrong. This wasn't anything to be afraid of.

But when he said, "Get one thing straight. You're not going to ruin this for me," she knew she had it right to be terrified.

He kept talking, "When I saw those fancy carriages lined up out front, I said, 'There's loot in there, and I'm going to get it.'" A snort came out with his grizzled laugh. "And who would have thought—in an orphan asylum?" Letting go of Sarah Emily, he aimed the gun at her head.

But it was his eyes that pinned her. They were intense and cold, but at the same time...?

"Now, here's how we're going to do this." His words snatched her focus off his eyes. From his rumpled coat pocket, he pulled a worn canvas sack splattered with rust colored stains and shoved it into Sarah Emily's hands. "You hold the sack, and we'll visit each one of these lovely ladies. First, they'll drop in their jewelry. Next, they'll get all the money from their purses and drop that in too. Understand?"

A gasp rolled in from every corner of the room.

The robber held the gun steady while he made slow deliberate roaming eye contact with each of the huddled women. "Good. Sounds like you understand."

Sarah Emily licked her dry lips and tasted the bitter smelling salts. She opened her mouth, all set to yell NO to this terrible man and his intentions, but it stuck in her throat like a spiky bone. Her mind whirled, *Where is Mr. Wilbur? Surely, he's getting the sheriff.* The nervous erratic breathing of the others in the room pulsated in her ears.

The gunman towered over her, his neck the size of a tree trunk. "Did you hear me? The others seem to get it; how about you, Green Eyes?" He shouted and pressed the gun's cold metal into her forehead.

Terrified into silence, she could only nod.

"Then let's get busy." He pushed her forward.

She had been holding herself so tight that, at his push, she stumbled forward.

"Okay, ladies. Let's do this nice and orderly, one at a time," he instructed them with deriding courtesy.

He started on the back row. The first lady let out a faint moan but sat motionless. He thumped her head with his knuckles. The room was so quiet, the whack sounded like a thump on a ripe watermelon. Her shoulders jerked, and she drew in a quick loud breath.

"Hey, lady, this is no game. Get those rings off your fingers."

Her eyes swarmed with tears, dusky ones, the kind that leak out from fear. But she slowly slipped off her gold wedding band and then from her right hand a large amethyst ring, dropping both into the bag Sarah Emily held in front of her.

"I'm sorry," Sarah Emily mouthed. This was all her fault. If she hadn't been so fired up to make these ladies look bad, they wouldn't be here. They would be off in their meeting hall having tea and . . . what *do* these ladies do? Why did she have to be so upset about not getting a hair clasp? She was shocked at the ramblings her thoughts could take at a time like this. "I'm very sorry," she silently formed the words again. If they got out of this, she would make certain she would find out how long it took water to boil.

"Shut your mouth." He dragged his fingers through his light brown hair. "You hear me, Green Eyes?"

She nodded and tried to swallow, but her mouth was still dry as dust.

"You can do this, Sarah Emily." Betsy's loud whisper drew her attention. Betsy's hands were tightly clasped at her chest. Not far from her, Timothy had taken the stance of a runner on the brink of springing forward, his right foot in front, a hand on each knee and his face dark and full of intent. Although Betsy looked anxious, she nodded a look of support. Sarah Emily's gaze slid toward the wall and found Cook's reassuring smile. Sarah Emily felt bolstered from all their transparent concern for her.

Yes, I can do this. I just know it!

"Not another word from anybody," the gunman yelled and pushed her toward his next quaking victim.

Down the rows they went, each lady giving up her jewelry—cameos, brooches, diamond earrings, watches—and money, while Sarah Emily held the canvas bag out to collect it all. Some cried softly; others glared at the man when their time came.

The gunman worked his way to Mrs. Hancock. He let out a long, admiring whistle. Like a midnight full moon suspended amongst glistening stars, a large opal pendant on a sparkling gold chain lay against her black velvet dress. "Get that off, and put it in the bag," he ordered.

She pressed her hand over the piece. "I'm *not* giving you my mother's opal."

The wallop he delivered to the side of her head seemed to get rid of her defiance, and she rocked sideways. "All right!" she shouted, rubbing the rising lump above her ear. Then, much softer, "All right." She unlatched the clasp and inched the opal and its gold chain over to the now-bulging canvas sack. In spite of all the color draining from her face, and the fact that she and the squirrel clinging to her hat were shaking nervously, her eyes fired anger.

"Good Girl." He smirked and patted her shoulder. "Now do the same with the money you've got in that fancy handbag."

Sarah Emily stared at the side of the gunman's face. Lines around his eyes were deep, and an angry pink dent of a scar jagged along his slightly upturned nose.

Mrs. Hancock opened her beaded purse and emptied her leather money pouch directly into the sack. The bills sank in soundlessly; the coins plinked and plunked as they hit the enlarging cache.

He moved on to Miss Percy. "Okay, last one. You, lady."

Miss Percy was bent over with her hands covering her face. She had been that way almost from the time the gunman had entered the dining room. When she sat up, the faint scent of rosewater spiraled into the tense, still-tinged-with-smelling-salts air—in spite of the window being opened. Her jeweled brooch sparkled in the last of the afternoon light coming through the window.

Suddenly, the gunman's face flushed. He turned an odd shade of gray. His expression contorted into a deathly mask. "That brooch . . . " His hand shuddered; strength visibly seeped out of him, and the gun listed forward. "That brooch, where did you get it?" His voice grew thinner with each word, and the gun hit the floor with a loud clunk. He backed up, his hands in front of him like shields. "No! No! I don't want to know where you got it." He made a run for the door, forgetting the gun and the canvas bag.

Outside, Mr. Wilbur groaned. When he stirred, his head felt several sizes bigger than before whatever had happened to him. Hesitantly, he opened his eyes. Ours hovered over him. "Move, girl," he said, shakily raising his hands and pressing on Ours's chest.

First, the dog licked his face before moving from her position of straddling him to taking a position right beside him. Still groaning, he rubbed the lump on the back of his head. Ours yipped, nuzzled and prodded his arm as if trying to get him up. His head throbbed, but his back was numb from the frozen earth he found himself spread out on. Staggering to his feet, he looked in the window and saw a man running toward the door. *The children!* A surge of new strength propelled him. "Come on, girl," he quickly whispered.

Mr. Wilbur and Ours barreled through the back door. Ours, all snarls and growls, took a well-aimed swoop, snaring the gunman's ankle in her teeth. He dropped to the floor like a sack of stones. Screaming and twisting, he tried to free himself, but Mr. Wilbur dove on top. In one fluid motion, Timothy slid across the floor and grabbed the gun.

Mr. Wilbur lay sprawled across the thrashing thief. "Timothy," he breathed in winded gasps, "is anyone hurt in here?"

"No." Timothy answered as he raised himself off the floor.

"Good. Then bring me the gun."

The second Timothy got close to Mr. Wilbur, the gunman gave a mighty thrust, tossing Mr. Wilbur upward and grasping toward Timothy for the silver weapon. Timothy darted out of his reach, while Mr. Wilbur grunted and slammed his full weight down, pinning the man again. Ours growled and sank her teeth deeper into the gunman's ripped leg flesh. The gunman wilted back to the floor, then lifted his head, staring at Ours. "Okay, okay. Just call that dog off."

Mr. Wilbur answered by jamming his forearm across the man's throat, forcing his head back to the floor.

Except for the gunman's sputtering howl of agony, everyone was silent. The panicked ladies tangled together like a knotted ball of yarn. The younger children squeezed into Cook the way puppies press against their mother. Some of the older ones stood shoulder to shoulder, their backs glued to the wall.

"Okay, Timothy," Mr. Wilbur said when he felt he had the man firmly pinned to the floor. "Let's try that again. This time, though, come around by Ours. I'd sure like this sorry fellow to give the dog a chance at his hand."

The gunman's response was a defiant scowl.

Timothy did exactly as he was told.

As soon as Mr. Wilbur had the gun, he aimed it at the robber's head. Then slowly rising up, Mr. Wilbur threw his weight backwards so he was kneeling above the gunman. With his eyes unswerving and his hands steady, Mr. Wilbur hoisted himself to his feet.

Ours stayed clamped onto the man's leg with no less determination than a thirsty leech.

"Make that dog let go." His face twisted in pain. "It feels like she's torn the flesh from the bone, and it's killing me."

Mr. Wilbur didn't move the cocked gun from its target between the frightened green eyes of the thief. The ladies and children were still silent, except for a shrill wail that discharged every few seconds. Without needing to look, Mr. Wilbur knew exactly who it was—Ophelia.

With the weight of the gun against his hand and the man

sprawled on the floor beneath him, Mr. Wilbur felt something balling in his throat. He tried to swallow, alarmed to find fear, a lot of it. He quickly looked at the orphans and their frightened faces and knew he couldn't let anyone see how truly scared he was.

He filled his lungs with air and, he desperately hoped, courage. He shoved himself up and locked his knees, staring at the prone man. "Ours, let go. Come here, girl."

Ours didn't budge, but growled a low rumble, as if to ask, "Are you sure, really sure, that's what you want me to do?"

"Yes, girl. Come here." Mr. Wilbur's eyes were still puncturing the man.

Ours released her hold and sprang to her partner's side, rumbles still coming from her throat. Her brown eyes also punctured the man.

"'Bout time you called that beast off. Ours. What kind of name is that anyway?" the gunman snarled.

The cockiness in his voice enraged Mr. Wilbur. "Shut up," he ordered, stepping closer. "If you say another word, I'll have her back on you. Now get up." Questions of why it was so cold in there and what the odd smell was briefly jolted across the back of his mind.

The gunman glared unspoken threats while lifting onto his elbows. He tried to raise himself from the floor, but his torn leg bent under him like a snapping twig.

If that wickedness in his eyes is any indication of what's inside him, and if he manages to get his gun away from me...Mr. Wilbur couldn't allow himself to think any further. The rush of rage the gunman had provoked in him would stoke him through this.

"Get behind him, Timothy," Mr. Wilbur spoke with authority. "Grab him under his arms and get this coward up." Then to the gunman he said, "When the boy touches you, if you try anything, the least little thing, I'll have this dog back on you while this gun makes holes in your head that can't ever be plugged. And if I find out you've hurt even one of these youngsters, I'll do it anyway."

"Ohhh," escaped from a lady.

"Shush," others said quickly.

"I'm scared," Caleb began to whimper. "I'm really scared." One finger tugged nervously at the corner of his mouth.

"It's okay, darling. Mr. Wilbur's here," Cook's soothing voice hushed him.

Mr. Wilbur could feel the muscles in his jaw tightening with the magnitude of the responsibility.

Timothy started toward the man, precisely as he had been instructed.

That boy is officially a man, Mr. Wilbur proudly thought as Timothy took long, confident strides, got behind the robber's head, squatted down and latched on to him under the arms. Slowly Timothy stood, dragging the gunman up.

"My leg. Watch it." The man dipped to one side. "That mongrel nearly chewed my leg in two."

"You'll live," Mr. Wilbur said gruffly, "unfortunately."

Timothy squeezed tighter and leaned his chest firmly against the man's back. "Do you still think you can do this with one hand tied behind your back?"

"I could have," the gunman said as he jerked his head toward Mr. Wilbur, "if this old man hadn't come to so quick after I knocked him out."

"Knocked out!" Sarah Emily hurried to Mr. Wilbur. "Are you hurt?"

"I'm fine. Nothing to worry about. But why is it so cold in here?"

"The window is open. A smelling salts bottle broke, and it was hard to breathe."

"Smelling salts? Well, how about closing the window now?" he said. "Then stand back 'til Timothy and I get this rat situated so the sheriff can come haul him off to jail."

"Timothy," Mr. Wilbur stretched out one arm toward the corner, "I want you to drag him over there. Prop him against the wall." With his other hand, Mr. Wilbur kept the gun pointed at the man's head.

Timothy heaved the gunman up a bit and checked his grip to make sure it was tight. Then he walked backwards, dragging the man, the gunman's boot heels etching a pair of squiggly lines as they scratched across the wooden floor.

"Sarah Emily, get me a chair," Mr. Wilbur called. He saw her lay a canvas sack on the table and take off for the kitchen while Timothy positioned the man in the corner. By the time she was back with the straight chair, the man was propped up and Timothy was a safe distance away.

Walking in front of the gunman, Mr. Wilbur pointed to a place on the floor. "Put the chair right here so I can watch every move this low-down scoundrel makes."

"Don't get too close!" Betsy's voice was tight.

"I won't. Don't worry," Sarah Emily said, staring the gunman square in the eyes as she put the chair down. "Mr. Wilbur—he's mean. Real mean."

"So, Green Eyes, your name's Sarah Emily?" The gunman met her gaze.

Mr. Wilbur bristled at the sinister sweetness of the man's words. "Don't talk to him," he told her firmly. "Timothy, run to the sheriff's office and tell him what's happened."

"Right away!" As though flames licked at his heels, Timothy hurried out the door without even taking a coat.

It won't be much longer now. Mr. Wilbur's shoulders ached to sag. But he didn't dare; he could see the wide-eyed fear on faces. *We've got to get him out of here. Whatever happened has everyone scared out of a month's growth.* He sat down and braced his wrist on his knee, keeping the gun pointed at the robber. With his other hand, Mr. Wilbur reached over and touched Sarah Emily's arm. "Are you all right, Sarah Emily Girl?" he asked, without taking his eyes off the robber, who was examining his ripped leg.

"I'm okay. Nobody got hurt, just scared."

He squeezed her slender fingers.

The robber's attention shifted from his wound. "Green Eyes already told you that I didn't hurt anybody." Having said that, he smugly settled back against the wall and dragged his dirty shirtsleeve across his mouth. "Just you, old man. And evidently not enough."

"I wasn't talking to you." Mr. Wilbur let go of Sarah Emily and leaned in closer with the gun.

Ours growled, baring her teeth.

"Listen." The man winced and grabbed his torn leg. "Listen, since I didn't hurt anybody," he waved his other hand toward the table, "and all the jewelry and money are in that bag, how about just letting me go? I'll leave town, and you'll never see me again."

"Sure, I'll let you go," Mr. Wilbur squinted his eyes, "when bears don't have hair! Now shut up."

Timothy barged through the door, wearing a brown leather coat. Sheriff Thornton was less than a quarter step behind him.

Mr. Wilbur exhaled a sigh of relief at the sight of his friend. "Yea!" the younger orphans shouted and clapped. Some of the older boys whistled. "The sheriff," the women breathed.

Long and lean with a coal-black, walrus moustache, the sheriff hurried closer with his revolver drawn. "Jenkins, Mildred," he made his way across the room staring at the crouched gunman, "what happened here?"

"I need the smelling salts," one woman said, her plea gliding past the sheriff's question as she kicked aside the shattered glass and, with her hanky, picked up the tightly rolled cotton wad that had been saturated with the ammonia mixture. She waved it under her nose and breathed in loudly. "Mildred, do you need this?" she asked, extending the yellowed clump.

"No, of course not." Miss Percy pushed away from the group of ladies and strutted importantly toward the sheriff, pressing her hair back, tucking a loose strand into the knot at her neck.

"Well, I do," the lady with the grapes on her hat extracted her hanky from her pocket and reached for the cotton.

Timothy spoke up. "Sarah Emily was the one in danger." He looked at Miss Percy with a sharp look that suggested she not try to make herself the heroine.

"Yes, yes," Miss Percy huffed in quick breaths. "He came in pointing his gun at us, and there was nothing we could do. I was so worried about Sarah Emily and the others." Laying a hand on Sarah Emily's shoulder she clucked and cooed, "Poor darling. I know she was terrified."

Sarah Emily pressed her lips together and dipped her shoulder away from Miss Percy's touch.

Mr. Wilbur glanced at Cook with her soft arms wrapped around the younger ones, while the others cuddled up near her. There's where they went for comfort, not to Mildred, he thought.

Turning to Sarah Emily, the sheriff lightly touched her chin with a finger, tilting her head up to him. "Are you hurt?"

"No."

"Is anyone else hurt?" He looked around the room.

"No."

"Well then, are you up to telling me what happened?"

Stepping away from Miss Percy, Sarah Emily said, "I most certainly am." With determination and anger girdling her words, she told the sheriff everything from the time the gunman stopped their party until his spine seemed to fold when he saw Miss Percy's brooch.

Then Mr. Wilbur filled in his part. "When I heard the horses acting skittish and saw a man's face in the window, I took Ours and went outside to check." He rubbed the back of his head where the lump had swelled to nearly the size of an egg. Since he had come back inside, he had forgotten about it. "This varmint here came up behind me and cracked me a wallop. I don't know how long I was out, but Ours must have brought me around." He dropped his hand to the dog's head and lightly scratched between her ears. "When I came to, she was straddling me, licking my face and whimpering. As quick as I rousted, she tugged on my sleeve 'til I got up, as if she knew danger was inside."

Ours's tail swished excitedly, and she looked at the sheriff like she had every right to be pleased with herself, and so should he.

"It was then that I looked inside and saw this snake. So, right away, Ours and I high-tailed it in through the backdoor."

"So you weren't in here during any of the robbery?" The sheriff glided his thumb and index finger over his glossy moustache.

"That's right." Mr. Wilbur nodded.

"Sarah Emily," the sheriff kept pressing his moustache, "tell me again about his reaction to Miss Percy's brooch."

"The girl must have misunderstood," the gunman quickly spoke up. "I realized I was doing wrong, and that's why I was leaving when the old man and dog attacked me. It didn't have anything to do with a brooch."

Anger ignited in Sheriff Thornton's blue eyes. "You'll have your turn to talk, but not now."

The gunman slumped back against the wall, but his gaze darted between Sarah Emily and the sheriff while she retold how frightened he became at the sight of Miss Percy's brooch.

When Sarah Emily finished, the sheriff said, "Mildred, would you mind taking it off so I can get a closer look?"

Her backbone went so straight, two of the finest crystal glasses filled with water could have easily balanced on her shoulders. "What does my brooch have to do with this robbery? After all, he said himself, he came in here because he saw the fine carriages outside."

"I know, but seeing your brooch rattled him, and there's something scratching at the back of my brain about a brooch."

"Mildred, if the sheriff has a notion that might help . . . " Mr. Wilbur touched her arm.

"Oh, all right." She removed it and slapped it into the sheriff's open hand.

Sheriff Thornton looked at the brooch, then at Miss Percy. "I need a lamp."

Suddenly, Mr. Wilbur realized evening had eaten away the afternoon light. The fire in the fireplace was waning, the gas lamp on the mantle had burned out and the few candles the wind from the open window hadn't snuffed out were nearly nubs.

"I don't see how my brooch has anything to do with any of this," Miss Percy said.

"A light—please, Mildred," the sheriff persisted.

She turned on her heel and disappeared into the kitchen, returning with a lighted lamp.

"Can you keep your eye on him for a minute?" the sheriff said as he looked at Mr. Wilbur.

"Like a cat perched on the edge of a fish pond."

"Thanks, Jenkins." The sheriff holstered his gun. Then, while

Miss Percy held the lamp, he studied the brooch front and back, back and front. Not a sound came from anyone until he finally looked up at her and said, "I'm going to need to take this with me."

"Whatever for?"

"Like I said, there's something scratching at the back of my brain. I'll return it to you as soon as I can." Without waiting for her approval, the sheriff pulled out his handkerchief from his right pants' pocket, wrapped the brooch in it and stuffed it back in his pocket.

Just then, Mr. Wilbur saw the gunman's face register panic.

"Jenkins, will you help me get him out of here?"

"Gladly."

"As soon as we get him locked up, I want you to stop by Doc Werther's and have your head checked." Then Sheriff Thornton turned to Sarah Emily. "Please bring me the canvas bag." And then to Timothy, "Keep the coat if you want," he said. "It's one my brother left on his last visit."

"Thanks. If you're sure, that would be great," Timothy stroked the lapel of the coffee-colored coat, as Sarah Emily retrieved the bag.

"You two have been a big help," the sheriff said when Sarah Emily handed the bag to him. "I'm probably going to need to talk to you again, though, to ask a few more questions. Can you do that?"

Sarah Emily slowly turned her head and fixed her gaze on the gunman. "Just let me know when."

Out of the corner of his eye, Mr. Wilbur saw Timothy slip his arm around Sarah Emily's waist, saying, "Name the time."

"Good! I'll be in touch." He held up the canvas sack. "Ladies, I need this for evidence right now, but you'll all get your belongings back." He may as well have been talking to Ours, because the women were all in a cluster, too engrossed in passing the smelling salt cotton around to hear anything he said.

The sheriff shook his head. "Mildred, as soon as they all decide they aren't going to faint, would you have each of them write down what pieces of jewelry they have in here and how much money."

"Do you need me to get the list to you today?"

"No, tomorrow's soon enough. Okay, Jenkins, let's go."

Chapter 14

few hours later at the jail, the gunman's story had been heard and the necessary papers filled out. Sheriff Thornton checked the sleeping prisoner, who lay on his back with a blanket stretched over him, breathing evenly, only his head and one arm showing.

The sheriff stood with both hands gripping the cell bars, examining the face of the sleeping man. He didn't remember ever seeing him before, but there was something... something about him. With his right hand he reached for the lantern hanging on the wall and held it against the bars. A wedge of light spread over the man's features. *Why do I feel I should know you?*

It was some time before the sheriff turned from the still-sleeping prisoner. He brought the lantern to his desk, setting it on the edge. He folded his wiry frame into the wooden chair and, with a single hoist, propped his feet on the desktop. Leaning back, hands behind his head, slightly rocking, he stared at the prisoner while mentally ticking off what he had said. *Says his name is Jack Gregory. Never been to Lander before. Just having a rough time and saw the carriages outside the orphan asylum. In a moment of weakness, decided it was an easy way to get a few dollars.*

Gregory snored a short burst. Without waking, he stuck his exposed arm under the blanket and rolled to his side. The cot squeaked and swayed. In this new position, the scar zigzagging down the side of his nose became clearly visible.

That's it! Sheriff Thornton swung his feet off the desk. They hit the floor with such a bam, he glanced to see if it woke Gregory. It didn't. The sheriff felt in his pocket for Miss Percy's brooch. Pulling it out, he laid the handkerchief on his desk and unfolded it. For several minutes he sat, not touching the piece of jewelry, only staring at it, tying a long-ago incident to the robbery today.

Suddenly, the strong jailhouse coffee gurgled on the wood stove and bubbled out the spout of the pot. He got up, and as he made his way to the stove, dusty memories began to emerge. Using the thick towel hanging on a peg next to the stove, he grabbed the hot handle of the coffeepot and poured himself a cup. He took a long drink and let his mind continue to connect details. By the time the second swallow was down his throat, he was sure who this prisoner was.

He set the cup on his desk so fast, the scalding brew sloshed onto his hand, but he didn't stop, just slapped his hand on his pants and kept going. Memories and anger propelled him like a tightly wound wind-up toy. *Anna Butler—would have been Anna Reece then. Had to be at least sixteen years ago.* He was hurrying toward the walnut filing cabinet in the corner.

He yanked open the third drawer. His fingers walked the tops of the folders and stopped at the one marked *Reece, Anna.* He wiggled the file out from the overstuffed drawer and slammed it shut.

Gregory moaned and slid under the blanket a little deeper, never opening his eyes.

Returning to his desk, the sheriff moved the handkerchief to the side, brooch and all. He sat down, slinging the file on his desk, and flipped it open. *October 1864,* it said on the first page. *Seventeen years ago,* he corrected himself. He read the notes he had made on that fall afternoon in 1864, the grim events beginning to surface again, one ugly one after the other. It was as if they had been poised, ready to step forward when needed.

He slapped the folder shut. "Lester," he yelled. "Lester, wake up."

The sleepy deputy came from the back room, yawning and stretching. "What's wrong?"

"Come out here and keep a watch on things. I'm going to the orphan asylum."

"Now? They'll all be in bed." Lester said, pouring himself a cup of coffee and yawning again.

"I'll take my chances. It's where I've got to start." Sheriff Thornton brushed the papers back in the file folder and scooped up the brooch.

***

Miss Percy stood by the stove, kneading her forehead and waiting for the kettle to boil. A cup of tea and some quiet moments to sort out the events of the afternoon was what she had planned before she could even think about going to bed. She was counting on her chamomile tea to spin her down into sleep. She pushed her hair from her shoulders, shaking it, letting it swish down her back. It felt good to have it out of its tight bun. She thought about how it used to be as black and shiny as a blackbird's wing. It was still black, she knew, but not nearly as thick or shiny. She closed her eyes and swayed gently, feeling her hair hanging long and loose. A whiff of the rosewater she had splashed on just moments before when dressing for bed fanned out around her. She wished she could wear her hair down all the time. She wished...

She jerked her head straight, and purpose came back. *Mildred, stop this frivolous wishing. Keep your senses about you.*

She exhaled, exhausted. Getting everyone settled down had been nearly impossible tonight. Surely, that water should be boiling soon. She picked up her mother's cup and saucer, trailing her finger over the tiny yellow flowers, skipping over the chip and around the cup again, deftly jumping the chip again. Her finger circled along with her thoughts, from the gunman, to her brooch and back. Had she seen him before? She searched her memory like rummaging to the back of a closet, checking every corner, every shelf and every box. She had done that all evening, and still, nothing—not even a remnant of a moth-eaten memory—could she find.

Then why did he react to her brooch?

"Mildred."

The sheriff's voice startled her and she jumped, rattling the cup on its saucer as he pounded on the kitchen door.

"Mildred," he called again.

"Coming." She quickly set the cup on the oak worktable and smoothed her hand down the front of her, making sure that the robe covering her nightgown was properly buttoned. "I'm coming." She hurried to the door while under her breath she huffed, "No need to wake everyone."

She rearranged her features into a more pleasant expression and said in her chirpiest voice, "Zeke, it's always good to see you. But, my stars, what are you doing here at this hour?"

"I know it's late, but I took a chance that maybe you were still up. And then when I saw the light in the kitchen, I'd hoped it was you."

"I came down for a cup of tea before going to bed. It's been a most difficult day."

"And for that, I'm sorry to have to disturb you, Mildred, but I've got to talk to you. You remember, I said that something was scratching at the back of my brain about a brooch?" He opened his clenched hand to reveal her flower-shaped brooch. "Well, I remember where I've seen this brooch before."

Her insides hitched a tad. She rubbed her hands together to keep her fingers from reclaiming it. It was hers, rightly hers. She saw him looking at her hands; they were nearly clawing themselves. "Oh, it's cold in here. I'll be glad when that tea is ready," she said, sounding too chirpy, bordering on absurd under the circumstances.

Just then, the kettle whistled. She tensed for a second to reign in her emotions and settle her voice at a more appropriate tone. "Tea, Zeke?" she said, sounding more like she wanted to.

"No thanks. Mildred, about your brooch."

"Let's talk in my office. Both Cook's room and Jenkins's are close. I don't want to disturb their sleep, and I have that list you needed of everyone's jewelry and the amount of money. You might as well get it while you're here. As far as the money goes, some of them weren't sure how much. You know, they couldn't count it before it went in the bag." She kept babbling, not able to find a stopping place. "You might as well get the list while you're here. We estimated how much money each woman thought she put in. You'll have to figure out a way to divide it up and make it fair." *Why, oh why, can't I hush?* she thought. *And why won't Zeke stop me?* She poured the boiling water into a teapot, set it on a tray along with her cup and started for her office.

The sheriff picked up the lighted candle and followed her.

Upstairs, once the lard-oil lamp in her office was lit, she blew out the candle. The sheriff began pacing back and forth in front of her desk, talking, his shoes swishing on the rug. She sipped tea— calmly sipped tea. At least, she hoped she appeared calm and intent on the story he was telling.

"That day in 1864 was horrible." He grimaced. "Every detail came back tonight, vividly—too vividly."

"In 1864?" she said. "Why, that was seventeen years ago. Doesn't ring any particular bell with me. Sit down, please, Zeke. A cup of chamomile tea might be just what you need."

"I don't need tea. Listen to me. The brooch belonged to Anna Butler, didn't it?"

She hesitated a moment. Then she nodded.

"Mildred, how did you get it?"

She set her cup on its saucer, slowly and deliberately placing it precisely in the little indented ring. "Zeke, just what are you saying?" Her voice wasn't the least bit chirpy now. It was controlled. For that, she was grateful.

"I'm not accusing you of anything. Sorry if I sounded like I was. Let's do it this way. I'll tell you about the day I first saw this brooch." Opening his fingers like a huge uncurling spider, he let the brooch sit in his palm a second before setting it on the desk in front of her. "Then you tell me everything you know and how you got it."

"Fair enough." She folded her hands together and rested them on her desk, her knuckles brushing the brooch, having no intention of telling him everything.

She could see his pulse ticking at his temple as he began. "That day in October 1864, Robert Butler burst into my office and nearly dragged me out. He took me to the house he'd bought for them to live in after they married. As I recall, this was just a week or so before the date for their wedding. Anna had been there on that day while he was at work to do some cleaning and hang curtains. When Robert arrived late in the afternoon, he'd found Anna on the floor, beaten and bleeding. He'd gone for the doctor before coming to get me.

"When Robert and I got there, the doctor was with Anna. Robert went immediately to her, and the doctor and I went outside so he could tell me what had happened."

Miss Percy saw the sheriff tighten his lips and quicken his pacing. "Sit a minute, Zeke," she said firmly. "I'm getting you a cup for tea."

She was thankful he submitted and sank into the red brocade chair facing her desk. She needed a minute to think, and walking to her china cabinet in the adjoining parlor would give her that. Her mind struggled to make the connection with what he was saying to her brooch. Nothing was fitting together, and really, all she wanted was her brooch back.

At her china cabinet, she chose the cup Mr. Wilbur usually picked—the cream-colored one with a dignified gold band. Men seemed to prefer that one. Returning to her desk, she said optimistically while pouring the tea, "Now, Zeke, I'm sure we can get this little matter straightened out."

"Mildred, it's not a *little* matter. The details have all returned with a vengeance; I can distinctly remember standing on that porch, that October afternoon." Then he went away behind the sharp planes of his face, drifting behind his blueberry-blue eyes.

"Take your time," Miss Percy said softly, refilling her cup. She sipped her tea noiselessly, not wanting to appear either concerned or anxious. Effortlessly, to the top of her thinking, drifted the memory from years ago of the day those blue eyes of Zeke's had rested on her, and he had asked her to the school picnic. She let her thoughts continue to drift on, imagining what her life might have been if she had accepted his invitation. Zeke had been sweet on her back then; she had no doubt about that, but she had to refuse him. What else could she have done? Dating him would have put an end to her own dream. So, after numerous rebuffs from her, he had set his attention on Deborah.

Several more long moments passed, and Zeke closed his eyes and shook his head as if he would like to shake the whole scene of what he was remembering from his mind. He set his cup on the edge of her desk and stood, resuming his edgy pacing. "When Doc and I stepped onto the porch, he said to me, 'A terrible thing has happened here. Anna has been beaten and . . .' Doc took off his glasses and rubbed his eyes. 'Well, beaten,' he'd said.

"Evidently, while she'd been working, a man pushed open the back door and rushed in. She wasn't sure what he stole, but he did take some silver forks and spoons. She was wearing her mother's brooch. He ripped it off her dress. At that point, Mildred, Doc stopped. He put his glasses back on and looked me straight in the eyes, and I knew what he was going to say next."

Miss Percy gasped. If she hadn't already been seated, her legs might have buckled, giving way to her plunging to the floor. The gasp was not for Anna, she realized, but for the horror of what Zeke was telling her. She should feel sorry for Anna, shouldn't she? She had been so detached for so long that sometimes she couldn't find "normal." *Have I misplaced it or have I ever owned it?* she wondered as she listened to Zeke plow forward with the story.

He said, "Doc told me, 'He raped her and then tried to kill her. Anna fought him. Being such a little thing, I don't know how she did it, but she got the brooch out of his hand and gouged it down the side of his face—she thinks near his nose, but she's not sure. It was then that he staggered out of the house holding his bleeding face and a canvas bag with the silver pieces and whatever else he took.'"

Miss Percy sat, her spine erect, her ankles crossed precisely under the desk and her hands folded on top in the very center. The tighter she pulled herself into a thin, straight line, the less of herself might accidentally slip out—like the strange stirring in her soul. She hoped it wasn't some sort of joy in what had happened to Anna. But, she had to admit, that's what it felt like. "Did she know who he was?" she managed to get out, thinking she needed to say something to interact with the story, keeping her eyes on her hands.

Surprisingly, her hands were speckled with age spots. When had they gotten so crinkled like crumpled paper that someone had tried to smooth out? She slid them off the desk and into her lap hoping Zeke hadn't seen how old they looked. Life was passing her by, and she hadn't noticed. Days had bent into years and years into decades.

As she sat with her hands in her lap, she feared her whole body was thrumming like a twanged string. Inside, she was; that was a fact. Had she been a fool to be so fixated on an unrealistic fantasy that she had let Zeke and a life as wife and possibly a mother get away?

"Mildred? Mildred," he called her back, his puzzled look suggesting she wasn't listening.

"Oh. Yes, Zeke, go on." She released a breath, realizing she hadn't in some time.

He waited a moment to see if she was listening before he went on. "No, Anna had never seen him in Lander before, but it was this brooch." He picked up the flower-shaped one on her desk.

"Zeke, I don't know about any of that." She was relieved that was the truth, and it took no thought or physical charade on her part. She was, all at once, unsure of her swimmy emotions or if she could keep them in check. "I remember the robbery but nothing about the brooch being involved. And certainly nothing about a . . . an assault." Squeezing her fingers tighter, she asked, "How did you keep it out of the paper, and even more impossible, the grapevine of gossip?"

"Since we couldn't find the man, Robert begged me, for Anna's sake, to keep the worst of it out of the news. We just said she'd been beaten during a robbery. Do you remember they postponed their wedding until early November and then moved straightway to Chicago?" The sheriff mindlessly stroked his moustache. "They tried to get on with their lives, but nothing ever seemed right again. When I'd heard they'd had a baby girl the next October, I hoped that would help. But even that didn't seem to bring the expected joy. Anna never seemed to fully regain her strength, though she tried awfully hard to make a good home for Robert and baby Sarah Emily."

"Yes. And Robert—" Miss Percy fiddled with the collar of her robe, breathing deeply to allow the rosewater scent to fill her, remembering aloud, "even after they moved back to Lander, I saw a sadness had settled on him as close and tight as skin." *And I thought, hoped, it was because he wasn't happy with Anna. Mildred Percy,* she rebuked herself, *you are a fool.* She began massaging one side of her forehead, switched to the other, then massaged both simultaneously.

"Yes. You're right, he's never been the same," the sheriff said. I guess it's been, what now, several years since I've seen him? I have no idea where he is. I thought maybe he visited Sarah Emily."

Telling him Robert was here as recently as month before last wouldn't change anything that had happened today—or seventeen years ago, for that matter. It really had nothing to do with anything, she reasoned. "No, he doesn't visit," she said.

"What a shame. Sarah Emily's such a sweet girl. Well, I need to know how you got the brooch. Obviously, after the way he reacted to it, the guy who did the robbery here this afternoon is the one who robbed and raped Anna."

"I feel dreadful about Anna, but I don't know this man, and I had nothing to do with either of these crimes." She reset her posture and spoke deliberately and cautiously. She might be a fool, but not a big enough one to let anyone into the secrets of her heart.

"Mildred, I never thought you were involved in a crime."

"I didn't see how you could. If you must know, Robert gave me this brooch when he left Sarah Emily here, but he never mentioned anything else." What she had said was the truth, and it was all Zeke needed to know. That was all she was going to say.

"I knew you had to have talked with Robert. His daughter is here, and you have the brooch. I was just hoping he'd told you more details—something to make it ironclad to charge this guy, Gregory, with that crime. Of course, we've got him on what he did here today. The brooch, his reaction to it and the scar down his nose should be evidence enough to link him to Anna. I'm going to wire the judge in River Bend tomorrow and see how soon he can get here.

"I felt such rage the day this happened to Anna, I remember thinking it was people who did that kind of awful thing who made me want to quit this job. But then I looked at Robert and Anna and realized it was people like them who kept me in it. It may have been nearly seventeen years ago, but I want to get this guy. I don't want him to get away this time."

"I understand. I'll do whatever I can," she said, trying to sound sincere. "May I keep the brooch?" she added carefully.

"You may—but not 'til after the trial. We might need it since Anna told me it's what she fought with."

"Okay." Miss Percy stood. "Are we finished for tonight? As you can imagine, I'm exhausted." She handed him the list she had pre-pared earlier.

"Sure. I can let myself out." He folded the paper and put it in his shirt pocket along with the brooch. "If you think of anything else that might help, you'll let me know?"

"Of course."

"Thanks for listening. Sorry to come at this late hour."

"Anytime, Zeke. Say hello to Deborah for me. Good night."

As soon as the sheriff was out of her office, she leaned back in her chair and breathed deeply of the rosewater that permeated her and the room. Briefly, she considered getting up and putting on more, but was too weary. She rubbed her eyes as if she could erase the disturbing day. One stubborn thought refused to be erased. She wanted that brooch back.

***

In the girls' dormitory, it had taken an extra long time for the girls to settle down and begin to drift off to sleep, but Sarah Emily was wide awake, sleep too slippery to catch.

A shaft of moonlight picked out the snow mounded in the cor-ners of the window panes. The wind screamed through the trees and howled its way through cracks, rattling the glass. She never had remembered to tell Mr. Wilbur about the gap around the window frame.

Even though she was drained, worn out and longing for sleep, the day insisted on reappearing in jagged images. She would have thought only the robber would be front and center in her thoughts, but it was an assortment of the day...the lady who arrogantly wiped her hand after touching her...Cora's theatrics...Betsy's beautiful voice and the invitation for her to sing at church...the gunman...the canvas bag...Timothy trying to protect her.

Her hand slid to her waist where Timothy had wrapped his arm while they talked to the sheriff. She stayed like that for a long time. He had never done that before. Finally, she pulled the covers tighter, yearning for sleep.

But her eyes stayed wide open. What was it about the gunman's eyes that haunted her?

Chapter 15

Two Sundays after the party, Sarah Emily stood on the snow-covered front steps of the orphan asylum shivering from the swirling icy air. It was so cold, it burned. Her arms were wrapped together, squeezed tight against her middle. Her neck was scrunched down in her coat collar. She stomped her freezing feet. Actually, the stomping was as much for the impatience of waiting as the cold. She wanted Mrs. Hancock to hurry up and get there. Betsy was sick, and Sarah Emily was anxious to deliver the message that they couldn't go to church this morning for Betsy to sing.

"Where are you, Mrs. Hancock?" Sarah Emily asked the empty street with annoyance, her breath freezing in front of her. She paced the porch, her gaze stretching up Lilac Lane. All she wanted to do was get back inside and check on Betsy.

Sarah Emily rehearsed in her mind the message Miss Percy had ordered her to say since it was too cold for Miss Percy to stand on the porch and tell Mrs. Hancock herself. Sarah Emily wasn't to leave out a word of it. Miss Percy had made that clear, very clear.

Out of the corner of her eye, Sarah Emily glimpsed a man with light brown hair running down the street. She gasped and grabbed the handrail. When she turned her head to get a better look, it was only Mr. Mitchell. His hat had blown off, and he was chasing after the wind-tossed black thing. *I'm too jittery since the robbery. I think I see him everywhere even though I know he's in jail.* She drew her coat tighter, wrapped her arms around herself and resolved not to let the thief, or his memory, steal one more of her thoughts.

Where was Mrs. Hancock? Sarah Emily didn't want Betsy to be sick, but she was just as glad they couldn't go to church. If church was anything like Mrs. Hancock and her bunch, Sarah Emily had no use or interest in it. Besides that, the church had never been interested in any of the orphans attending before now.

Finally, Mrs. Hancock's carriage arrived, the driver coaxing the two perfectly matched, gray-speckled horses to a smooth stop. He jumped down and opened the door. Inside the carriage, Mrs. Hancock and another woman sat cozily wrapped in warm furs with heavy blankets covering their laps.

"Where's Betsy?" Without giving Sarah Emily time to answer, Mrs. Hancock turned to the woman next to her. "Lillian, this is one of the orphans."

"Is this the one Florence taught the hymn for church today?"

"No, that's Betsy. This is Sarah Emily Butler." Mrs. Hancock's eyebrow jutted upward when she said 'Butler.' She joined her hands together and rested them atop her self-padded stomach.

"Ah, Anna Butler's girl?" Lillian also cocked an eyebrow as if a cryptic code was passing between the two.

Those horrid women. A white fury pumped in Sarah Emily. *How dare they say my mother's name like that?*

"Yes. Anna Butler's girl." Mrs. Hancock laid a gloved hand on Lillian's blanket-covered knee. Then she turned her attention to Sarah Emily. "Now where is Betsy? We don't want to be late."

Sarah Emily swallowed, forcing burning bile down so she could answer and get inside, away from these churchgoers. "Betsy's sick so we can't go."

"But she's learned the hymn, and everyone is expecting her," Lillian said, skipping past Betsy's illness, giving a huffy twitch of her shoulders. "What will we tell the people who've come to hear her sing?"

"She's *sick,*" Sarah Emily repeated, ever so precisely, as if Mrs. Hancock and her snuggly-warm companion were slow witted. "Miss Percy says to tell you thank you for inviting us." Purposefully, she left off part of what Miss Percy had said to say— and please ask us again after Betsy gets well. Sarah Emily left that unsaid, hoping they would never ask again.

Mrs. Hancock scowled and was drawing up air from her rigidly corseted middle to speak again, when Sarah Emily turned to run inside.

"Orphans. One simply can't depend on them," Mrs. Hancock said and nodded for the driver to close the door.

"I see that," Lillian replied in the manner of pure disgust of those beneath her, and Sarah Emily thought she seemed practiced at it.

The carriage door closed. For a second, Sarah Emily considered whirling around, yanking open the door and telling them just what she thought, but decided not to waste the time. Betsy was far more important than either of those women.

"Betsy?" she called out a minute later, opening the dormitory door.

There was no answer, just cottony-thick silence.

The covers on Betsy's bed were rumpled and shoved aside. Everything's fine, she tried to convince herself. She had to stop being so jumpy. Betsy was probably feeling better and went down to breakfast, that's all. And anyway, this didn't have anything to do with the gunman. *He is not going to continue to frighten me,* she vowed again. Voices eked out from the far end of the hall.

They weren't from the sick room; they couldn't be. You only went there if you were contagious or very, very ill. The last time someone went to the sick room, it was Josephine. Sarah Emily had heard her moan and cry, and she watched Doc Werther come several times each day and sadly shake his head as he walked out after each visit. In less than a week, Josephine died.

Sarah Emily made a frenzied dash out of the dormitory, not wanting to believe Betsy could be sick enough to be moved there.

She pushed open the door of the dark, stuffy cubicle. "Betsy?" Sarah Emily said softly, starting to go in.

"Don't come in here," Miss Percy screeched. "Close the door and go downstairs!"

Sarah Emily stopped, but frantically tried to see if Betsy was in those suffocating shadows. Brown windowless walls encased the room. A cot, with Betsy on it, was pushed against one wall. Extra benches from the dining room were stacked against another wall. A small burning candle was perched on the top of the stack. Miss Percy and Doc Werther were standing on the remaining narrow slit of floor. Miss Percy's handkerchief was smashed tightly to her mouth and nose.

"Betsy has The Fever. Get out. Now!" Miss Percy ordered, her eyes equaling the sternness of her words.

Sarah Emily backed out of the room, but closed the door only part way. The spoiled fish stench of the room, that dank sick smell merging with rubbing alcohol and other medicinal odors, escaped, making it harder to stifle her anxious breathing and rapidly beating heart so she wouldn't be heard. *The Fever. People die of The Fever!* She hid just outside the door, pushing her spine and palms flat against the wall, and listened.

"Mildred," Doc Werther was saying in hushed tones, "there isn't any more I can do except order the medicine from Chicago."

The wall behind Sarah Emily felt like it was moving, becoming a soft, billowy curtain that wouldn't hold her up. She would fall backwards and spiral down into . . . she didn't know what, only that it was not someplace she wanted to go.

"That's completely out of the question," Miss Percy snapped back. "It costs too much." She cleared her throat and softened her tone. "I just don't have that kind of money."

"Yes. Yes, of course. I understand," he said, without any surprise at all.

"If I did, you can be certain, I'd have you order it right now."

There was that silky voice. How could it come from a heart of moth-eaten, scratchy wool? Sarah Emily pushed harder on the wall, finding, with relief, that it had turned into a wall again. Miss

Percy could get the money. She had gotten it for the cakes to serve Mrs. Hancock and the cinnamon for her buns and the cider. Truth be known, Sarah Emily didn't doubt Miss Percy had a wad of it stuffed in her underpinnings right now.

"She must have the medicine. There's nothing else I can do for her," Doc Werther's voice trickled out into the hall. And then Sarah Emily could hear him gathering his things, snapping his black medical bag shut and walking toward the door.

Miss Percy would be furious when she found Sarah Emily lurking between the shadows in the hall. But Sarah Emily didn't budge, not even when Miss Percy came out of the sick room and stood directly in front of her, glowering.

"I told you to go downstairs!"

Sarah Emily could feel the burn of Miss Percy's eyes, but refused to meet them. Ignoring the headmistress, she spoke directly to the doctor. "How much does the medicine cost?"

Miss Percy drew in a loud, aggravated breath, and then Sarah Emily felt searing pain as Miss Percy pinched her shoulder in a spot that caused such agony her knees buckled.

In that instant, as Sarah Emily's mind fixed on Betsy, she did the unthinkable. She shoved Miss Percy aside and straightened her legs. "How much does the medicine cost?" she again demanded.

Miss Percy stepped forward. "I'll get you—" She snapped her mouth shut, apparently to dam up the rest of her overused insult from escaping. She slid her hands against her head and pressed her black hair down, the muscles in her jaw jerking.

Sarah Emily knew exactly what Miss Percy wanted to say—I'll get you, you little orphan brat—but she wouldn't dare in front of the doctor.

"Sarah Emily," the doctor laid his hand on the shoulder Miss Percy had pinched and massaged it gently, "It costs one dollar. Don't you be concerned, though."

"Order it!" Sarah Emily whirled around and bolted down the hall toward the dormitory. "I'll get the money," she called over her shoulder, not giving the doctor or Miss Percy a chance to respond.

Kneeling beside her bed, she pulled out the cardboard

container that held her beloved mahogany box. When she lifted it out, she didn't rub it lovingly like she usually did. She knew this time she had best not stop to think about what she was doing. Betsy *had* to have the medicine. That was all that mattered. She opened the hinged top and took out the photograph of her parents, which she carefully laid in the cardboard container, put the lid on and slid it back under the bed. She grabbed her coat.

Holding the mahogany box and trying to wiggle into her coat, she nearly tripped as she rushed down the back stairs. Quickly, she steadied herself and darted through the kitchen and out the door.

By the tool barn, Timothy, wearing the coat Sheriff Thornton had given him, was throwing a stick for Ours. Tail wagging, the dog jumped and caught it in her mouth, then seemed to spin in the air before her paws ever touched the ground.

"Look at her, Sarah Em. If I didn't know better, I'd say she's smiling," Timothy said as Ours proudly dropped the stick at his feet. "Good girl!" He rubbed her affectionately.

Sarah Emily's heart heaved, and she was nearly dizzy with grief. She leaned back against the tool barn to steady herself and clumsily mopped at spurting tears with her coat sleeve. *Ours, I love you so much. Please understand why I have to do this.*

Timothy stooped to pick up the stick and was in position to throw it again. When he saw Sarah Emily, he let it fall. "What's the matter?" He started toward her with Ours bounding ahead.

"We're going to have to sell Ours to get money so Betsy can have the medicine she needs," Sarah Emily said through her sobs.

"What are you talking about? Medicine for Betsy? Aren't you two supposed to be at church so Betsy can sing?"

Dropping to her knees, she set her prized box on a tree stump beside her. Her chin was clamped to her chest, dripping tears forming puddles on the polished wood. She picked up the hem of her coat and dried the box. Then she scrunched the chunk of coat into her hand, squeezing as hard as she could to fight back any imminent tears. She lost. A fresh batch erupted. Sarah Emily buried her face in the dog's thick fur and cried so hard that Ours joined her with a pathetic whimper.

"What's wrong with Betsy?" Timothy asked, squatting beside her, the leather of his coat squishing delicately.

She lifted her eyes to him. "Betsy's got The Fever," she said, jerky breaths shuddering her body.

"The Fever!" Timothy emptied his lungs in one explosive gust. "Are you sure?"

"I heard Doc Werther and Miss Percy talking." Sarah Emily sniffed, and her chin quivered. "She needs medicine, and Miss Percy won't buy it. I told Doc Werther to order it."

"What? How much does it cost?"

"One dollar."

"Wow!" He whistled through his teeth.

"I'm going to sell my box and Ours so I can pay for it." She waited for him to respond, knowing his need to think things through.

He pulled Ours into a tight hug, as if that was his answer.

"Timothy," she pleaded, laying her hand gently on his shoulder, "these are the only two things I have to sell. Surely they must be worth a dollar. Betsy can't die."

"You're right, of course. Betsy can't die," he said, a crack ripping at his voice. "I'll help you," he said and sprang to his feet.

She rose from the ground and faced him, grateful, that again, he understood her. This time, he didn't call her idea a scheme or try to talk her out of it.

"Wait here, I'll be right back," Timothy said, and left, the tail of his coat flapping out behind him as he ran.

He came back with two lengths of rope and wearing his old coat. He handed her the one from the sheriff. "Here, your coat is too thin to be out in this kind of weather."

She gratefully put it on over her coat. The handsome brown leather coat hit Timothy mid-calf but on Sarah Emily it dragged on the ground.

He handed her one of the ropes. "I figured the coat would be too long. Tie this around your middle so you can hitch it up some."

"Thanks," she said. "Are you going to be okay?"

"Sure. My old coat is in better shape than yours."

It wasn't. It was in worse shape than hers.

After the rope was fixed around her, and the other was looped loosely around Ours's neck, Timothy picked up Sarah Emily's mahogany box and handed it to her. Silently, they started walking. Sarah Emily clutched her mahogany box, Timothy held the rope and Ours trustingly trotted between them.

They skirted around the side of the building so Miss Percy wouldn't see them leaving. Once out front, Sarah Emily and Timothy didn't need to discuss where they were going. Orphans were not welcome at the rich end of Lilac Lane, but they held their heads high anyway and walked with purpose.

Chapter 16

$\mathcal{S}$arah Em, I always imagine these houses to be the finest in the whole of Illinois. What do you think?" Timothy said, sweeping away the silence they walked in.

"What? Yes. I think so too," she mumbled and pushed the unruly lock of hair from her eyes. His question, she knew, was a ploy to get her mind off the task ahead. He was right in thinking that her mind was filled with Betsy's illness and having to sell her two most precious possessions. So, to divert her thoughts, she let her gaze roam ahead of her steps.

Lilac Lane. The wealthy residents loved the spring lilacs that lined the streets and perfumed their yards so much that they planted summer ones as well. Now, the street was bare of those thick, purple bunches that made Lilac Lane a favorite place for romantic souls. Old and young liked to stroll in the moonlight or families to gather on their lawns and visit on sunny afternoons.

Five houses, pretty as a painting, all snug against the cold with velvet smoke luxuriantly twisting from the chimneys, gave the street a winter beauty. Positioned grandly in each yard, with neat steps luring visitors to front doors, were the homes in fashionable, yet ever so tasteful, colors of frosty white, buttercup yellow and Wedgwood blue.

They stopped in front of the first house—the Mitchell home, and Sarah Emily asked, "Don't you just know the family is all gathered 'round a blazing fire on such a cold Sunday afternoon?" Wrapped around her question was her yearning for a home and a family of her own. "And they're playing games and laughing together and—"

"Sarah Em, stop it. You're always picturing things you don't know anything about."

"—and they're drinking hot cocoa," she went on, paying Timothy no heed, "and eating cookies. I just know it." They hadn't waited for lunch, and her stomach grumbled at the mention of food, but she disregarded that emptiness. "Let's try here. Since he owns the mercantile, Mr. Mitchell should know that Ours and my box are worth a lot."

"At least, now you're talking sensible."

"Imaginings are sensible! It keeps your mind full of the nicest pictures." She tossed her head, and the lacy vapor from her words swayed in the frosty air.

"What about *this* picture?" Timothy asked, a touch of playful taunting in his voice, as they started up the walk. "You know Mr. Mitchell wastes no time wasting time. So you'd better state your business pronto when he opens the door, and act like you know what you're doing."

"Well, if you think you can do a better job, Timothy Marshall, you do the talking."

"I will, then. Sit, Ours," he ordered. But the dog twisted around to face Timothy, and her wagging tail beat against the door— thump, thump, thumping.

In mere seconds, Mr. Mitchell jerked open the door.

"Do...do you want to buy a box and a dog?" Timothy blurted out.

"No! And what are you orphans doing on *this* end of Lilac Lane?" Does Miss Percy know you're here?" Not waiting for an answer, Mr. Mitchell slammed the door.

Ours growled.

"I'm sorry, Sarah Em. Old Man Mitchell flung open the door before I was ready, before I even knocked."

But Sarah Emily was bent over laughing so hard she had to wait until she could catch her breath to speak. "When you go calling, Ours will do your knocking. That's what we'll tell people why they need to buy her. She can do that for them." She dissolved into another ripple of laughter. "When you go calling, Ours will do your knocking," she sing-songed again.

"Yeah. I heard you the first time—very funny! I'm glad *you* can laugh." But by the time they got to the end of the walk, his laughter exploded into the icy air, blending with hers to make its own lyrical sound. Ours danced between them. Then Timothy looked at Sarah Emily. Their laughter subsided, and they became sober. "Come on, Sarah Em," he said softly. "We've got work to do."

When they stood at the next front door, Sarah Emily made sure the hair was out of her eyes and the gold clasp on the front of her mahogany box faced outward. Timothy ran his hand down Ours's back, smoothing flying fur. Sarah Emily and Timothy looked at each other and adjusted the tilt of their chins upward. Timothy confidently banged the enormous brass knocker that was the centerpiece of the burgundy-colored front door.

"This house looks regal," Sarah Emily whispered. "It's just the right place for a fine dog like Ours to live." The second the words were out of her mouth, a rock the size of a cabbage dropped into her stomach at the thought of Ours not living with her anymore. *Betsy has to have medicine!* she reminded herself, standing erect and stoically facing the door.

The heavy drapes pulled away from the edge of the window, just enough for one eye to peer out, then a freckled-faced boy of about ten years old opened the door. The moment Sarah Emily started to tell him about her wonderful dog and beautiful box, he turned around and yelled into the house, "It's two orphans and a dog."

"Tell them to get off our porch," an unseen voice yelled back. "And get to *that* end of Lilac Lane."

The boy turned to Sarah Emily, Timothy and Ours. "You

heard." He smiled, cruel pleasure seeping from the smile, and the dots on his face scrunched into one rusty blob.

The door slammed shut so fast and hard, Ours skittered backwards, nearly dragging Timothy off the porch. Sarah Emily burned with shame and anger. They walked away in silence.

"This should be a friendly place," Timothy said brightly as he pointed to the front columns on the third house. "Since pineapples are the symbol of welcome, they've got a whole plantation of 'howdy' carved right into the porch."

Sarah Emily ran her fingers along the deeply carved fruit on the wooden posts. "And just where did you learn about what a pineapple means?" That was a ridiculous question, she thought as soon as she had said it.

"I read it in a book about Colonial symbols."

"Well, just knock, Mr. Pineapple."

When Timothy knocked, a woman squinted through the large oval leaded glass in the center of the door. "Are you orphans?" she bellowed.

Sarah Emily and Timothy looked at one another, then back at the woman in the oval frame. Sarah Emily moistened her lips with her tongue and spoke up. "Yes, ma'am, we're orphans. But...we...we have a fine dog and a beautiful mahogany box for sale." She thrust the box closer to the glass in the door. "Won't you come out and look?" She willed more bravado into her voice than she felt in her spirit.

"No! Now, shoo or I'll get the broom after the lot of you."

The woman's words clubbed Sarah Emily. Her arms fell like weights in front of her. The box slammed against the top of her legs. She could feel herself dangle between hope and despair. In a flash, she chose to latch on to hope. *Betsy! I've got to keep trying for Betsy.*

Timothy led Ours away from the door. "Well, so much for the welcoming pineapple." He patted a column of the spiky fruit, letting a pathetic laugh trail him off the porch.

Sarah Emily ran past him and down the front walk. She spun around to look at Timothy and Ours. "I'm not giving up."

"I know, Sarah Em. I'm not either."

Sarah Emily turned toward the street and walked swiftly. Timothy and Ours caught up and fell in beside her.

"I've always wondered why these people moved out so soon," Timothy said as they neared the next house. "Seems like they didn't live here more than two or three months at the most."

"I know why they moved," Sarah Emily answered, never taking her eyes off the empty house that looked as dark and cold as the day.

"How'd you find out something like that?" Timothy tugged the rope to keep Ours from racing forward.

"You remember last summer when the farmer on the south side of town had those extra watermelons and brought them to us?"

"Sure, I remember. That was about the best slice of watermelon I ever had, but you didn't get any because Miss Percy sent you to your dormitory for taking too long on an errand." He turned to face her fully. "You never did tell me what that was all about—and what does it have to do with this empty house?"

"I'll tell you what it has to do with this house." Sarah Emily breathed in the frosty air and felt it stab her lungs. "Miss Percy sent me to Mitchell's Mercantile for some chamomile tea. She said we'd all jangled her nerves raw."

"That's nothing new," Timothy said.

"Yeah. But with the mercantile just around the corner, I should have been right back. But I wasn't."

"Then what took you so long?" Timothy stepped over the dog that had lain down between them.

Memories emerged. Sarah Emily could smell the green of the grass and feel the heat of that past August afternoon, although her cold feet now crunched in the snow as she walked to the edge of the front porch and set her mahogany box there. She went to the center of the frozen yard, threaded her dangling hair behind her ear and faced Timothy and Ours. Neither had moved an inch.

"That afternoon," she began, "right here where I stand, there was a tent made of gauzy white fabric with giant pink bows. The bows had to be this big." She put her arms up over her head and stretched her fingers, touching the tips together and making large circles. "The bows tied back the fabric at each corner.

"Women in frothy lace dresses with enormous hooped skirts were holding fancy parasols against the heat and smiling while they watched young girls covered in lace and ribbons play on the thick grass." She held out her arms level with the ground and twirled around on the snow-covered yard. "There was music and laughter flitting all around like butterflies."

While Timothy stood still and listened, Sarah Emily walked over to a row of spindly lilac bushes. "These were big and full, so I hid like this." She knelt behind the spent branches and pushed some aside. That winter day the ground was icy, and the wet cold numbed her knees, but it was a summer day she was feeling.

Ours stood up and tried to pull toward Sarah Emily. "Not now, girl," Timothy said quietly. "Just listen to Sarah Em."

The dog sat down.

"From here, I could see into the tent." Sarah Emily stared through the opening she made in the now leafless lilac bushes. "There were big baskets of fresh-cut flowers with colors to rival a rainbow. A long table was spread with a white cloth, and each corner was held down with pink bows to match the ones on the tent, only smaller. Right in the middle of the table was a tall cake." She spread the branches farther, as if to let Timothy see what she had seen that summer day. "The cake was covered with pink frosting and tiny white flowers."

The summer scene was vivid in her memory, every detail sharp. "At one end of the table were fancy glass pitchers full of lemonade—with slices of yellow lemons and fat red cherries floating on top. On the other side of the table were shiny silver platters, piled with tiny sandwiches."

"Didn't anybody see you hiding there?"

She shouldn't have been aggravated because that would be the question any orphan would have asked. Any orphan would know better than to linger in front of the houses on Lilac Lane. Sarah Emily let the branches snap back. She stood up and walked to Timothy and Ours. "I didn't even think about that," she said and *was* aggravated because she longed for Timothy to move past what an orphan *should* have done and see what she *had* seen that day.

"Just listen," she said. "Mothers and daughters were dressed alike. Timothy, I saw a mother look at her daughter with love pouring from her eyes. And then she laid her hand on her daughter's shoulder so gentle and natural—like it had been there a million times before." Sarah Emily put her hand on Timothy's shoulder. "What would it feel like to have your ma's hand resting on you with such love?"

"I can't even conceive of such." Timothy's voice was no more than scratchy air.

They both stared at Ours, stretched out between them. She knew Timothy was trying to imagine, just as she was, how wonderful it would be to have a ma.

"What happened next?" Timothy finally asked.

"I was still hiding in the bushes when I was nearly scared out of my skin by a girl asking me, 'Do you live at the orphan asylum?' I sprang up from the ground and told her I did, but I was on my way to the mercantile. I said I was sorry I'd been looking at her party and would leave right then."

"What'd she do? Weren't you scared?"

"Yeah, I was scared. But listen, you won't believe this. The girl had the sweetest smile and told me not to go."

"You're right, I don't believe you."

"As if that wasn't enough of a surprise, she asked me if I wanted something to eat."

"You mean her party food?"

"Yes, her party food. When she went to get it, I was sure it was a trick. This girl was going to get her mother who'd grab my ear and drag me back to Miss Percy and her leather strap. I was fully aware I needed to be getting out of here and on to the mercantile, but I couldn't take my eyes off the party."

"You were taking a big chance by staying."

"I know. But I couldn't move." Sarah Emily tilted her head and looked through the wintry air back to the summer scene. "It was the mothers."

"Mothers." Timothy drew in a long breath and his shoulders sagged when he exhaled. "Go on with the story."

"This girl had on a creamy white dress with a peach satin ribbon tied around the middle. Her mother wore one with the same colors, except it was made different because she was going to have a baby. The girl's hair came down to her waist, and it was all silk and shine and tied back with another peach ribbon. I've never seen hair that color. It was the gold and red of a sunset all mixed together. I think she might be the prettiest girl I ever saw—prettier than the porcelain doll in the window at Mitchell's Mercantile. And there I stood, plain as a bean."

"You aren't plain, Sarah Em," Timothy's voice was soft and his eyes held hers. "But if you're a bean, then you're a lima bean."

"A lima bean?"

"Yeah. A lima bean." Timothy scratched the back of his neck and grinned crookedly at the ground. "Because they're my favorite."

Sarah Emily felt the flush that crept up her neck and warmed her face, while her toes twitched. She quickly put one foot on top of the other, trying to quiet them. She swallowed hard, planted her hands on her hips and cocked her head to one side, anxious to divert his attention from her feet. "Do you want to know why they moved away, or do you want to keep talking about your silly old lima beans?" And all the while she talked, she kept thinking, *Lima bean. That's the sweetest thing he's ever said to me.*

He shuffled his feet in the snow. "Go ahead. Tell me why they moved."

She kneaded her cold hands together, her shoulders curled forward. If she was cold in two coats, she knew Timothy must be freezing. "Let's go sit on the edge of the porch and get out of this wind, and I'll make the rest of the story short. We need to be on our way."

Timothy lightly tugged on the rope, and Ours lumbered to her feet. "We've only got one more house to try. But Miss Percy isn't going to be pleased when she knows what we've done with Ours. Besides, my stomach is so empty it's about to fall to my feet."

"I know. Mine too."

They ran up the front steps to the edge of the porch. Timothy and Sarah Emily sat with their legs dangling over while Ours lay down behind them.

"Go on from where she brought you some food," Timothy said, leaning back against the dog.

"She brought us both a plate piled with the prettiest and best tasting food I'd ever put in my mouth. Little sandwiches all cut to look like diamonds and flowers and stars. I ate mine, every single crumb, in jig time, but she ate in dainty little bites and still had lots of food left." Sarah Emily leaned back against Ours and turned to Timothy. "You'll never guess what happened next."

"With this story, I couldn't possibly guess."

"She gave me her plate."

"You mean with food still on it?"

"Yeah. She said there was plenty, and she'd get more later."

"What'd you do?"

Sarah Emily playfully socked Timothy in the shoulder. "What do you think I did? I ate it—every crumb!"

Timothy sat forward and rubbed the spot she had hit. "Just 'cause you're a girl, you think I won't punch you back. One of these days, you're going to be surprised when I haul off and wallop you a good one."

She answered the laughter in his eyes with, "Do you want me to go on? Or are you hurt too bad?"

"No, I'm not hurt. And I've listened this long, so you may as well finish."

Sarah Emily closed her eyes and remembered the summer afternoon. "After we ate, Melody and I, we sat talking like I was somebody who lived in one of these grand houses." She opened her eyes and turned to Timothy. "Her name was Melody. Isn't that about the prettiest name you ever heard?"

He nodded.

"Melody said her ma named her that because she hoped she'd have a nice singing voice. When I asked her if she did, she said, 'No I can't sing a note.' I asked if her ma was disappointed. But she said, 'Of course not. My mother doesn't mind a bit.'"

Sarah Emily put her hand on Timothy's arm and looked directly into his eyes. "Can you imagine what it must be like to have a ma who loves you that much?"

"No," Timothy breathed.

"This next part is what hurts and where I try to stop remembering. The problem is, I usually can't shut it off." Sarah Emily scooted a little closer to the edge of the porch, flattened her hands beside her on the wooden floor and leaned slightly forward on her stiffened arms. "Melody and I were having such a good time. It was her fifteenth birthday party. She didn't know it, but I was pretending she was my friend, and I lived in that green and white house next door. Melody was being so nice, not seeming to care at all that I was an orphan. She never once said a thing about my clothes or hair."

Sarah Emily took a deep breath, let it out slowly and rocked a few times on her locked arms before she could go on. "We were talking, like I said, having a great time, when we heard this frightful scream and jumped up. I knew from the scream that something was wrong, terribly wrong. It was Melody's mother, and she was bent over and two of the other mothers were on each side of her, practically carrying her up these front steps, rushing to get her inside. They were saying the baby was coming too soon, and someone should get the doctor."

"What did Melody do?"

"She got this scared look on her face and ran inside too. I waited and waited, but when no one came outside, I went on to the Mercantile to get Miss Percy's chamomile tea. When I came back by, Melody was standing on the porch. As soon as she saw me, she ran out and told me Dr. Werther was there, but her ma was doing poorly. Anyway, before she went inside, she grabbed hold of my hand and asked me to come back the next day."

"Let me guess." Timothy shook his head. "You came back."

"Yeah, I did. I got up early and sneaked down here before breakfast. It was the saddest thing I've ever seen. Melody's face was red and swollen. Her beautiful long red hair was all tangled. She was still wearing the same dress she'd worn to the party, but by then it was wrinkled and dirty."

Sarah Emily stared into the gray air, clasped her hands in her lap and squeezed her fingers together. For a minute, she just squeezed and released, squeezed and released. "The baby died." Then with her gaze steady on nothing, she said, "And so did Melody's ma."

"Died." Timothy's word faded. "Died," slowly, he said it again.

"I've never told a soul any of this, but since that day, I've thought a lot about what it must be like to lose your ma when you're fifteen years old. In some ways, I think Melody was better off than me, and in other ways not. She got to know her ma and feel what it was like to be loved."

Timothy sighed. "But think how she must miss that."

"Yeah. That's why I don't know which way is easier. And there's something else I've thought a lot about." She chewed her bottom lip for a minute. "Her pa kept her," she whispered. "He didn't put her in an orphan asylum." *And neither did Betsy's pa;* the words were right there to be spoken, but at the last second, she didn't.

Timothy's hand covered hers. "Is that why you never told me about Melody? It hurts to think about her pa keeping her and yours not?"

"Yes." Her voice was barely a whisper, her eyes taking in his hand, her heart spinning. "Don't you ever wonder about your ma and pa?"

A gust of frosty wind whooshed around them. "Sarah Em, I know what you're thinking. Melody knew her ma, and even though she died, Melody is still living with her pa. And, most important, she knows who she looks like. So according to your way of figuring, she knows how she'll turn out."

"Why do you always sound like that can't be true?" Her words were as icy as the wind, and she tried to jerk her hand out from under his.

He tightened his grip and wouldn't let go. "Here's how I see it. It would be great for everyone to know about their parents, but some of us just don't. And that's the fact of it. Cook told me one time, 'A body chooses what kind of person they want to be—good or bad.'"

Sarah Emily wriggled her hand until she got it out from under his. She pulled her coat sleeves down, curling her cold hands up inside like retreating turtles' heads. "I guess I just want to know why Pa didn't keep me. And why when he came to see Miss Percy, and I saw him that day outside the school building, did he run?"

"I know, Sarah Em. I know that's real important to you."

"And Betsy's what's important right now." Sarah Emily couldn't bear to talk about her pa or Melody any more. She twisted her hands out from her sleeves and stood up. "We've got one more house."

Timothy reached for the rope around Ours's neck and grinned. "See, caring about Betsy the way you do, you're already a good person."

"Good *and* fast." Springing down the steps, she called back to him. "I'll race you next door."

As she tore off toward the next house, the gunman's face, his eyes and jagged scar forced themselves into her mind. She hated the way they intruded, uninvited and unwelcome. She had tried to keep those thoughts caged up like mean dogs, but they barked and growled and snarled, clawing and chewing until they escaped. She rubbed her eyes, determined, once and for all, to blot out the image of that day in the dining room.

"What's wrong? Snow get in your eyes?" Timothy asked.

"Yeah...snow..." she said and ran faster toward the last house on the block.

Chapter 17

arah Emily held her breath at the next and last house while Timothy knocked on the door, and Ours scratched behind her up-ear, making a white rocking chair bump back and forth.

No answer.

Timothy knocked again, and Sarah Emily pushed out her breath in a nervous swoosh, puffing her cheeks, wondering about the people who had recently moved into this house.

Sarah Emily loved the way the forest green shutters and front porch stood out against the dazzling white of the house. She had pretended this was the house she lived in the afternoon she was with Melody because if she ever had a home of her own, she wanted it to look just like this. She would give anything for a peek inside.

But all she could see were heavy drapes. So many nights her dreams took wings and let her live in this house—until dawn came and Miss Percy appeared.

Disappointed that she couldn't see, she turned from the window, swiped the hair out of her eyes and reached for the back of the rocker to stop its wobbling. The door opened.

Sarah Emily thrust her box forward. "Would you like to buy a dog and a…" Her words were arrested by the woman's welcoming smile and dazzling blue dress.

"Well, glory be. Do come in. It's much too cold to be standing outdoors."

The sound of the lady's voice caused Sarah Emily to reclaim her wits. "Thank you, ma'am, but we came to offer you these fine two things, this dog and box. We're willing to sell them for only a dollar for the both."

Timothy jostled against her as he labored to hold the rope to keep Ours from bounding into the house where wonderful aromas of food meandered out to the porch.

"You must be freezing. Come in." The lady opened the door wider.

Sarah Emily's gaze jumped from the vivid blue dress to the foyer. Her thirsty eyes guzzled in the splendor. Light glittered from a large ornate kerosene fixture that hung from the high ceiling. The pedestal table in the center of the room sat on a round blue rug and held a shiny brass bowl that was flanked by tall candlesticks. The wallpaper had bouquets of spring flowers, each tied with delicate blue bows that swayed toward the next bouquet as if blowing in a soft wind. It was every bit as grand inside as she had ever dreamed—actually, grander.

"Please, come in," the lady urged them again.

For a moment, the invitation tipped over Sarah Emily's reason for being there. "We can't come in." She quickly uprighted her thinking, pried her stare from the captivating foyer and put her hand on Ours's head. "But would you buy this dog and box? The dog is much smarter than she looks."

"Yes, much smarter than most dogs," Timothy added.

Swishing her exquisite blue skirt to one side, the lady swept her hand back into the entry hall. "Well, if you'll come in, we can talk better where it's warm," she said with such kindness that Sarah Emily's heart trembled.

But she and Timothy stood, dumbfounded, as surely as if their shoes were nailed to the floor with dozens and dozens of foot-long spikes—not Ours, though. She had one large wooly paw already in the house, and her nose was up, wriggling to capture the delicious smells of good things to eat.

The lady touched Sarah Emily's arm. "Please, come in."

Timothy glanced at Sarah Emily, and she saw his questioning expression.

She didn't understand this lady's insistence that they come in either. But Sarah Emily knew she wanted to—more than anything else, she wanted to go inside. She and Timothy traded shrugs of surprise and then of acceptance.

He bent down by a wicker chair, and started tying Ours to its leg.

"Oh no. You can't leave her out here." The woman shivered and hugged her arms as white snow puffs churned across the porch. "It's much too cold for me to examine the dog to see if I want to buy her. Bring her in too."

Now, Sarah Emily couldn't have been any more surprised if the lady had suddenly become an elephant and offered them a ride on her enormous gray back.

With an astounded stare at Sarah Emily and then another bewildered shrug, Timothy stood, looped the rope around his hand, and the three stepped inside.

Sarah Emily heard the heavy door close and then felt the lady's hand on her back.

"Let's go into the parlor. We have a fire in there."

Sarah Emily glanced into the brass bowl as they passed the round table. It was filled with flower petals of all colors. They gave off the scent of a summer garden, and here it was wintertime. How could that be?

Sarah Emily supposed that since the lady was new on this street, she probably didn't know they were orphans. Something surged in Sarah Emily's chest, something hot and painful. *She'll throw us out as soon as we tell her. I just know it.*

But before Sarah Emily could think of a way to hide the fact they were orphans, the lady steered her into the parlor, her hand still pressing lightly on her back. As they entered, Sarah Emily and Timothy gasped together at the beautiful room that was as wide as a lake.

"I wondered who was at the door." A tall, plump man sitting near the fire rose from his chair and steadied himself, then stepped toward them, limping on his left leg. "And who are our guests?" he asked, his smile crinkling eyes brown and sweet as raisins.

Sarah Emily liked him instantly.

"Oh my. I didn't ask their names." The lady clapped her hands together and let out a little laugh that tinkled like golden bells. "Where are my manners? I haven't even introduced myself."

"Then let me." The man's booming voice was as large as he was, but it filled the room with a light merriment. He hooked a hefty thumb onto a tiny pocket on his gray vest. "We're Mr. and Mrs. Neal. And who might you three be? Where do you live?"

Sarah Emily's chest tightened again. *Now they're going to know we're orphans.*

"She's Sarah Emily Butler; I'm Timothy Marshall." And gesturing to the dog, whose nose hadn't stopped sniffing at the tantalizing aromas, he answered, "Her name is Ours."

Quick thinking, Timothy, Sarah Emily thought, answering the name part, but ignoring the address.

"Nice to meet all of you." Mr. Neal held his hand out toward the sofa. "Please sit down and tell us why we have the privilege of your company this afternoon."

Privilege? No one on this end of Lilac Lane ever thought it was a privilege to see orphans. Not knowing what else to do, Sarah Emily sat down next to Timothy, and Ours sprawled out on the rose-colored rug at their feet.

Mr. Neal returned to his blue chair that faced the blue and rose sofa. Mrs. Neal patted the curls around her face as she settled into the matching chair next to his.

Sarah Emily became embarrassed by her own unruly shank of hair that was still insisting on sliding into her eye, but as she pulled it back and twisted it around her ear, she caught sight of rows and rows of the richly colored spines of books. This would be a paradise for Timothy, she thought.

Then her gaze traveled on to the blue porcelain vase on the edge of the mantle. Her hair was forgotten as she remembered all the blue in the front hall, and she quickly took in this room. The blue satin cloth over the side table, the blue design in the drapes, edged by rose-colored fringe, the blue flowers in the sofa fabric and Mrs. Neal's blue flowing dress—yes, this lady must love blue.

"That's an exquisite box you have there," Mr. Neal spoke, again filling the room with his jovial voice. "Mahogany, isn't it?"

The Box! Betsy! Quit your gawking and be about business, Sarah Emily gave herself a mental slap. "Yes, it is." Sarah Emily shifted the box in her lap so the gold clasp faced the Neals. "This box and dog are for sale."

"For sale?" Mr. Neal arched one of his grand gray eyebrows that had wisps of inky black hairs, obviously left over from younger days. "Why would you want to sell such a lovely box and nice dog?"

Timothy leaned forward. "We need the money for something really important, or we wouldn't be selling either of them."

"Can you tell us what that is?" Mrs. Neal asked and delicately folded her hands in her lap. Her movements were the graceful smoothness of a small bird fluttering to a tree limb.

"Our friend, Betsy, is sick, and we need the money for medicine," Sarah Emily said.

"Medicine?" Mr. Neal's eyebrow arched again, but his eyes still spoke of gentleness.

"Yes. Betsy has The Fever, and Doc Werther says the medicine will cost one dollar."

"And why are you buying your friend's medicine?" Mr. Neal asked. "Doesn't she have parents?"

"Dear," Mrs. Neal broke in, touching her husband's arm. "Sarah Emily, Timothy, do you live at the orphan asylum at the end of the street?"

Mr. Neal winked at Mrs. Neal, "Of course," his mouth moving soundlessly.

"We'll be leaving now." Sarah Emily sighed and started to stand. It was out. They couldn't hide who they were. At least she got to come inside, if only for a few minutes. That was some consolation.

"Leave?" Mr. Neal said, springing forward in his chair. "Why? You just got here."

"You *want* us to stay?" Timothy stared at Mr. Neal.

"Even though you know we're orphans?" the words popped out of Sarah Emily's mouth. She expected Mr. Neal's kind expression and dark eyes to change at the word *orphans*. She watched carefully. They stayed exactly the same.

"Certainly, we want you to stay."

This was a perplexing place, but Sarah Emily eased back onto the sofa, keeping a close watch on his eyes. Their sweetness would sour.

"We were about to have something to eat when you arrived. Won't you join us? Mrs. Neal and I have been to church this morning, and we're hungry."

Church? That alarmed Sarah Emily. If these people were anything like Mrs. Hancock, she didn't want to stay.

"And while we eat, we can talk about the dollar you need. You are hungry, aren't you?" Mr. Neal smiled, and his chin disappeared into his collar.

Hungry? The breakfast oatmeal had long ago left her stomach hollow. She looked at Timothy, and their eyes screamed, FOOD! The thought of leaving was gone.

Mrs. Neal stood. "I'm going to tell Opal to set two more places at the table. And I'm sure we can find something for Ours. While we eat, you must tell us how she came to be named Ours. What delightful ears." She leaned down and rubbed the dog. Her beautiful blue dress whispered around her, and she painted the air with the smell of summer lilacs. Then, just as she was leaving the room, she turned back. "Dear, would you put another log on the fire?"

"Yes, and tell Opal that I'm unusually hungry and to put out plenty of fried chicken, and we'll need extra big slices of her chocolate cake for dessert." Mr. Neal winked at Timothy as he moved toward the fireplace.

He sure does a lot of winking with those nice eyes. Sarah Emily watched the fire snap and pop as it accepted the new log into the flames.

This time, Mr. Neal limped on his right leg.

And she wasn't cold anymore.

And Mr. Neal's eyes were still kind.

And she could still feel the soft imprint of Mrs. Neal's hand on her back.

For sure, this was a perplexing place.

In no time, Mrs. Neal reappeared. "Everything's ready. Come to the table."

"What will we do with Ours?" Timothy asked.

"Why, you bring her too." Mrs. Neal waved them forward with a lively gesture. "We have a place all set for her."

A place for Ours? Sarah Emily wasn't sure she had heard correctly. But, right then, she decided that for now, she would lay aside thoughts about Betsy's sickness, about how angry Miss Percy was going to be and the robber. She would simply let herself crawl into this unexpected adventure of being and eating in this grand and glorious house with these grand and glorious people

"I know, I'm ready to eat." In three long, limping strides, Mr. Neal was across the room.

Timothy, Ours and Sarah Emily followed him to the dining room.

This room was as lovely as the others Sarah Emily had seen, but it was the preserves in here that commanded her attention. She heard Mrs. Neal tell Timothy where Ours's food was—on the floor next to his chair. Mr. Neal touched her shoulder, directing her to her seat. She heard another woman's voice telling Mrs. Neal that the rolls would be out of the oven in a minute, and she felt the table jiggle when Ours bumped it as she lapped up her food. Her gaze had skimmed the huge bowls of mashed potatoes, green beans and carrots, a platter of fried chicken, and the applesauce, pickles, and gravy. But the preserves—two kinds—strawberry and a deep purple one, maybe blackberry—were what enthralled her. Her tongue quivered. Preserves.

Finally, she looked at Timothy, his mouth open, his eyes round as they darted in sharp lines from food to food.

"Sit, sit," Mr. Neal said. "Everyone sit."

Sarah Emily slid her box under her chair. Mr. and Mrs. Neal took their places at the ends of the oval table, and Sarah Emily sat across from Timothy. She touched the edge of the blue and white china plate, then let her fingers glide across the silverware—a fork, a knife and a spoon. She had never been at a table set like this.

Sarah Emily looked up and saw Mrs. Neal take her napkin from the table and place it in her lap. Mr. Neal did the same thing.

Following the Neals' actions, Sarah Emily draped her napkin over her lap. When she saw Timothy's still beside his plate, she slid down in her chair and flung her leg under the table until she kicked him.

His head jerked up, and he scowled at her. She scooted back upright in her seat, lifted her blue napkin slightly above the edge of the table, and nodded toward his. Timothy pulled it into his lap, but looked distracted.

"We usually just eat from bowls." Timothy's words tumbled out. "Are those mashed potatoes? We have soups mostly." He seemed unable to stop the rushing stream. "Those are mighty big pieces of chicken. When we have chicken, it's usually soup, and the chicken doesn't do much more than sit on the edge of the pot and swing his hind legs through it a couple of times."

Mr. Neal threw his head back and laughed in large, generous bursts; his whole face seemed to be weathered by many past smiles. "Well, today you're having fried chicken, young man." He reached a thick hand over and wrapped it around Timothy's arm. "And you can have a *hind* leg or any piece you want, as many as you want." He winked and then folded his hands. "But first, let's pray."

Pray? Sarah Emily's arm jumped and knocked her knife clattering to the floor. *Oh, great, fine guest I am.* Mortification burned her cheeks, but she bent down to retrieve it.

"Just leave it, dear," Mrs. Neal said. "Don't worry. Opal will bring you another."

Sarah Emily uncurled herself and looked across the table. Timothy's eyes were closed, and his head was bowed just like Mr. Neal's. *He's eager to get on with the praying so he can get on with the eating,* Sarah Emily laughed to herself. She knew Timothy wasn't any more used to praying than she was. It was then that she caught sight of a large framed portrait on the wall. She quickly studied the faces—Mr. and Mrs. Neal and two teenagers—probably their children.

"Dear Heavenly Father," Mr. Neal's voice thundered out.

Sarah Emily closed her eyes.

"Thank you for this Lord's Day and for your many blessings in it. We are especially grateful for our visitors who are here to share this meal with us."

Grateful for our visitors? Sarah Emily opened one eye. Timothy's eyes were squeezed shut. Mrs. Neal's hands were in her lap, eyes closed. Ours had finished eating and was asleep in the corner, a satisfied snore flapping her lips now and again. Sarah Emily closed her eye.

"We know you have each of us in your mighty hands, and we thank you for your plan for our lives," Mr. Neal continued.

I don't think I'm in anyone's hands, but I'd like to get my hands on this food, Sarah Emily thought.

She breathed deeply of the mingling aromas that rose from the table and imagined the sweetness of the preserves that glistened from the crystal dish that was divided into two sections by a tall silver handle.

"This food we are about to eat was provided by you and your bounty to us."

I thought that lady named Opal cooked it.

"In the name of Jesus Christ we pray. Amen."

Mr. Neal sighed. "I'm hungry. Let's get started." He handed Timothy the platter heavy with fried chicken.

"Have that big piece on top for starters."

Timothy took the platter with both hands and held it woodenly in front of him like it might disappear if he breathed or moved.

"Go ahead, my boy, that big one has your name on it."

Without any more cajoling, Sarah Emily watched Timothy take the piece nearly the size of his hand. If Betsy weren't too sick to eat, she would figure out a way to get a piece of that chicken back to her.

"Would you like some mashed potatoes?" Mrs. Neal spoke into Sarah Emily's thought.

Sarah Emily seized the bowl, sunk the spoon in deep and came up with a huge mound all before Mrs. Neal got her hands off the bowl. With the overflowing serving spoon hovering above her plate, Sarah Emily looked at Timothy's mountain of potatoes with gravy running down in great gullies. She looked at Mrs. Neal's plate, and although Sarah Emily wanted the same amount Timothy had, she shook about half of the potatoes back into the bowl to come closer to the diminutive serving of Mrs. Neal.

Then Sarah Emily took a fat roll and slathered it with butter since the preserves hadn't moved from the other side of the table, and she wasn't sure how to get them. Just as she pushed a large portion of the bread into her mouth, she saw Mrs. Neal put a pat of butter on her plate using the knife on the side of the butter dish. She replaced the knife, broke her roll in half, then broke the half in half and buttered just one piece with her own knife.

Sarah Emily took another roll and did likewise. She liked the way that looked—elegant and mannerly. *I have to remember to tell Betsy the proper way to butter and eat a roll.* She sat up straighter and began to feel very elegant herself as she patted the corner of her mouth with her napkin, like Mrs. Neal.

But all the time, Sarah Emily kept her eye on the preserves.

Finally they were passed, and Sarah Emily ladled generous mounds of both kinds onto her plate along with servings of all the other food. While everyone ate, she was amazed at the easy chatter that crisscrossed the table, bouncing from subject to subject. Timothy easily could keep up with Mr. Neal on nearly anything he brought up. Sarah Emily surprised herself on how well she could enter in also. Again, Timothy's urging her to learn had paid off.

She liked this sitting in a chair instead of on a bench. She liked eating with a fork, not just a spoon. She liked holding the glass—water goblet, Mrs. Neal had called it—not a heavy cup. She liked the way Mrs. Neal put small bites of food into her mouth, and she especially liked her graceful movements. Was this what it felt like to be a lady? If this was, Sarah Emily liked it.

Sarah Emily yearned to know how to make a home smell of enticing foods and a flower garden all at the same time with no vinegary smell. She wanted to know how to place pretty things in a room and make it colorful and inviting with no gray walls. She wanted to fix her hair in a decidedly feminine way, not stretched back into a tight bun or whacked off.

Yes, Mrs. Neal knew these secrets.

At last, Sarah Emily felt stuffed-sausage full. On trips to town she had watched the skilled fingers of the butcher push the ground meat into the casing until it looked like it wouldn't hold another bit; then he would slide his fingers down the smooth sides, making room for a little more. She eyed the last roll and thought she could make room. She put another spoonful of strawberry preserves on her plate and took the lone roll out of the polished silver bread bowl.

Just as Timothy reached over and speared another piece of chicken, Mr. Neal said, "We'd enjoy hearing how Ours got her unusual name."

She felt a prick remembering that she was here to convince them to buy Ours. Putting her fork down, she cleared her throat, wiped her mouth with the napkin and pushed the long flopping piece of hair from her eyes. "I named her Ours—" She paused when Ours lumbered over and sat down beside Sarah Emily, dropping her head into her lap.

"Ours heard you say her name," Mr. Neal laughed. "She must love you very much."

Sarah Emily rubbed the dog, looked into the adoring eyes and felt that prick even stronger. An image of Betsy huddled on the cot in the sick room shoved aside her own grief at losing Ours, and she began to enthrall them with stories about her extraordinary dog. She told how Ours found Miss Percy's brooch, how she helped Mr. Wilbur apprehend the gunman and how she got her name. And ending with what couldn't be told in an anecdote, but what truly was the best thing about Ours—she was a loving, affectionate friend.

Opal appeared with a tray laden with slices of chocolate cake which Sarah Emily had totally forgotten were still to come. During Sarah Emily's stories, Opal had cleared the dishes. Now she circled the table, leaving a plate in front of everyone. Sarah Emily saw that Mrs. Neal's was the smallest piece while the plate Opal put in front of her had a slice as large as Timothy's. On this, Sarah Emily had no desire to copy Mrs. Neal's daintier portion. Sarah Emily simply pulled herself up straighter in the chair and wondered just how far a sausage casing could be stretched.

All through dessert, Sarah Emily and Timothy laughed easily with the Neals. *If it weren't for the reason we're here, this might be the best day of my life,* she thought. What was even better than the food and Mr. Neal's funny stories was the fact they didn't seem to care that she and Timothy were orphans. In fact, it didn't seem to bother them at all.

After a while, she realized she had done exactly as she had wanted—to crawl inside this experience and enjoy it, forgetting everything else. But when the clock chimed two, she knew it was time to climb out.

She pushed her empty cake plate toward the center of the table, leaned down and got her box from under the chair and set it in front of her. Her fingers tightly gripped it as she looked first at Mr. Neal and then Mrs. Neal. "This visit and food have been wonderful—you can't even imagine how wonderful. But Timothy and I are here to see if you'd buy Ours and my box." She went on to explain in detail why they needed the money.

After she finished, Timothy flashed her a *great—you did a great job* look.

With hope pressing against Sarah Emily's throat, she looked at Mr. Neal.

He winked at Mrs. Neal who nodded and smiled. "Why don't you three go into the parlor, and let us talk about this. We'll be along shortly."

Sarah Emily searched their faces for a clue as to what they were thinking, but they only smiled at her. She smiled back, hoping they would understand how important this was. Timothy reached for Ours's rope. As Sarah Emily stood, she saw him swipe his finger across his cake plate and get a last dab of icing.

"Thank you for the food," Timothy said.

In the parlor, Sarah Emily settled in front of the fire, which by now burned low and warm. It crackled inside the hearth, sending swaying black shadows over the walls and above the bookshelves.

Timothy sat beside her, his hands clamped between his knees. A few minutes later when the Neals came in, Ours was yawning and stretching out for another nap.

Mr. and Mrs. Neal took their places in their matching chairs. Mr. Neal leaned forward. "This is what we'd like to do. We'll buy your box, but you must take Ours home with you. She's a fine dog, and we'd love to have her, but she wouldn't be happy with anyone else. She clearly loves you both. We'll check with Dr. Werther today and make sure he orders whatever medicine Betsy needs."

Sarah Emily slid off the sofa and put an arm around Ours. She didn't know how to feel. She was thrilled to keep Ours, but afraid if the Neals didn't take both Ours and the box, they wouldn't get Betsy enough medicine. "Don't you want both? The medicine is going to be expensive," she said, half-afraid they would change their minds and want Ours too.

"No, we want you to keep your dog." Mrs. Neal smiled. "But don't worry about your friend. We'll make sure she gets all the medicine she needs."

"There's nothing else we have to sell." Sarah Emily held her open empty hands out. She wasn't sure if she was supposed to offer something else in place of Ours.

"Oh, no. We don't want anything else. You must be very worried about Betsy." Mr. Neal looked at her with those kind eyes. "But I'll tell you what you can do. Why don't you come back tomorrow and help with some chores if you're concerned about us not buying Ours?"

"Yes, please come back," Mrs. Neal said.

"Chores—we can do chores—anything you need done," Timothy piped up.

It would be hard for either of them to get back here, with Miss Percy hiring out Timothy and Sarah Emily's own afternoon chores at the orphan asylum, but if the Neals would get the medicine for Betsy, she would find a way.

Sarah Emily stood and held the box out to Mrs. Neal as if entrusting a child to someone. "We thank you both." She felt a tight band around her chest when Mrs. Neal took the box, Sarah

Emily's only possession of her mother's.

But Betsy was worth it, and for that Sarah Emily felt genuine gratitude. "Thank you. Betsy is so sick."

Mrs. Neal set the box on her lap and reached out to cradle Sarah Emily's hands in hers. "I can tell this box is special to you. We haven't talked about where you got it, but when you come tomorrow, I want to hear all about it."

On their way to the front door, Mrs. Neal set the box on the pedestal table in the foyer, next to the shiny brass bowl that filled the room with the sweet scent of summer flowers. Sarah Emily trailed her hand across her box and felt a tear squeezing into the corner of her eye. But at the same time, she hurried her mind forward to Betsy being well and out of that depressing sick room.

"Then we'll see you tomorrow after school," Mr. Neal said.

"Don't worry about your box, sweetheart. I'll take good care of it," Mrs. Neal whispered, as she encircled Sarah Emily's waist with one arm.

As they left, Sarah Emily had never known such caring people, other than Mr. Wilbur and Cook, in all of Lander. The Neals had fed her food and kindness, both in generous servings. Mr. Neal had made her laugh, and Mrs. Neal was everything Sarah Emily always pictured a lady to be.

Tomorrow. Her thoughts excitedly repeated over and over. *Tomorrow. They asked me to come back tomorrow.* Sarah Emily went off the porch backwards, not wanting to miss a moment of those extraordinary people. She knew, even if she never got a hair clasp, this was the best Christmas present. There was only one thing that could make this any better—for Betsy to get well by Christmas.

But that was only four days away.

Chapter 18

he next morning, Sarah Emily hovered between being asleep and awake. With her eyes still closed and the blanket pulled under her chin, she floated on the silky smooth surface of the most marvelous dream. She and Timothy had been invited into that beautiful house at the end of Lilac Lane, her favorite house, and they had been treated like people, not orphans, and she had eaten so much preserves that it could only have happened in a dream. She flinched and her eyes popped open. This wasn't a dream; it was a nightmare, because the reason they had been there was that Betsy was sick.

As wakefulness emerged more fully from sleep, Sarah Emily realized that it was all true. The dream had really happened with the Neals, but sadly, the nightmare of Betsy's illness was equally true.

She jumped up, dressed and made her bed before the other girls' feet landed on the floor. She zipped out of the dormitory and down the hall to the sick room, hoping, since it was early, that Miss Percy wouldn't be there.

As soon as Sarah Emily opened the door to the dark, little room, the sweet scent of rosewater hit her. Her hopes drained away. There was Miss Percy, green towel pressed to her mouth and nose, standing with her back pressed against the stacked-up benches as far away from Betsy as possible.

At the sight of Sarah Emily, Miss Percy's eyes ignited. She rushed across the room, her heels stomping, and jabbed two stiff fingers into Sarah Emily's chest, backing her into the hall.

It was amazing that such spindly fingers attached to such a slight body could inflict such a powerful poke. Sarah Emily clenched her teeth, determined not to let on that each jab felt like a horse's kick. Miss Percy wouldn't be allowed that pleasure.

Once in the hall, Miss Percy jerked the towel from her face and pointed back into the sick room. "Contagious. I don't want an epidemic." The words snapped like a whip. Then she aimed one of those spindly fingers toward the stairs, and Sarah Emily understood its order: leave—now.

Just as Miss Percy turned back to close the door, Sarah Emily took a quick long stride behind the headmistress. Looping back, Sarah Emily stuck her head in to see Betsy, and sang out as fast as the words would come, "Hi, Betsy. It's Sarah Emily. Get well. I sure do miss you."

And then she bolted for the stairs with Miss Percy leaning over the railing, yelling, "You orphan brat. You've started my day off with a headache. If I had my strap ... "

Downstairs, in the noisy dining room, Sarah Emily caught her breath and tried to, but couldn't, dismiss the worry that the Neals took her box, but wouldn't get the medicine for Betsy. She should have insisted they give the dollar to her, and she give it to Doc Werther herself. Was their being nice just an act to get her box? *One of these days, surely, I'll learn to think before I not only come up with plans, but also when I make important decisions. How long does it take water to boil anyway?*

She moved to the food line and watched for Timothy while she got her oatmeal. Only seconds after she sat down, she saw him get his breakfast and come toward her.

With one fluid motion, he raised a long leg to step over the bench, plunked his tray on the table and sat down across from her. "Was that you Miss Percy was yelling at a few minutes ago?"

"Yeah. It was me. I tried to see Betsy."

"How is she?"

"I don't really know because I didn't actually get to see her. Miss Percy wouldn't let me."

"I wanted to check on her before school too. But I guess I'd better scratch that idea."

"Yeah. I don't think there's much chance of you getting in the sick room either. Miss Percy is keeping it locked, afraid of The Fever spreading." Sarah Emily laid her spoon down and pushed the long string of hair from her face. "I hope Mr. and Mrs. Neal took the dollar to Doc last night. We can trust them, can't we?"

"I think so," he said slowly. "You notice they called him Doctor, not Doc?"

"Yes, I heard that too. But can we trust them?"

"It's hard to know. We don't have too much to go on since last night's supper was the first nice thing anyone at *that* end of Lilac Lane ever did for us. And that was a mighty nice thing." His lopsided smile was huge.

"Sure was. I woke up this morning thinking that maybe it had been a dream, but then I remembered how delicious those preserves were."

"I know. I did the same thing, only for me it was the fried chicken."

"And chocolate cake."

He grinned. "Okay, the whole meal." As quickly as the grin came, it faded. He leaned closer to her. "I guess we'll know soon enough if it was a trick to get your box when we see if Betsy gets the medicine."

"I heard Doc say yesterday the medicine had to be ordered from Chicago. I don't know if it would be here on the next day's train or not. The other thing that keeps worrying me about the Neals is that they go to church—so does Mrs. Hancock and her bunch. I wouldn't trust Mrs. Hancock with so much as my stained-up, worn-out, everyday apron, let alone with something like my box or getting Betsy's medicine."

"I know, the church thing bothers me too. Don't worry though, Sarah Em. If they didn't do what they said, we'll think of something else."

"Yeah. You're right. We'll think of something." She picked

up her spoon and stabbed at her oatmeal.

Timothy shot her a reassuring smile.

There, he'd done it again, trying to help her make things work out. March was getting closer. What would she do without him? She couldn't even imagine—didn't want to imagine.

"Did Miss Percy say anything about us being gone yesterday?" Timothy asked while pouring a cup of milk.

"Nope. Not a word. Since the Neals didn't keep Ours, and she won't miss my box, it looks like we squeaked by without being caught."

"I'm not sure how we did that with being gone so long." Timothy reached into the breadbasket and then laid three thick slices on his tray. "At least the bread rations haven't gotten smaller," he said, eyeing the thin oatmeal in his bowl. "I'd like to go back to the Neals' today, but Miss Percy has me hired out, which means I'll miss school again and won't be back until supper or maybe even later. I hate for you to have to do whatever chores they want done by yourself. Do you still want to go?"

"Sure do. I'm keeping my end of the deal, and hope they've kept theirs. Don't worry about me. I can handle whatever they want." She reached for the milk pitcher, but Timothy touched her hand and lowered it to the table.

She looked at him.

"Sarah Em, I'm awful sorry that you had to sell your ma's box. I know how much it means to you." He flattened his fingers on her hand, and his eyes stayed on her. "Maybe someday, I can earn enough money to buy it back for you."

At that moment, she was unable to say anything. She didn't want to move her hand, and she couldn't move her eyes. Under the table her toes twitched.

Sarah Emily had no idea how long they sat that way. She knew it could only have been seconds, lovely seconds, before he lifted his hand, or someone would have seen them, and laughing and jokes would be flying through the dining room.

She finally said, "I can't get my ma back by keeping the box, but maybe it can help Betsy." She raised her shoulders and let them fall in a heartfelt shrug, as much to clear her head of the confusing yet wondrous feelings that Timothy's words and touch had caused, as to expel the sadness of having her box gone.

"You're a very special person, Sarah Em, to be so generous," he said. Then his attention was drawn to something behind her. "Hey, Doc is here."

Sarah Emily turned around to see.

"We'll ask him about Betsy's medicine." Timothy stood and called out, "Doc Werther?"

"Ah, Sarah Emily. Timothy." The doctor smiled at them and came over. Sliding onto the end of the bench next to Timothy, he set his medical bag beside the breadbasket. "I've only got a minute because I need to see Betsy. And I was looking for Miss Percy. Do you know where she is?"

"Haven't seen her since I came in here." Sarah Emily pushed the breadbasket out of the way.

"Well, I'm glad I found you first. I wanted—"

Sarah Emily stopped him. The doctor's eyes told her that he knew all about yesterday. "You won't tell Miss Percy about us going to the Neals', will you?"

"Of course not."

"Did they give you any money?" Timothy asked

"Yes. First, I want you to know how impressed I am with your concern for Betsy." Doc Werther looked at Sarah Emily and then at Timothy. "But listen, you two, as soon as I left here yesterday, I wired Chicago for the medicine to be sent on this morning's train." He opened his bag and pointed to a skinny brown bottle. "And here it is."

"That's wonderful." Sarah Emily clasped her hands together, peered in the bag and breathed a breath of relief.

"Yeah. Thanks, Doc." Timothy awkwardly reached to shake the doctor's hand.

"You don't think I'd just do nothing about Betsy, do you?" Doc Werther latched shut his bag. "I only wish we had a hospital here in Lander. My clinic is full up with people sick with The Fever or I'd take Betsy there." He took off his glasses and rubbed two fingers against his eyelids.

With that gesture, Sarah Emily was aware of the weariness straining his eyes, thinning his voice and stooping his shoulders.

He put his glasses back on, adjusting the gold wires over his ears. "Anyway, the Neals offered to pay for all the medicine Betsy might need. They're fine people. I met them last year, unfortunately enough, though, under tragic circumstances."

"Edward, I'm so glad to see you," Miss Percy tore into their conversation as she hurried to them, balancing a pile of cinnamon buns on her pink plate.

Clearly, the cinnamon was holding out, Sarah Emily noticed.

"Edward," Miss Percy said in a sprightly voice. "So good to see you."

"Let me handle this. Your secret is safe with me," Doc Werther quickly whispered to Sarah Emily and Timothy as he slid out from the bench and stood. "Mildred, good morning. I was looking for you when I saw these two sitting here."

"Yes." She flashed them a cold stare. Then, looking at Doc Werther, she smiled and waved her plate toward her small table in the corner. "Let's go sit over there. I was just coming in to eat my breakfast, and I saw you so I had Cook give me extra. She's going to bring you a cup of coffee, and we can share these. We haven't had time to just sit and visit in ages."

"And I don't have time for that now. I'm here about Betsy."

"Oh, yes. Why, of course, Betsy." Miss Percy arced her head down and clucked. "Precious Betsy. Yes, yes, of course. I was just up to see the dear, sick one a few minutes ago."

Sarah Emily's gaze locked with Timothy's. He rolled his eyes in disgust. Sarah Emily inwardly groaned at Miss Percy's feigned concern.

"I've got the medicine and need to give her the first dose." Doc Werther patted his medical bag.

"Medicine? But how . . . too much money . . ."

"All taken care of." Doc Werther raised a hand to stop her sputtering protests. He scanned the pink plate of delicious-smelling buns and then the thin oatmeal in Sarah Emily and Timothy's bowls. "In fact," he said, "why don't you leave these for them, and come help me." Prying the plate from her, he set it on the table.

Stunned, Sarah Emily watched Miss Percy's eyes flit from the plate to the doctor and back to the plate. "My...my...buns—"

"No need to worry. They won't go to waste. I'm sure these two will enjoy them." Doc Werther put his hand under Miss Percy's elbow and steered her across the room.

Just as they got to the door, he looked back with a smile, a giant triumphant smile.

Sarah Emily even thought a new spurt of energy rushed over him.

Timothy snatched the plate off the table, hiding it on his lap. "Reach under here," he whispered, looking around the room. "I'll hand these to you, one by one, and you put them in your apron pockets. We'll go eat them under the stairs."

Moments later, they settled back in the darkest corner under the slanted-ceiling alcove beneath the stairs.

"Since I can't see in here, hold out your hand, and I'll give you a cinnamon bun." After giving Timothy one, she felt in her pocket and brought out one for herself.

"You know, Sarah Em, I've been thinking a lot about something," Timothy said through the darkness.

"What?"

"Doc Werther is getting up in years. He's been doctoring all our lives and long before. I'm wondering if what I'm about to say sounds like the craziest thing you've ever heard." But then he didn't say anything.

"I won't know if it's crazy if you don't tell me."

She heard a shuffle as if he needed to rearrange himself before he could speak again.

"I want to be a doctor," he said matter-of-factly, letting the new idea hover over them in the inky air.

She waited, thinking he might say something else, something to explain this astounding pronouncement of an orphan thinking about becoming a doctor.

After some time, he sounded anxious, but he asked, "Well, what do you think?"

"Timothy, I think it sounds wonderful. You're smart enough,

that's for sure."

"But I can hear some doubt in your voice," he said, a touch of disappointment in his.

She wasn't sure what to say. The very idea of Timothy being a doctor was exciting, and he would be good too. She was certain of that. He was caring and smart enough. But there were two problems, the way she saw it. How could he ever afford to go to school to learn medicine? And he didn't know who he looked like, so how could he know if he could be a doctor? He would get upset if she said that, so she reached into her pocket and said, "Have another bun. Where would you get your schooling?"

"I don't know." He took the bun. "Doc Werther got his in Chicago."

"How do you know that?"

"Because a few months back when I was there for our checkup, I made a point to look at his certificate on the wall."

That was the day she had overheard the mothers and told Timothy how to tell what kind of person he would be. No wonder he was always so adamant about that not being true. He had made up his mind to be a doctor, and he knows nothing about his parents. Then she thought about what he had just said. Chicago! That was twenty-eight miles away. He always said he would stay close. When would she see him? She sent her apprehensions slinking back to wherever they came from. Now was not the time for them to show up. "Timothy, you'd be the best doctor ever," she said.

"Really? Do you think so?" He sounded relieved. "I was afraid you'd laugh at me or say something ridiculous about not knowing who I look like."

She gulped soundlessly in the blackness of the alcove. This talk of being a doctor was important to him, she could tell. "Have you talked to Doc Werther or anyone about this?" She felt the stickiness of the bun she was holding, matting her fingers together. Talk of his leaving had cinched her stomach so she couldn't eat.

"No, not a word to anyone. You're the first person. It's just something I've been going over in my mind. But I kept thinking it was too ludicrous for me to even consider—an orphan becoming a doctor. You know, Miss Percy's been hiring me out a lot lately, and she always says I've had all the schooling I need. One day I was cleaning out Mr. Mitchell's horse barn, and his kids were running around doing nothing and treating me like I was nothing. And I got to thinking, how come Miss Percy gets to make the decision if I've had all the schooling I need?"

Timothy sounded so determined, so much like a man, so sure of himself.

"I don't mind cleaning out a horse barn; in fact, I kind of enjoy being with the animals and getting away from this place for a few hours. But once March 17 comes, and I turn eighteen, I can't live here anymore. So I got to thinking about what I want to do with my life, and doctoring keeps shooting up slick as grease in my mind. I want to help sick people. It's not just because of Betsy; I've been thinking about this long before she got sick."

A little shudder came up from inside her. Timothy had been thinking about this, and she didn't know it. Maybe she didn't know him as well as she thought. She could feel, even in the dark, that Timothy was waiting for her to respond. "Then you need to talk to Doc Werther. See what he says. Find out how you go about becoming a doctor. I know he'll help if he can."

"Do you think so?"

"Yes. I definitely think so. And Timothy…"

"What?"

"I'm really proud of you." She meant it.

"I know you're wondering why I never told you."

"Well, yes. Why didn't you?"

"I didn't because it was something I needed to be sure about. And then when I was, you got so taken up in this notion about who you look like…" His words trailed off like he didn't know what else to say.

"I'm sorry. Really sorry."

"That's okay."

Neither said anything else about that. Her stomach relaxed a bit and she nibbled on the crumbled bun she had been holding, and, evidently, he had been holding his too, because she heard him eating.

"Betsy would surely like one of these, if she wasn't so sick," Timothy said.

"She surely would. I'm so worried about her. You know, she's about the best friend a girl could have."

"Well, what about me?" In the dark, Timothy sounded playfully hurt. "I thought I was your best friend."

"Aw, now don't go feeling sorry for yourself, Timothy Marshall. I mean she's my best girlfriend. Here's another cinnamon bun."

As he reached for it, she felt his hand bump her arm in the darkness. Her toes twitched.

"Okay, if Betsy is your *girl*friend." He drew out the word girl. "That would mean I'm your best *boy*friend. Is that what that means, Sarah Em?" Now his tone sounded more serious.

Glad that he couldn't see the color she felt rising in her cheeks or her vigorously twitching toes, she tried to sound annoyed. "Here, you can have the last bun." She got up from the floor and scooped up the tail of her apron, wiping the stickiness off her hands. "You've got to go to work, and I'm going to school. I can't be talking about boyfriends right now." Tossing her head, she sauntered out of the unlit closet, struggling to get the toes on her right foot to quit their baffling twitching.

But inside, she had the sensation of warm honey gliding down. *I do believe he likes me in a special way.* She could feel the color rising in her cheeks again and hoped no one else noticed as she hurried down the hall. Her thoughts stayed on Timothy, despite her best effort to unfasten them.

He was kind. He smiled often. His hair had a nice wave in the front. He helped her with what he called her schemes. And she had to admit, usually, he took her ideas and made them better. He was good at numbers, and she wasn't. He loved Ours and got along great with Betsy. He missed having a ma, so he understood that she did too. And there was that time when Marjorie told her the orphan asylum was no place for dreaming. But Timothy had assured her that dreaming could be done anywhere, so she should go ahead and dream all she wants. And now he was dreaming of being a doctor.

Yes, Timothy Marshal. Maybe, someday, I'll let you be my boyfriend. And her toes twitched more furiously than ever.

Chapter 19

*L*ater that afternoon, after school, Sarah Emily hurried down Lilac Lane, scrunching deeper inside her coat, lifting the collar to act as a shield against the icy wind that bit at her. Snow had buried Lilac Lane in silence.

About halfway to the Neals', she met Mr. Mitchell, his down-turned face clenched against the cold. "What are you doing on *this* end of Lilac Lane so soon? Weren't you just here yesterday?" There wasn't any neighborliness in his tone or words. After all, she thought, they were neighbors. The wind sent his coattails skipping, and he clamped his hand on top of his black wool hat.

"I'm visiting the Neals," she said proudly—probably, she knew, a bit too proudly.

"Humph," he mumbled and swiftly walked past her going toward his house.

Visiting the Neals. She could hear the words repeating in her head and wondered what in the world she thought she was doing. And neighbors? Just because she had eaten one meal in one of these houses, it didn't make her a neighbor. She lived at *that* end of Lilac Lane.

The Neals didn't want her back for a visit. They wanted her back to work. But, even so, they *were* the most polite folks she had ever known, not the fake polite of Mrs. Hancock and her group. The Neals evidently had done what they said about getting Betsy's medicine. They even told Doc they were willing to pay for all she needed, and they had never met Betsy.

Maybe, just maybe, they truly were good people. Trying hard to believe that, a twinge of excitement sped up her feet to the beautiful white and green house on the corner. At the front door, she boldly knocked.

Opal opened the door and a huge smile stretched across her face. "Oh, Miss Sarah Emily, come in out of the cold. Mrs. Neal's been helping me get the pantry organized today. With just moving in, there's still lots to do. We'd lost tract of time and just a few minutes ago we realized it was about time for you. Mrs. Neal is upstairs waiting for you."

That's the reason the Neals wanted her to come back—to help them with all the chores of moving in. A momentary letdown wormed its way into her happy mood. *Get a hold of yourself, silly girl.* For whatever reason they wanted her was okay. They had bought Betsy's medicine, and who wouldn't want to spend time in this house? She looked around the beautiful foyer and hoped for lots of chores that would keep them wanting her to come back. She wasn't sure how she would manage without Miss Percy knowing, but she would think of something.

Then her eyes rested on the round table where Mrs. Neal had put her mahogany box last night. It wasn't there. *It's not my box anymore,* Sarah Emily rebuked herself. Mrs. Neal can put it anywhere she likes.

"But Mrs. Neal said when you got here," Opal was still talking, "to show you upstairs to the room with Miss Amy's things. Let me have your coat."

"Miss Amy? Who's that?" Sarah Emily's mind raced on with what else she thought she had heard: Did Opal call her *Miss* Sarah Emily? Was Opal going to hang up her coat?

Then, as if to confirm her thought, when Sarah Emily twisted out of her coat, Opal immediately took it. "Miss Amy is the Neals' daughter. Didn't you know?" she said, draping the coat on one of the bright brass hooks on the polished wood rack.

Leading Sarah Emily to the family portrait in the dining room, Opal explained that the Neals had two children, Amy and Nick. "They were both killed last year in a train wreck—such wonderful children. We all miss them something fierce. I'd been with those young 'uns since they were born."

"I'm sorry. I know what it is to lose someone you love."

"Yes. I'm sure you do," Opal said gently. The late-afternoon light caught her tears shimmering like glass splashed with rain.

"But the Neals seem so happy." Sarah Emily stared at the portrait she had seen last night. Sometimes parents die, and sometimes children die. If children without folks are called orphans, she wondered, what are parents without children called?

Laying a hand on Sarah Emily's shoulder, Opal said, "The Neals were devastated in losing them in that awful train wreck. They can smile because they know Amy and Nick are in heaven, and one day they'll see them again."

See them again? Sarah Emily's heart raced with the confusing, exciting, new thought. Did that mean she would see her ma?

"Let's get upstairs." Opal started out of the dining room. "Mrs. Neal has been expecting you, and I imagine she heard you at the door."

There, Opal said it again. She had said it when Sarah Emily first arrived—and now she had said it again; Mrs. Neal *was* expecting her. Sarah Emily inwardly smiled; she felt relieved about coming and thrilled at being wanted, even if it was just to do chores.

Opal ushered her upstairs. At the top, Opal pushed open a slightly ajar door. "Mrs. Neal. Look who's here." Opal stepped back for Sarah Emily to go into the sunny bedroom, fragrant with the scent of summer lilacs.

Mrs. Neal, wearing another beautiful blue dress, turned from the tall chest where she was putting things in the drawer. Sarah Emily's gaze quickly saw there was a rocking chair next to a magnificent four-poster bed, covered in a white counterpane with intricately embroidered bouquets of lilacs scattered over it.

"I'll be in the kitchen getting things ready for later," Opal said, turning to go back downstairs.

"We won't be long here," Mrs. Neal answered.

Sarah Emily presumed she meant they would be right down to get started on whatever work needed to be done, but she didn't mind.

"I'm so glad you came, Sarah Emily. I was hoping you would."

"Yes, ma'am. I told you I'd come back and help with chores. I'll do anything. Tomorrow, too, if need be. I'm so grateful you got the medicine for Betsy."

Mrs. Neal smiled, reached out and drew Sarah Emily into a hug. Sarah Emily was taken aback by that gesture, but the hug felt so good, she was sorry when it ended.

"We talked to Dr. Werther last night, and he assured us he's doing everything he can for Betsy. We'll be glad to pay for whatever she needs. As far as chores go, I'm sure we can find something for you to do, but first come sit with me." Mrs. Neal took Sarah Emily's hand and led her to a dressing table topped with a mirror and pulled out the bench covered in lavender satin—the exact shade of summer lilacs. Mrs. Neal extended her hand toward the seat.

How did Mrs. Neal make her movements flow with such ease? Sarah Emily decided that was something she and Betsy would practice together when she got well. Sarah Emily lowered herself onto the bench, and Mrs. Neal sat beside her.

As soon as she was seated, Sarah Emily saw her mahogany box in the center of the dressing table. Her heart lurched. Then her hand. She wanted to touch it, to rub her fingers over her precious box again. But she forced her hands to stay in her lap, stiffening her back, clenching her jaw. It didn't belong to her anymore. How long was it going to take to get that through her head? It did puzzle her, though, why Mrs. Neal had it in here—in Amy's room.

Sarah Emily's attention was drawn from her box to Mrs. Neal pulling a tiny gold knob the size of a pea on the dressing table. A drawer opened. From it, she lifted out a beautiful hair clasp covered in tiny pearls.

"Oh," Sarah Emily gasped and immediately reached to touch the lovely thing, but drew her hand back fearing again that this also might be something Mrs. Neal wouldn't want her to touch. The hair clasp must have been Amy's.

"You may have it, dear. It belonged to my daughter, Amy. I saw you struggling with your hair yesterday and thought you might like this." Mrs. Neal gently gathered the long, unruly shank of Sarah Emily's hair and fastened the dainty clasp around it.

Slowly turning to see herself in the beveled glass, Sarah Emily let her fingers glide over the smooth pearls, then across the wave in her hair the clasp had created. She didn't know what to say. Finally, still staring in the mirror, she stuttered, "It's . . . it's beautiful." It was beautiful, more beautiful that any of the hair clasps the Ladies' Aid Society had ever given out.

Patting Sarah Emily's knee, Mrs. Neal smiled and said as she stood, "And so are you."

Sarah Emily studied herself in the mirror. She had never thought of herself as beautiful, and the only beautiful thing she saw now was the hair clasp. Still looking in the mirror, she found Mrs. Neal and watched her walk around the room. "These were Amy's things. She loved lilacs and wanted her whole room done in them. You can't imagine how delighted she was when she knew we were buying this house—on Lilac Lane. Of course, we weren't buying it just because of the name of the street, but it delighted that daughter of mine anyway."

Sarah Emily turned around on the bench to get a good look at the room, not just a narrow mirrored reflection. The drapes were covered in lilac blooms. There was a large painting of lilacs in a gold frame hung on one of the lavender walls. A crystal bowl, beside the bed, was full of dried lilac petals. The room was absolutely lovely. Sarah Emily drew in a quick short breath at the thought of anyone actually getting to sleep in such a room. It was a far cry from the bleak, gray dormitory she had slept in for twelve years. *Dormitory!* Was only Amy going to sleep in here? Just one person in this big room? How sad that Amy never got to enjoy it. As Sarah Emily let her gaze glide over the room again, she wondered if Mrs. Neal would say anything about Amy's death.

Mrs. Neal settled her slender frame back into the rocking chair and fluffed her blue skirt around her. "Now, tell me about your exquisite mahogany box," she said, and the rocking chair began a rhythmic *swish, swish.* "I put it in here for safekeeping."

Sarah Emily was surprised Mrs. Neal referred to it as "your mahogany box." Maybe that meant it would be okay to hold it. Sarah Emily reached around and tenderly picked up her beloved treasure. She looked at Mrs. Neal—not a trace of displeasure on her face, so Sarah Emily nestled it in her lap.

She caressed the box with her fingers. "This belonged to my ma. She died a long time ago. I figure she must have kept special things in it, although I don't know that for a fact. I only know that when I was four years old and my pa left me at the orphan asylum, he said Ma loved this box. And he gave it to me. There was a picture of them inside." Sarah Emily stared, unblinking, at a far corner of the room to keep tears from splashing out.

"I'd love to see the picture of your parents sometime. Does your father visit you often?"

"No ma'am." She kept focusing on the corner, the way the two walls came together, the way the molding at the top slid around the top and separated the lavender walls from the white ceiling, the tiny crack that looked like a bumble bee. But the scene in the schoolyard of her pa running from her took over anyway. She tightened her fingers around the mahogany box. "He came to the orphan asylum once, not too long ago. But he... he only talked to Miss Percy."

Sarah Emily's shoulders trembled as she struggled to hold back the flood of hurts and rejection that squeezed up from the bottom of her heart and pushed at her throat. She had worked so hard to keep those feelings inside—*locked* inside. Some had slipped out that day her pa left her for the second time, but she had managed to get them pressed back down. Now, why had she allowed Mrs. Neal's niceness to wedge that place open?

Still staring at the corner of the room, Sarah Emily heard the rocking chair stop its swaying, Mrs. Neal's dress rustle, and then her soft footsteps as she came and sat beside Sarah Emily on the satin-covered bench.

Mrs. Neal eased Sarah Emily's head onto her shoulder and

gently wrapped a loving arm around her. They sat, slightly swaying together, while Sarah Emily emptied out onto Mrs. Neal's blue dress the deluge of tears that had been stuffed in, piled up and buried in the bottom of her heart for so many years. When her crying subsided, Mrs. Neal drew her lace hanky from her pocket and wiped Sarah Emily's swollen eyes.

"There, there, dear. I'm so sorry." Mrs. Neal rubbed Sarah Emily's back. "I had no idea asking if your father came to see you would bring that kind of response."

"I...I didn't either." Sarah Emily sniffed, drained and limp, her breath coming in jerky spasms.

Did Mrs. Neal understand how important it was for Sarah Emily to know who she looked like? Sarah Emily stared evenly into Mrs. Neal's eyes.

Startled, Sarah Emily saw something like she had seen in the mother's eyes at Melody's birthday party—like she had dreamed of someone looking at her. Confused, she touched the hair clasp. Sarah Emily's heart pounded, suddenly afraid that grief had caused Mrs. Neal to lose her grip on reality. "Do you think I'm Amy? Is that why you're being so nice to me? Is that why my box is in here?" Sarah Emily searched Mrs. Neal's face.

Mrs. Neal smiled. "No, dear, I'm not trying to replace my daughter."

"I didn't mean...it's just..."

"Just that you're not used to anyone showing you love?"

"Not by someone who looks like a ma. At the orphan asylum there's Cook and Mr. Wilbur; they love me. They love all of us. But there's not a ma sort of person."

Sarah Emily had to ask, "Mrs. Neal, do you understand what it means to look like someone, and then you can be certain how you'll turn out?"

Mrs. Neal slightly tilted her head in a questioning look.

"You know, if you look like your ma or pa, you'll be like them?"

"Wherever did you get that idea?" Mrs. Neal laid her hand on Sarah Emily's.

Sarah Emily would have to tell Mrs. Neal what she had heard on the street corner. How else could she explain what she meant? It was as clear in her mind as the day it had happened three months ago. She had caught every detail then and mentally recited it so many times that not one moment of that encounter was fuzzy.

"I was on my way back from Doc Werther's office. Miss Percy had taken a group of us for our yearly checkups. Until you're sixteen years old, she makes you hold onto a rope so we stay together when a group leaves the orphan asylum. That day, I was at the back of the rope when we were about to cross Main Street onto Lilac Lane. I saw these two women standing at the corner. One of them had her baby in a pram; the other leaned down and looked at the baby and said, 'I certainly can tell she belongs to you. Her mouth—why, it's just like yours.' Those were the very words the mother said.

"I've studied the photograph of my ma and pa over and over, but I don't see any likeness of them in me. Of course, I can't tell what color their eyes are, so I don't know if one had green eyes like I do. But I don't see my upturned nose either." Sarah Emily faced sideways so Mrs. Neal could get a full view of her profile. "I've got to know who I look like."

Without another word, Mrs. Neal stood and went across the room to the tall bureau. She picked up a large black book and returned to the bench. Opening the book, she said, "It's right... hmmm," she slid her finger down the wide columns of words on the page and stopped. "Ah, yes, it's right here." Mrs. Neal shifted the book so that half of it was in Sarah Emily's lap. It covered the mahogany box that she still clutched. A few of the gold-edged pages fluttered, then settled down.

"Look what it says." Mrs. Neal put her finger under black words on the thin paper, and read, "So God created man in his *own* image."

Sarah Emily didn't want to hurt Mrs. Neal's feelings since obviously she thought this was important, but she felt like screaming, *What do the words in this clumsy old book have to do with me? Can't you see, I'm not a man?*

"Hasn't anyone ever told you about your heavenly Father, God, and how much He loves you?" Mrs. Neal said.

"I don't know if it's the same God, but once Betsy told me to call out to him when I was in the shadow of death."

"Yes. I'm sure she meant the same God. That's in this book too." Mrs. Neal smiled. "Sarah Emily, God loves you so much—more than you can ever imagine—more than anyone else no matter how much they love you. And you're made in *His* image, *His* likeness. He's your wonderful Heavenly Father."

What *is* she talking about? Sarah Emily watched Mrs. Neal's mouth move and she could hear the words as they came out, but not one made any sense.

Sarah Emily's confusion must have been apparent because Mrs. Neal said again, "Sarah Emily, you're made in God's image, and He loves you and wants to be your Father."

This time, a few of the words squirmed their way into her understanding. Even so, she could only respond with a few disjointed ones. "My father? Love me? His likeness?"

"Yes, all of that—and more." Mrs. Neal closed the book, laid it on the dressing table behind them and wrapped gentle arms around Sarah Emily. "It's true," she whispered.

"Hey, I thought fudge . . . " Mr. Neal and his booming voice came through the door. "Oh. I'm sorry," he said. "I didn't realize there was serious girl talk going on in here."

"It's all right, dear," Mrs. Neal said. "We've just been discussing a few things."

As Mrs. Neal talked, Sarah Emily saw Mr. Neal's gaze weave to the book then back to his wife. "I see." He limped on his right foot into the room, smiling, and the corners of his eyes crinkled with the same good-natured merriment Sarah Emily had seen last night.

"You be thinking about what I said," Mrs. Neal said as she brushed her hand across Sarah Emily's cheek. "We'll talk more about this when you come back tomorrow. For now, how about you helping Opal in the kitchen?"

Come back. Mrs. Neal wanted her to come back tomorrow. Sarah Emily's thoughts spun and twisted, tangling themselves around God, likeness, love, tomorrow—*and what was Mr. Neal saying about fudge?*

"Of course, I'll help in the kitchen. That's what I came for, to make up for your not buying Ours." Also, she thought, a break to take in what Mrs. Neal said would be good.

Moments later, in the sparkling white kitchen, Sarah Emily helped Opal gather fudge ingredients. Then she perched on a tall stool while Opal stirred the heavy pot that was bubbling with a thick, brown glossy mixture. They talked and laughed like making fudge together was a familiar activity. It didn't seem possible that this was a chore.

"Opal, can I ask you something?"

"Sure—as long as it's something I can answer." Opal touched Sarah Emily's shoulder. "First, sit back. Don't let this boil up on you. Now, what did you want to ask me?"

"Why does Mr. Neal limp on his right foot sometimes and sometimes on his left?"

Opal laughed out loud. "You've seen it too. Well, it's like this— he hurt his foot months ago—nothing serious. But Mrs. Neal pampered him and made on over him like he was mortally wounded. Of course, she pampers him all the time. I declare, those two are regular love birds."

"Is he still hurt?"

"Not one tiny bit. He just loved her babying him so much that he kept on limping 'til it became a habit. The funny thing is, Mrs. Neal and I noticed right off that he can't remember which foot was hurt. So he just limps on either one. He's such a dear man, neither of us has the heart to tell him we're on to his little charade, though I suspect he keeps doing it just to keep up a joke. With that man, his good nature fits him as naturally as a finely-tailored suit of clothes."

"Oh. Well, I was just wondering about his limp." How enjoyable, Sarah Emily thought, it must have been for Amy and Nick to have such a fun pa.

Opal lifted the spoon from the pot and let a string of the chocolate drizzle into a cup of cold water. She squeezed the chocolate with her fingers and then held the cup for Sarah Emily to see the small brown marble. "Soft ball stage. Perfect. Let's get it off the fire."

Opal pulled the big pot to the worktable beside the stove and tilted the pot toward her. With a long wooden spoon, she began beating and beating the chocolate. "It'll be fudge before you know it. Have you ever made fudge?"

"No. I've heard of it but never made it or tasted it."

"Never tasted fudge? My, oh my. We'll do something about that today, but it'll have to cool first, or it'll burn the hide right off your tongue." Opal laughed again.

What a joyful house! The joy was even more amazing since Sarah Emily knew about the tragedy with Amy and Nick.

Opal gave one last swirl of the spoon through the chocolate. "Get me that pan over there." She nodded toward another cabinet.

Sarah Emily spotted a long, shallow pan that had been smeared with butter. She jumped off the stool and brought it to the work-table. Opal held the kettle at just the right angle for Sarah Emily to scrape the gooey chocolate out onto the buttered pan.

"Now comes the hard part." Opal wiped her hands on her apron.

"Hard? Looks like the work's done."

"Hard because we have to wait while it cools out on the porch."

While Opal went to the porch, Sarah Emily looked around the kitchen. What a wonderful place to be...it was sunny, bright and warm, even on such a cold winter's day...it smelled of fudge...it was filled with joy...it was just about perfect. It would be perfect, she thought, if Timothy and Betsy were here, too.

Opal closed the porch door behind her and scrubbed her hands up and down the tops of her arms. "Brrrr. It's cold enough out there that the fudge should be ready in no time. But I'll tell you what we'll do while we're waiting. How about a piece of fried chicken left from yesterday? Would you like that?"

Like that? Before Sarah Emily came today, she hadn't dared even hope for something to eat. This was too good to be happening again. She had been sure last night had been a one-time treat.

Opal, not waiting for an answer, bustled about filling a blue and white plate. She set it on the kitchen table and motioned for Sarah Emily to sit down.

Sarah Emily's gaze circled the food. There was a plump chicken leg, a piece of bread covered with those wonderful preserves, an apple and a tall, blue glass filled with cold milk.

"Go ahead. Eat. You do like my cooking, don't you?" Opal

fixed her hands on her spacious hips. An exaggerated look of hurt puckered her face.

"Of course, I love your food. It's just that I wasn't expecting..."

"Then if you like the food, eat." Opal flapped her hand as if to say 'enough talk.' She swung up the fudge pan from the worktable and plopped it in the sink.

Sarah Emily ate. Opal washed dishes and sang. "Great is thy faithfulness. Great is thy faithfulness." Opal's voice was like liquid penetrating a dry place in Sarah Emily.

"Who are you singing about?" Sarah Emily put down the piece of chicken.

"God."

Was Opal made in his likeness too? Come to think about it, if that were true, what Mrs. Neal said couldn't be right. Not only did Opal have brown skin, but also her eyes were brown, not green, and Mrs. Neal's eyes were blue. Mrs. Neal must have said that to try to make her feel better like she tried to make Betsy feel better when she came to the orphan asylum. Sarah Emily and Betsy both knew it wasn't true that she would get used to living there. Mrs. Neal knew they weren't all made in God's likeness.

Sarah Emily wasn't sure if she was pleased Mrs. Neal had tried to cheer her up or disappointed that it wasn't true. She wasn't made in God's likeness. Sarah Emily sighed and finally asked Opal, "Do you know much about God?"

Opal twisted around to see Sarah Emily as she talked, her hands still immersed in the suds-filled dishpan. "I know enough to know He loves me and I need Him. There are lots of other things about God too, but if you get those two—that He loves you and that you need Him—then you've got the most important."

Sarah Emily looked down, jiggling the apple back and forth on the table. "Do you know..." she said as she slowly raised her head, "do you know if He loves orphans?"

Opal pulled her hands from the dishpan, shook off the frothy white soap foam, lifted the tail of her apron and as she dried her hands, walked to the table. "Orphans. Kings. Beggars." She touched her chest. "And cooks. Everybody. Miss Sarah Emily,

God loves everybody."

"Mrs. Neal said I'm made in His image and His likeness."

"That's true. Did she tell you about His Son?"

"No."

"Well, I'm sure she will another time." Opal talked on about God, while Sarah Emily finished every morsel, even nibbling the apple core so close that she nearly swallowed it. Sarah Emily's stomach filled, along with her heart.

The clock chimed out five o'clock. "The fudge should be good and cooled by now. I just want it to cool, not freeze out there." Opal started toward the porch door. "Put your plate in the sink and pour yourself another glass of milk. Milk and fudge go real good together."

In the next few minutes, Sarah Emily ate the glossy, smooth fudge until her stomach swished and swirled. Never had she tasted anything like it.

"Too much can make you sick."

Sarah Emily popped another one of the velvety chocolate pieces in her mouth.

"Can't say you haven't been warned." Opal laughed. "If there's any left, would you like to take some back to your young man?" she asked, with the knife poised above the candy.

"My young man?" Sarah Emily nearly choked.

"Yes. Timothy. The young man who was here with you."

"Timothy's not *my* young man."

"Well, he looks at you like you're his young lady. I took note of that yesterday."

Sarah Emily's toes twitched.

"Do you want to take him some fudge or not?" Opal grinned playfully.

Sarah Emily tried not to look flustered. "Yes. That would be nice."

Opal cut and wrapped six generous squares of fudge. "Here's enough for you to share."

Just as Sarah Emily was about to put the fudge in her apron pocket, Mr. Neal walked in—not limping on either foot. He held Sarah Emily's mahogany box out in front of him like an object bursting into flames, but he didn't know whether to drop it or hurl it outside.

Mrs. Neal was beside him, her hands twisting around each other. "Opal we need to have a private word with Sarah Emily."

"Surely, ma'am."

Sarah Emily felt sick. Was it from too much fudge or the look on the Neals' faces?

Mr. Neal swallowed hard and licked his lips. "Sarah Emily, after you came downstairs, I happened to see your box and was reminded of one I'd seen years ago. Please sit down. There's something I want to show you." There was no twinkle in his eyes, only seriousness.

Her mouth went dry. Her tongue stuck to the roof of her mouth. Was her box worthless, and had he decided not to buy anymore medicine for Betsy? She put the package of fudge down and backed herself into the chair, not taking her eyes off Mr. Neal. Her body quivered inside and out. Everything about this house had been too good to last. She should have known that.

Mrs. Neal sat down next to Sarah Emily and took her hand. *What was happening?* Sarah Emily gasped to be able to breathe.

Mr. Neal continued to stand. "Sarah Emily, a long time ago, I saw a box like this in a specialty shop that I visited. What made me remember it after all these years was that the shop owner showed me a secret compartment. Did you know about that?"

"A secret compartment? There's no secret compartment," Sarah Emily said, feeling Mrs. Neal's hand tighten around hers.

Mr. Neal picked up the box and unscrewed first one, then two, then the third and fourth perfectly round feet. The bottom fell out. He turned the box so Sarah Emily could see a tiny drawer that was tucked underneath.

He opened the drawer. In it lay a tightly folded square of paper. "When I first found this letter, I should have asked you before I looked at it, but I was so excited to have found the secret compartment that I didn't wait. I thought maybe you had simply forgotten to take the paper out. I apologize."

"Letter?" Sarah Emily said, her voice husky.

"Yes, a letter. A letter from your mother."

Sarah Emily went numb.

Chapter 20

While everyone ate breakfast the next morning, Sarah Emily hid in the farthest, darkest corner of the alcove under the stairs. She couldn't face Timothy. She slumped to the floor, and a sharp corner of the letter in her pocket pricked her thigh.

The letter. How she wished Mr. Neal hadn't found it. She wished she had never heard those mothers and learned that who you look like is who you are. She despised who she looked like, and even more, who she was.

She pulled her knees up to her chest and clasped her arms around them, pulling herself into a ball so tight she could have kissed her own knees. Trying to comfort her crushed spirit that writhed in pain, she rocked back and forth. What *was* she going to do?

She hated herself. She had always hated being an orphan. Now she hated herself. "Sarah Emily, you're worthless," she whispered into the blackness. She clinched her knees tighter and dug her fingernails into her arms, hard enough, she hoped, to give her something else to think about. She dug harder. It wasn't working.

Drowning in despair, she lost track of time. But when she heard the others scuffling by, voices climbing over one another, she knew it was time for school. She didn't want to go. Of course, keeping her mind on her studies would be impossible, but the real reason for not going was she couldn't face anyone—especially Timothy.

Suddenly, she released her digging nails and stood. She wouldn't go to school! She had never skipped school before, but today's decision was made without any thought as to how others would view her abnormal logic. While she waited for everyone to get outside, she devised her plan, in spite of Miss Percy's predictable fury. In a flash, she jerked her shoulders back and shoved a rod of I-don't-care down her spine. *I'm spending the day in the woods where no one will find me.*

As soon as the hall was silent, she slipped out of the building and ran toward the woods. Immediately, she realized the mistake of forgetting her coat, but she wasn't going back. Freezing to death might be a blessing. The wind prowled as if doing its part. The leafless trees stretched out their spindly bare arms without offering any comfort or warmth. Her eyes squinted against the snow and cold. She crammed her hands into her apron pockets, but the cold stung her face and ripped through her dress and apron. Raw, bone-chilling wind sucked her breath as she bolted deeper into the woods, one hand squeezing, crumpling the letter.

Her whole body was folding in on itself from the cold. Running with her hands in her pockets tilted her off balance, but she kept going, stumbling and tripping, rising and staggering. Brittle twigs snapped, flinging up to scratch her. Snow pelted her, freezing her tears on her eyelashes and cheeks. It burned to pull in the least bit of breath.

She yanked her hands out of her pockets and folded them across her chest, tucking her hands under her arms and continuing to run. Finally, her breath froze in her lungs and her legs buckled, tumbling her to the icy ground.

She pushed off the ground enough to sit up, scrunching in on herself, her shoulders meeting her earlobes. The words of the letter in her pocket were chains whipping themselves tightly around her throat, threatening to choke her at any moment.

The cold stung her legs and bottom like the bites from a thousand ants. She lumbered to her feet as clumsily as a newborn calf. Now what? If she had eaten breakfast, maybe she wouldn't be so cold, or if she had brought the parcel of fudge Opal had fixed for Timothy, she could eat that. But she had run out of the Neals' house so fast, she had left it there.

The wind tore through the naked woods in great gusts, shaking the branches, bending treetops, piercing like needles between every thread of her insufficient clothing. The sun was out, but the hard bright light wasn't giving off any more warmth than a picture of it would. Rubbing her hands together, she scanned the woods for a place that would give her some shelter. She either had to find a place or go back.

She couldn't go back—not yet—maybe not ever.

Hunching her shoulders forward and blowing on her hands, she turned around searching for a hiding place. The shed. It leaned with the wind and looked as menacing as ever.

There had to be somewhere else. She continued to blow on her hands as her eyes roamed the woods, but her breath just froze in white, cold clouds instead of giving any warmth. Her teeth chattered so hard, she was afraid they might clink out of her head. The rest of her hurt, plainly hurt, from the frigid air, and the shed was the only shelter she saw.

Surely, she could stand it just long enough to warm herself. Then, after she warmed up, she would be able to think of something else. She set off as fast as her frozen feet and wet shoes would go, reminding herself that she had spent a day in there and survived, and she could do it again.

Once inside, she closed the door, and as her eyes adjusted to the dimness, she went to where the huge pile of rags had been. As usual, Miss Percy had started gathering another bunch, although this one was smaller than when she had been in there before. Despite how smelly and rat infested they were, her intention was to burrow down in them for some warmth, but the door swung open, hit the outside wall and then banged inside, slamming into the trunk behind it. One hinge was hanging loose, slapping as the wind rocked the door. The remaining hinge, itself loose, wasn't tight enough to keep the door closed against the roaring weather.

Sarah Emily sifted through the rags until she found one of the wooden boxes that held their ruined records and scooted it against the door. Then she poked a rusty nail into the hinge to keep it from swinging out again. As soon as the door was secured, she held her breath, jumped in and tunneled down, swaddling herself with the filthy rags. She tried to ignore the awful smell and just hoped she didn't land on a nest of rats also trying to find a warm place.

She lay on her side, drawing her feet up close behind her. So far, no rats. Yanking a fistful of rags over her hands, she clenched them together under her chin and tried to figure out what she was going to do. What could she do? She didn't want to know who she looked like anymore. She didn't want Timothy to know how worthless she was. Here she was, under a pile of retched smelling castoffs. She wasn't even worth as much as a worn-out old shoe. At least a worn-out old shoe had once had a use. She was worse than that. She shouldn't have been born. She was useless—less than useless—she was repulsive.

If only she could shut off her thoughts for a little while, long enough to let her body rest. There must be some way to turn her mind off, to have it go blank. She tried not to move, so she would create an envelope of warmth. But the stampede of wild horses rushing through her thoughts, across her heart, wouldn't let her lie still or stop thinking.

She sat up and dug through the pile of assorted fabric around her looking for something to put on. She found a man's suit coat, undoubtedly a castoff from the Ladies' Aid Society, but the sleeves had been cut out. Even so, the wool over her back and chest would feel good. She wiggled her arms through the huge rough-cut holes and overlapped the front across her. Next she found a woman's dress that was a sturdy fabric and pulled it like a shawl around her arms. Then she straightened the lumpy wads of material covering her legs.

Sarah Emily took the crinkled letter from her pocket. She flattened it on her outstretched legs and slowly read it. She read it again and again—so many times, she lost count. Each time the heart-bruising words seeped deeper until she knew that the place she'd set aside in her heart for the pain of her past was over-flowing. It couldn't hold another hurt, certainly not one this big.

There was a scratching on the door, and it clacked against the heavy box. She heard whimpering. Ours! Sarah Emily kicked off the rags, stuffed the letter into her pocket and ran to the door. She pushed the box aside and let in a tail-wagging, snow-covered Ours.

"Oh, Ours, I'm so glad to see you. You never leave me alone in here, do you?" She had to smile. Ours was the first thing that day to make her even think about smiling. "Come on, let's lie down and keep each other warm."

The dog followed her to the place in the rags where she had been. She pushed more aside to make room for Ours. Once down, Sarah Emily snuggled in beside the dog and pulled rags over both of them. Then she worked her arm under the rags and over Ours. Having Ours with her made the crude cocoon warm more quickly and not seem so lonely. Together they drifted off to sleep.

"Hey, Sarah Em. Where are you? Sarah Em?"

Timothy's insistent calling woke her, and she bolted up. She had to get out of the shed before he found her. She flung off the rags, shoved the box away from the door, and she and Ours ran outside into the woods. Ours yelped beside her as they ran. "Sshhh, Ours. Please. You don't understand how much I don't want him to find me." She ran faster despite the bitter cold.

"Hey, there you are, wait up. Wait up!"

She let Timothy's words bounce off her back while she ran from him, farther into the woods. *Timothy, please go away. I don't want you to know about me.*

Catching up with her, Timothy grabbed her arm, forcing her to stop. "What's the matter with you? I know you could hear me." His words were as thin as a thread from running so hard.

A haze of guilt settled over Sarah Emily as she watched him search her face for a clue to her strange behavior. Sliding her hand into her apron pocket, she clutched the letter. Since Mr. Neal had found it yesterday, she had read it so many times that she could clearly see the page in her mind. Every flourish of her ma's beautiful penmanship. Every phrase of tenderness. Every word of shame. *No! It's never to be told. Not even to you, Timothy.*

"You weren't at supper last night. I figured you'd gotten to eat at the Neals' again. But then, you weren't at breakfast." His tone turned uncharacteristically abrupt. "You didn't come to school. I've been looking everywhere for you, and I find you out here, wearing a...what is that?"

She hadn't taken the armless man's suit coat off. It must have made her look like a person gone mad.

He touched her cheek, and his expression melted from scolding to concern. "You're freezing." He took off his wonderful leather coat and helped her get into it. She was so stiff from the cold, she could barely bend her arms. "This isn't like you," he said while he helped her button it. "What's wrong Sarah Em? I was so worried about you."

His last words hung in plumes of frosty vapors in front of her. She had the sudden urge to grab them out of the icy air and put them in her pocket. That way, she could bring them out to hear again and again every time the contents of the letter barged into her thinking.

"If you're not going to tell me what's wrong or even speak to me, you're at least going to come inside and eat supper," he told her while rubbing his arms as he began to shiver. Timothy commandingly marched Sarah Emily to the dining room with Ours by her side.

She had become too cold, tired and hungry to fight him, but letting him coerce her into coming in didn't mean she would have to tell him what was in the letter.

"You'd better take that...that other thing off before Miss Percy sees it," he said, helping her out of his coat. Once the man's sleeveless coat was off, he wadded it up to hide inside his.

Thankfully, when they went into the dining room, most were finished eating so the room was nearly empty. As soon as she was seated at the table, with a steaming bowl of potato soup in front of her, she realized just how hungry she was. She had eaten so much fudge at the Neals' yesterday and then nothing today that most of the morning and afternoon she had felt like dozens of fish were diving and somersaulting in her stomach. Maybe something warm would help her feel better and think more clearly.

After she had eaten two bowls of soup and five pieces of bread and had drained her third cup of milk, she saw Timothy examining her over the rim of his gray milk cup.

"Okay," he said finally. "You've got gullies in your forehead, worry clouding your eyes, heaviness bending your shoulders and if I could see your gizzard, I'd wager it's tied in knots. Even more telling to me than all of that is you haven't said one word since I nabbed you outside. Not one word. What gives?" He crossed his arms, propped them on the table and leaned toward her, waiting.

She knew she had to say something. He wasn't going away. At once, it came to her. She would tell him what she had learned about God. Maybe she could make him think she was confused about that. "All right. I'll tell you what's wrong." She pushed aside her tray and mirrored his posture—arms folded on the table, leaning toward him. "Mrs. Neal told me I'm made in God's likeness. Can you believe that? She even read it to me from a book."

Sarah Emily chewed her bottom lip a moment to regroup her thoughts. She had to sound bothered about this so Timothy would believe it was the reason for her torment. "You know, Miss Percy always said that any talk about God is nonsense because He never answers any of her prayers. I just don't know who to believe." There, that sounded convincing enough. She uncrossed her arms and sat straight.

Timothy's eyes studied her...and studied her...and studied her.

Sarah Emily squirmed...and squirmed...and looked away.

"I don't know anything about you being made in God's likeness, but I do know that you never give merit to any other of Miss Percy's thoughts or ideas." He leaned even closer. "So, what's really gnawing at you?" His brown eyes swathed her with caring.

Sarah Emily's resolve for keeping her secret crumbled. The threat of tears lurked beneath her eyes. She covered her face with her hands and gritted her teeth. *How can I tell him?*

Lowering her hands, she looked around. Miss Percy was at her table in the corner, drinking tea and absorbed in a book. Evidently, she hadn't been told that Sarah Emily had been absent from school that day. Miss Dickens probably hadn't even noticed. Marjorie and a few others were huddled in a hushed conversation, two tables away. Cora was busy wiping off the empty tables. And Timothy's gaze was still fixed on her—full of tenderness—but unmoving. She squeezed her eyes shut to round up her courage as she fished her hand into her pocket and fingered the letter.

"Timothy." She opened her eyes. "I found a letter from my ma. It tells about how I came to be born." She saw the muscles in his jaw tighten, his only visible reaction. "It's shameful. Real shameful," she said in hushed, clipped syllables.

His quiet face and brown eyes remained steadfast on her. "Sarah Em, there can't be anything shameful about *you*. I don't know about this letter or how you got it, but I do know what kind of person you are. And probably, if the truth were told, there's some shame in everybody's past from one place or another."

"Not like this." She scraped her nails across the letter.

"Don't you think everyone in this orphan asylum feels like the reason they're here is worse than anybody else's?" He touched her arm for a moment. "Can I see the letter? You know I won't tell anyone what's in it."

She knew he wouldn't. Timothy could be trusted with anything, but this, she didn't want him to know. If Timothy was ashamed of her . . .

"Whatever this letter says, it's obviously too much for you to handle alone. Let me help you. Isn't that what friends are for?" He held out his hand for her to put the letter in. "Please, Sarah Em."

Chapter 21

$\mathcal{S}$he drew the crumpled paper from her pocket. Lifting it to the table, she was a tangle of push-pull emotions, clutching the letter so hard her fingers ached. The seconds tiptoed past, and the letter stayed in her hand.

"Please, Sarah Em," Timothy whispered again.

At last, she let go, and he took the letter. Carefully unfolding the paper, he laid it in front of him, smoothed the wrinkles out with his palm and began reading softly aloud.

My Darling Sarah Emily,

I love you. I must tell you that first even though I've told you I love you many times, kissed you, hugged you and adored you since the moment you were first laid in my arms. My greatest desire is for you to know what a joy your life has been to me.

I'm writing this letter while sitting in the maple rocker beside your bed, the rocking chair where I've cradled you against me each night and sung you to sleep with lullabies. Right now, you're sleeping, and I hope dreaming of ponies and blue skies and wildflowers and bread and preserves—your favorite food.

Today has been, by far, the most difficult day of my life. The doctor told me that I probably won't be here for your third birthday, just two months away.

I'm going to miss all the nights of tucking you into bed with stories and tales. I'm going to miss the special days—birthdays, first day of school, your wedding day and the day your first child is born. I look at you now, snuggled up to your favorite doll, your long brown hair spread in soft ringlets across your pillow, smelling of soap and baby love, and I want this night to go on forever. Leaving you, Sarah Emily, is hardest of all, which brings me to the reason for writing this.

Please understand, as you read and through whatever you will experience in the years after this night, that Robert Butler is a good man. The events I'm about to tell you have wounded him so deeply that his scars have crippled his thinking and judgment. You need to understand that.

I want you to know your beginnings. But I also want you to know that, to me, you are precious.

I don't know a good way to say these things, so I'll just say them and pray that the love I feel in my heart for you as I write will stay with this letter, no matter when you read it.

One afternoon, right before I was to be married, I was working in the little house we would be living in. A robber forced his way in and grabbed some silver and my mother's brooch. Then he did the unthinkable. He raped me.

He was going to kill me. But I somehow was able to snatch my mother's brooch out of his hand and gouge his face. That's what drove him away.

Robert Butler and I were married, but we soon realized I was expecting a child. We knew the father was the thief because of how far along I was. A wise woman came into my life and showed me in the Bible that what Satan intends for evil, God makes good. Sarah Emily, you are more than good. You are a wonderful gift.

Robert didn't want anyone to know all that happened. He truly thought he was protecting you and me. So we moved to Chicago before anyone in Lander knew I was going to have a baby and stayed there for nearly a year after you were born. Then when we came back, Robert insisted that your real birth date, July 26, not be used, but that we make up one to look like you were born ten months after we married. I regret that I went along with his plan, but Sarah Emily, remember he really is a good man. It's just that his world was crushed.

I developed a relationship with Jesus through this experience and found peace. Sadly, Robert refused and has been constantly tormented.

The brooch that saved my life is beautiful, shaped like a flower with rubies and emeralds. It belonged to my grandmother. Just the day before the man tried to kill me, my mother had given it to me. And Sarah Emily, someday I want it to be yours.

There are four things I pray everyday for you. I may not be there with you, but I have complete confidence in God that my prayers will follow you.

I pray for you, my precious Sarah Emily, that there will be someone in your life who will love you with a mother's love. I know my parents will care for you, but they are old and their years are limited. I want you to know a mother's love.

I pray the brooch will be a treasured heirloom that will speak of your heritage from the Reese family. May it always bring blessing into your life.

I pray you will find a godly husband—one who will not only love and cherish you, but will protect you by his faith in God—one who will stand with you in hard times as well as easy.

And the most important thing I pray for you is that you will know God as I do, to know Him as a Friend, Father, Comforter and Savior.

You will have found this letter in the secret compartment of my mahogany box. I'm putting it there so you won't find it until you're old enough to understand these things. I will ask Robert that the brooch and mahogany box always be yours, and when you are old enough, he'll tell you where to find my letter.

Now, I'm going to blow out the candle. And then kiss you on your soft check. You are my joy. Take my love with you always.

Sweet dreams,
Your loving mother, Anna

Timothy tipped back at the waist and sucked in half of the room's air. "Oh, Sarah Em, this letter has so much about who you are—not shameful things, but good things. Your ma must have been a wonderful woman. And she loved you. She loved you."

His eyes scanned the page again. "Your mother believed in God. That should make you feel better about what Mrs. Neal told you. And the brooch..." He looked up from the letter. "It's the one Miss Percy has, isn't it? I wonder how she got it."

"I don't know," Sarah Emily said sharply as frustration mounted in her. "How can you talk about the brooch now? How can you say the letter is full of good things? My pa is a thief and a...and a...terrible man. That's who I look like. That's how come I don't see myself in the photograph I have. That's who I'll be like— someone who does awful things to people." A thousand kinds of anger collided in her, all looking for a way out.

"Miss Percy. Miss Percy," Cook yelled, exploding into the room. "We need Doc Werther, and you'd better come. Betsy's gotten worse. I took some soup up to her, and she's burning up with fever and don't know her own name."

Miss Percy scraped her chair back, her book falling to the floor. "What do you mean?"

"We need Doc Werther," Sarah Emily screamed, scrambling up.

"I'll get him." Timothy was on his feet and out the door.

"How can she be worse?" Miss Percy said, taking the time to pick up her book. "The doctor started her on medicine yesterday. I'll see for myself how she is." She headed for the back stairs, and Cook followed her.

"You stay right here." Miss Percy thrust a finger toward Sarah Emily. "I don't need you in the way when the doctor gets here."

Sarah Emily's chest heaved, and she laid a hand on it to hold her heart inside. She knew the final signs of The Fever were a high fever and talking out of your head. She couldn't lose Betsy. *Your pa's a thief and a rapist.* The words galloped faster and faster in her mind. *Betsy is dying. Your pa's a thief and a rapist.* She sat down and clamped her hands to her ears, trying to smother the words.

"I heard Timothy read that letter."

Startled by Marjorie's voice behind her, Sarah Emily jerked and then snatched her letter off the table.

Marjorie's famous grin of malicious delight twisted her lips. "Too bad about your pa. And now Betsy. Sounds like the God your ma asked those special things for you isn't listening. Probably doesn't have much time for orphans."

"How did you...you're a terrible person!"

Marjorie raised her hand to cut Sarah Emily off. "No need fussing about me hearing the letter. I heard it. Can't undo that. And doesn't seem like there's much you can do for Betsy either. But I do know something you can do, since you've got a good dose of thievery in you."

Sarah Emily felt Marjorie's awful words slam against her. She crammed the letter in her pocket and stood.

Marjorie squeezed Sarah Emily's arm as tight as a bear trap and shoved her back down on the bench and slithered in beside her. "Sit down and listen to me. Tonight there's going to be a robbery just down the street. I want you to come help."

Sarah Emily was astonished to realize a part of her wanted to do what Marjorie said. She had always stayed clear of Marjorie, but it was true—a hot anger passed through her. Marjorie was right; she did have a good dose of thievery in her blood. That feeling of hatred toward herself swelled up again. Sarah Emily listened to Marjorie, strangely calmed by the thought of the daring crime she laid out.

"You know the guy who robbed us at the Christmas party, Jack Gregory? He's busting out of jail tonight, and we're going to help him rob a house."

"How do you know that?"

"I've got my ways. Just listen. He's going to get into the house. I'm to meet him at midnight, and we need help. Be ready. Go to bed with your nightgown over your clothes." Marjorie pushed herself away from the table and stood.

At once, Sarah Emily knew she couldn't do this. It was true, she didn't like who she had found out she was, but she wouldn't be a part of any robbery. "Leave me alone. I'm not doing that," she said angrily and stood to leave.

"Not so fast, Miss Goody-Goody. I heard *everything* in that letter."

Sarah Emily stopped, stunned.

Marjorie's eyes were cold and hard. "I'll tell it all, and I mean— all. Your pa is more than a thief. He's a rapist."

"How can you be so cruel?"

"Easy. I do whatever it takes to get whatever I want." A wicked laugh twisted her mouth. "Midnight—or everyone is going to know what happened to your ma—and what you are. There's a name for your kind." She turned and left the dining room.

Sarah Emily felt a hard lump forming in her heart. It was hard to breathe with Marjorie's threat, her ma's letter, her pa's crimes and Betsy's condition ready to choke her.

Then, out of the corner of her eye, she saw Cora and Sarah Emily turned to face her.

Cora's face was tight. "Please, Sarah Emily, don't do what Marjorie says." She threw the wet cloth down on the table; it landed with a squishy thwack and Cora ran from the dining room.

❦

That night, Sarah Emily lay in bed, wide awake, rigid beneath the blankets while the moonlight danced in eerie shadows on the wall. She heard the clock in the hall bang nine times. She had been in bed for an hour but couldn't lull her thoughts to sleep. She was angry with Marjorie, but she was angrier with herself. Then like sewing a dress, the pieces of her life began to come together in her mind. No wonder Robert Butler never came to visit her. He wasn't her pa. What was her name? It wasn't Butler. And she was born July 26, 1865, not October 26. The life she was piecing together was ugly, made of mismatched, torn pieces, and the seams were inside out and crooked.

The brooch! She remembered that day in the schoolyard when Robert Butler was talking to Miss Percy, and she kept covering it with her hand. And what about the morning in the kitchen when Miss Percy said she had no claim to the brooch? Could it really be her mother's?

She rolled over knowing that dreadful letter was under the bed in the cardboard container that used to hold her mahogany box and now held the pearl hair clasp from Mrs. Neal. That was the only place she could think to hide the letter. Later, she would have to find someplace better.

The clock banged ten times. How could she have considered

being part of Marjorie's plan? Sarah Emily twisted under the covers, trying to pull her twisted nightgown down, but it was hard to maneuver it over her dress. She looked at Betsy's empty bed, the moonlight magnifying the emptiness so that she couldn't stand to look at it. Sarah Emily rolled over the other way. Her thoughts sped back to right before she had come to bed when she had learned that Betsy's fever was down, but just barely. She was so seriously ill, she still might not make it through the night. Doc Werther was staying with her. Sarah Emily felt like the bottom had dropped out of her life and she was falling, falling, falling...

The clock banged eleven times. Going with Marjorie would be wrong; she knew it. But Marjorie would tell everything if she didn't. Betsy might not live. Sarah Emily shouldn't even be alive, and wouldn't be if it hadn't been for a terrible vicious act. *Rape. Rape. Rape.* She silently mouthed the word over and over wanting it to become an odd gibberish sound as words sometimes do when you said them repeatedly. But *rape* stayed *rape,* every letter forming the word that meant shame to her.

What kind of life did she have? A life in an orphan asylum. *Timothy.* For a second, the thought of him caused a tiny bit of comfort to touch her. She pulled the covers tighter under her chin and watched clouds clot in front of the moon. He wasn't disgusted with her when he read the letter, but when he really thought about it, he wouldn't want anything more to do with her, not with the kind of man her pa was. The comfort vanished. Sarah Emily lay still while time slunk by. The night felt enormous, and she was lost in it.

The clock banged twelve times. She heard a bed creak. Blankets being pushed back. Feet brushing the floor. A cloud moved and the moon lighted the dormitory. Marjorie was up and looking her way.

Sarah Emily pushed her blanket back, put her feet on the floor and pulled her nightgown over her head. She slung the flannel garment on the bed, grabbed her coat and followed Marjorie.

Outside the cold air blasted her. Without a word, Sarah Emily walked with Marjorie down Lilac Lane in the moony whiteness of the night.

Marjorie turned into Melody's yard.

Sarah Emily stopped short. "I can't go in this house."

"And why not?"

"Because the girl who lived here was nice to me. Besides, her ma died. I just can't go in there and steal from them."

"Of course you can. So, she was nice to you? Nobody's lived here for months. The house and everything in it is being sold. That girl's father is going to an asylum for the crazy. They say he saw a woman walking down the street who was going to have a baby, and she had the same color hair as his dead wife. He just went totally crazy."

"How do you know that?

"I told you before, I have my ways."

Sarah Emily's heart broke remembering the beautiful red-haired Melody and her sweetness. Life made no sense.

Marjorie grabbed Sarah Emily's arm and shoved her forward. "Get in the house before somebody sees us."

The front door was already unlocked. Marjorie somehow found two candlesticks and handed one to Sarah Emily. Sarah Emily struck a match, and when she touched the wick, the candlelight spread a slice of yellow over the room. Chairs were inverted on chairs. Large pieces of cloth covered large pieces of furniture, looking like massive grotesque animals in the shallow light. The match burned low, Sarah Emily flinched and flapped it out. Fear suffocated her. She wanted to run out of this house and back to her bed.

"Well, so now we've got Green Eyes on our team."

Sarah Emily whirled to face Jack Gregory. His mouth twisted into a sneering grin, expressing amusement at seeing her.

She locked her knees to keep from dropping to the floor. How had she been so foolish to have gotten mixed up with him? How could she have been so stupid to let Marjorie badger her into this?

"Here, Marjorie." He held out several pillowcases. "You know what to do. Start upstairs."

"Sure!" Marjorie took the pillowcases and ran from the room.

Gregory caught Sarah Emily's arm. Turning her to face an enormous china cabinet, he flipped open the glass doors. Then he let go of her. "Here's where you start, Green Eyes." He forced a pillowcase into her empty hand and nodded toward the huge collection of silver pieces. "Fill it." His eyes showed no amusement now, only threats.

His eyes! Green. Just like hers. Her mind coiled to when he had bolted at the sight of the brooch on Miss Percy at the Christmas party. What had her ma's letter said? *I was able to get my mother's brooch out of his hand and attack his face.* Sarah Emily's gaze locked on the jagged scar that crawled beside Gregory's upturned nose. Upturned. Just like hers.

Her legs went liquid, and she slumped against a bookcase, nearly dropping the candlestick. *This can't be my pa. Oh, please. No. It just can't be.*

Gregory jerked the candlestick out of her hand and set it on an empty shelf of a bookcase. "What's the matter with you? Did you think you came here for a party? Now get that silver in here." He tugged on the pillowcase.

Her fingers gave way, and it fell to the floor, landing in a pasty white pool at her feet. She wrapped her hands into a fist and clamped them to her mouth.

The hinges on the front door squealed. A blast of cold air whipped into the room, snuffing out the candle.

In the dim moonlight, Sarah Emily saw Gregory snatch a gun from his belt and aim it with precision straight at the door.

Cora was standing there.

"Cora!" Sarah Emily screamed and raced forward, knocking Cora to the ground. Sarah Emily felt the force of the bullet plunge into her back. She fell forward.

In a swimmy distance Sarah Emily heard Gregory yelling, "What's a kid doing here? I thought it was the sheriff coming in."

She felt him roll her to her back. He leaned over her. She stared up into Gregory's face.

Her pa's face.

Suddenly, Mrs. Neal's words flashed across her mind in capital letters—GOD, FATHER, IN HIS LIKENESS.

Her eyes were closing. She heard her blood gurgling in her ears.

Chapter 22

Sarah Emily swallowed what her mushy, watery brain identified as dust and dead bugs. She tried to lick her lips, but her tongue dragged on hard, cracked lumps. She attempted to coax her eyes open, but only one slightly cooperated, opening about the depth of a coin. The sunlight zoomed into the wedge of her opened eye and stung. She snapped it shut. She seemed to be propped over on her side, but she wasn't sure. She flexed a single muscle to begin to shift positions. *Ouch.* Some sort of growl she had never heard before came out of her mouth. A searing pain ripped across her shoulder.

"She made a noise," she heard someone say in an urgent way. "I think she's coming back."

Sarah Emily felt a warm hand on her arm.

"Sarah Emily. Wake up."

Doc?

"She's stirring. Oh glory be."

Mrs. Neal?

"Law, child, open your eyes and look at us. Please."

Is that Cook? Sarah Emily's mind was jumping about like a small bird popping from tree branch to tree branch. Besides hearing people, she smelled lilacs. Where was she? Rubbing only her fingertips on the sheets, she felt their soft creaminess—nothing like she had ever slept on before.

"Sarah Emily, wake up." This time, the warm hand gently patted her cheek.

She lifted her thick eyelids. But, again, the sun stung, forcing them shut.

"She's back." Doc Werther let out a great whooshing sigh. "I need to examine her. Will one of you help me?"

"It's been what I've been living for," Cook spoke up immediately.

"I'll go tell Joshua and Opal that Sarah Emily's awake," Mrs. Neal said.

Sarah Emily heard scuffling feet; the door opened and then closed.

"I'm so grateful our girl is waking up." Cook's voice was hushed, but full of emotion.

Sarah Emily cautiously lifted her eyelids again. This time she was able to keep them open as she took in lavender walls and drapes covered in lilac blooms. *How could I be in Amy Neal's room?* As she twisted to get a better look at where she was, the pain ripped through her again. A moan splattered in her throat.

"Hey. Lie still. No squirming around." Cook laid a soft hand on Sarah Emily's head and smiled. "You gave us quite a scare. This has been a mighty woeful three weeks."

Three weeks? She couldn't mean that I've been here for that long.

"Sarah Emily, can you tell me how you feel?" Doc Werther leaned in close.

She wasn't sure how she felt. She didn't know how she got in this bed or why her shoulder hurt like a railroad car had been dumped on it, and she wasn't sure she could talk. So, she said nothing.

"I heard you moan. Can you speak?"

She lay silent.

"Can you wiggle your fingers for me?"

That she could do. And, she did.

"Well now, that's a good sign. Now turn your head, but slowly."

She did that too, though he didn't need to tell her to do it slowly.

"Great!" His excitement was mounting, and she could hear it in the way he said "great" immediately.

She decided to try to force her dry throat and mouth to cooperate and tell him that she hurt. "Back and should..." She grimaced, her cracked lips ripped apart instead of separating, and each word grated against her throat. Her speech was so garbled that she doubted he had understood her.

Cook fished in her pocket for a hanky and dabbed it at each eye. "Law, it's good to hear this girl talking again. Can I get her something to drink? She sounds dry."

A drink sounded wonderful to Sarah Emily—something to wet her lips and mouth.

"Not just yet," Doc Werther said to Cook. Then to Sarah Emily, "Your back and shoulders hurt? Is that what you're trying to say?"

She was surprised he knew, but she nodded her head with the least motion possible.

"I know they do. But you're going to be fine." He said it with such relief, she thought he might have been worried before that she wasn't going to be.

Doc Werther opened his medical bag.

"Thirsty...real thirsty. What happened?" she croaked out, her voice rough and frizzy, but not as garbled.

"Sarah Emily, do you remember getting shot?"

Shot? The whole horrible incident rushed in like a flood through an open door. Her heart seemed to stop. "Cora?"

"Cora's just fine." Cook tucked her hanky into her apron pocket. "She wasn't hurt at all, and she has you to thank for that. You can thank her that you are alive."

She wasn't sure what Cook meant, but relief that Cora was okay sent her heart beating again.

"And she's eager to see you and make sure you're all right." The doctor lifted a roll of gauze bandage from his bag. "Now I need you to turn onto your stomach and let me check your wound. Cook will help you. She knows just what to do since she's helped me many times with this."

Cook pulled back the sheet and gently grasped Sarah Emily, well below her shoulder, closer to her waist.

"Wait!" Sarah Emily said before Cook eased her over. She was almost afraid to ask, but she had to. "Betsy?"

"Doing better." Doc Werther laid a pair of scissors and a tin of ointment on the bed. "She's still very sick, though, but she's going to be all right. I'll tell you what, you two girls have kept me mighty busy these past weeks." He smiled. "Now, let's get this wound dressed."

Betsy was going to get well. Cora wasn't hurt. Relief again rushed over her. It outweighed the pain Sarah Emily was feeling. She gritted her teeth and allowed Cook to help her roll flat until her cheek rested on the smooth sheet.

Then, as Doc Werther peeled off the old bandage, Cook held her hand.

"Beautiful. This is healing beautifully." Doc Werther rubbed ointment on the wound. "The bullet went into your back and lodged next to your heart. It was tricky getting the thing out without damaging your heart. That's why you were unconscious for so long—the wound is deep and you lost a lot of blood during the surgery."

"Surgery? I had surgery?"

"Yes, you did." Cook squeezed her hand. "Right here on this bed in this room."

Sarah Emily could feel the pressure as he applied the fresh bandage.

"And you're healing nicely," he said. "Cook, let's get her back on her side, and then get some water for this thirsty girl."

Cook and the doctor gently repositioned her. "Water coming right away," Cook said, patting Sarah Emily's leg.

When Cook left the room, Doc Werther sat down on the chair beside the bed and pulled out his stethoscope, wiping it with a cloth soaked in wintergreen oil. That sweet scent merged with the pungent scent of the ointment he had smeared on her back. As he listened to her heart, a wave of nausea and weakness rolled in, and she screwed up her face.

He saw her. "You're probably feeling shaky right now," he said. "Although we've been moving you to change your bandage, you haven't known it. All this movement now, the light and smells, are a lot to deal with when you first wake up after such a long time. On top of that, you haven't had anything solid to eat, and you probably have a thousand questions buzzing in your head. That alone is enough to make an inquisitive young woman like you light-headed." He laughed and put the stethoscope back in his bag.

"How about while we wait for Cook," he said while sitting back in the chair and crossing one ankle over a knee, "I tell you some of what we know happened? Maybe it'll answer some of your questions."

She tried to eke out a smile.

"From what we can piece together," he began, "Cora overheard you and Marjorie talking, and, well, you know how Cora adores you. She was so frightened, and although it was midnight when you left with Marjorie, she followed you. That little girl is one sharp cookie and brave, too, I'd say. As soon as she knew where you were, she took off to get the sheriff. He told us that Cora ran out of his office ahead of him and toward the house where you were so fast that he had a hard time keeping up with her. He arrived mere seconds after the shooting happened, and he sent Cora to get me. She knew I was with Betsy.

"Since the Neals were next door, I brought you here. I couldn't take you to my clinic, not with The Fever outbreak keeping it full. I couldn't take a chance on you catching that along with your bullet wound. The Neals were not only glad to take you in that night, but have been wonderful about keeping you these weeks."

"Does that mean I have to go back now?" Sarah Emily asked in a hoarse whisper.

"I don't think Mrs. Neal would let you out of here until she knew you were completely well." Doc Werther patted her arm. "I'm sure she's already talked to Miss Percy about you staying until your wound is healed. And...well, Miss Percy is...well, let's just say, Miss Percy isn't feeling well herself. In fact, Opal has been taking special food to Betsy and sitting with her some in order to help Cook. Those two have become great friends."

"Does Miss Percy have The Fever?"

"No."

"Now back to you, Sarah Emily. The sheriff has questions he wants to ask you. I guess we all do, but not until you feel strong enough. There's no rush."

She knew he didn't understand why she had gone to Melody's house with Marjorie that night. Looking back on it, she wondered herself why she had caved in under Marjorie's threats. But if Betsy was going to be okay, and Cora was fine, the rest she could handle.

"Here's your water." Cook arrived, carrying a tray. "Opal fixed you some broth. Mrs. Neal says to tell you that she'll be up shortly. She's real anxious to see you with your eyes open. That woman sat by your bed for a big part of these past weeks."

"And somebody else took her share of turns by this bed." Doc Werther nodded toward Cook, then stood, picking up his medical bag.

"And Opal too," Cook said, setting the tray on the dresser.

"Those three women didn't want you to be left alone for a moment. So someone would be with you when you decided to take a notion to wake up, they took turns round the clock. With Betsy being sick and also Miss Percy being down, they have taken on a huge load—might have to hire them all on as nurses."

"Shush now. Wasn't anything we didn't want to do." Cook picked up the water and a spoon. "Want to start with water since you're so thirsty?"

The doctor patted Cook's shoulder. "Just give her a few sips of that water and broth. Too much too fast isn't good for her. She can have some more in an hour or so." Turning to Sarah Emily, Doc Werther brushed the long hair off her forehead. "Don't you worry. We'll hear what you have to say about that night when you feel up to it."

A gleam scampered across his eyes. "By the way, there's a young man who every single day has pestered me for nearly hourly updates. He's been here so much, I'm sure the Neals think they have a new piece of furniture in the parlor. I'll let Timothy know you're going to be just fine, and he can come by to see you tomorrow." As he left, he said, "Remember, Cook, just a few sips."

Only minutes after Cook had given Sarah Emily some of the water and broth and had gone downstairs, Mrs. Neal came in with a silver bell in her hand. "This is a grand day for sure. Here you are—awake and taking some liquid." She set the bell on the bed-side table beside the mahogany box. "You ring this whenever you need or want anything, anything at all, and someone will be right up."

Sarah Emily hadn't noticed the box until just now. It sat on its four perfectly round feet. She guessed Mr. Neal must have put it back together with the tiny drawer tucked inside, out of sight. She stared at the box, thinking about the last time that she had seen it, and Mr. Neal had opened the secret compartment to reveal her mother's letter, hidden for so many years. Then she remembered that she had left the letter under her bed in the cardboard box. Had anyone found it?

"Sarah Emily, are you all right?"

"Oh, yes. Thank you for the bell. And thank you for taking me in. It's hard for me to imagine I've been here three weeks. I don't remember a thing. But Doc Werther tells me that you, Opal and Cook sat with me the whole time. Has Miss Percy or Mr. Wilbur been here?" She was suddenly exhausted and sagged deeper into the mattress.

"Mr. Wilbur comes by several times a day, every day, to check on you. Dear man, he's had his hands full trying to help Cook since Miss Percy isn't feeling well."

"What's the matter with Miss Percy?" Sarah Emily couldn't recall her ever having more than a cold. "Doc says she doesn't have The Fever."

"No, she doesn't. I'm sure she'll be fine."

Why was everyone acting so strange about Miss Percy? Couldn't they say what was wrong with her? If Sarah Emily weren't so weak, she would push for an answer.

"You concentrate on getting yourself well and strong," Mrs.

Neal said. "But Miss Percy does ask about you every time I see her."

"Really?"

"Opal and I have been taking turns checking on Miss Percy and Betsy, trying to help Cook and Mr. Wilbur as much as we can. Actually, they didn't really need us. The two of them had everything under control, but we enjoyed being involved anyway."

"You've been busy if you've been going down there and taking care of me too. I really do appreciate being able to stay here. I understand Doc even did surgery in here."

"He needed to get you someplace fast where he could tend to your bullet wound and where you could stay and recuperate."

Mrs. Neal adjusted the curtain so the sun didn't irritate Sarah Emily's eyes. "Cook said you were able to sip a little broth."

"It tasted wonderful. I was so thirsty."

"She's gone back to get supper ready, but Opal or I will give you some more later. Don't be surprised to see Cook back here after supper along with Mr. Wilbur. Those two are very fond of you."

"And I of them." Sarah Emily winced as a pain seared across her back.

"Try to lie still. You've been doing entirely too much talking. Dr. Werther says you'll be sore and tender and very weak for a while." Mrs. Neal fluffed the pillow behind Sarah Emily's back and added another for support. "You have to stay on your side until Dr. Werther says you can lie on your back. Can I get you anything, dear?"

"No, thank you. Just being here is enough." An uncontrollable tiredness began creeping over her, and enormous yawns swelled in her throat.

"Well, then, if you don't need anything, I'm going to go out and let you get some rest. I'll be back and check on you later. Remember, you ring the bell if you need us."

The next thing she knew, Mrs. Neal was opening the curtains and saying, "Good morning."

"Morning?" Sarah Emily stretched her legs and did a little half-roll in bed. Pain stopped her.

"Yes, it's morning. And don't roll over any farther. Dr. Werther is coming in a few minutes to check on you and change your dressing. Remember, you can't lie on your back."

"I don't think I could. It hurts just to move my shoulders. How could I have slept all afternoon and all night?"

"You've had lots of practice the past three weeks," Mrs. Neal smoothed the hair out of Sarah Emily's eyes. "Cook, Mr. Wilbur and Timothy—all of them—came to check on you last evening."

Sarah Emily was disappointed not to have seen them, especially Timothy. There was so much she wanted to tell him. There was so much she needed to sort out and hoped he would help. Most of all, she wanted to know if he was angry with her for going with Marjorie—or, if by now he knew she was Jack Gregory's daughter.

Mrs. Neal was saying, "Since Mr. Wilbur and Timothy hadn't seen you awake for so long, they wanted to verify that you really had come back to us. But you were so soundly asleep that no one wanted to wake you, and Dr. Werther said to let you be. That little bit you were awake yesterday afternoon would have been very exhausting for you, he told us."

"Do I hear my words being quoted," Doc Werther's voice boomed out.

Sarah Emily couldn't see him, but heard the clacking of his heavy-soled boots coming up the stairs.

"Morning Edward," Mrs. Neal said brightly as he entered the room. "Our patient just woke up."

"For the next few days, sleep will be her main activity. And that's fine."

"Opal slept in here with her most of the night," Mrs. Neal said, "just in case she woke up and wanted something to eat. She still hasn't eaten a thing, since you can't call those few sips of broth yesterday afternoon eating." Mrs. Neal looked at Sarah Emily. "Do you think you could eat some breakfast?"

"I think so, maybe a little something," she said, honestly thinking that she was starving, but afraid that Mrs. Neal would send her back to the orphan asylum if she thought Sarah Emily might eat too much.

"Some more clear broth would be tender on her tummy. Start her out with that for now. By tonight, try her on a small amount of soup.

Why don't you tell Opal to fix her something while I check her over?"

Maybe soups and broth wouldn't cause them to send her back.

"Edward, how about some breakfast for you?" Mrs. Neal asked. "Or, at least, a cup of coffee? Joshua is about to eat and would love for you to join him."

"Now you're talking. Tell that husband of yours I'll meet him in the kitchen when I finish here. Just coffee for me though. I can't stay long—too many patients to tend to."

Mrs. Neal nodded, and a shadow of her lilac scent stayed behind when she left the room.

"I have a message for you from Betsy," Doc Werther said, pulling out a bandage roll from his bag.

"From Betsy!"

"Yes, my dear, from Betsy. When I saw her last evening and she heard you were awake and talking, she was so thankful, I could hardly keep her in bed. She wanted to run down here and see for herself. Now let's get you rolled over on your stomach. As I said, she was so excited. She knows you sold your box to get her medicine and would have sold Ours, and she loves you for caring so much about her."

"You promise she's going to get well?" Sarah Emily asked with her cheek and half of her mouth squished on the pillow.

"I try not to make promises when it comes to medicine since there's only so much I can do. But in this case, I'd say it's safe to promise. She's definitely over the worst part and getting stronger every day."

"I'll bet she loves the Neals." She could feel Doc Werther taking off the bandage.

"Well, I would suppose so. They're wonderful people and have done so much these last weeks. They've made sure she had all the medicine she needed along with plenty of food. They don't talk about it, but they've had whole grocery orders delivered from the mercantile so Cook would have plenty to fix for everyone. They wanted everyone to stay strong and healthy so they didn't catch The Fever." He removed the lid from the ointment tin.

"They are . . ." she said, searching for the right word to describe these unusually nice people. *Ick.* She scrunched her nose. The smell of the ointment wasn't any better today than yesterday.

"How about generous?" Doc Werther suggested.

"Yes! Generous, that's the word. They are that. I wonder why some people are that way, and others like Miss Percy are so greedy. You'd think with the Neals' losing Nick and Amy, they would be bitter and wouldn't want to help anyone so soon after their own tragedy."

"You would think that, wouldn't you? I'm always amazed at the amount of good in some people and just amazed at how much bad can be in others." He finished applying the fresh dressing. "Okay, back on your side."

She didn't want him to roll her over and look at her. *Amazed at how much bad can be in others,* he'd said. Could anyone have more bad in them than Jack Gregory? And that was in her. Sarah Emily felt such shame that she wanted to bury her face and never, never have to look at anyone again.

"Sarah Emily, let me help you roll back to your side," Doc Werther was telling her.

She realized she'd stiffened her body. "Oh, sorry," she said as offhandedly as she could. Did she think she could stay there with her face smashed into the pillow forever?

"Now, gently, back onto your side. I know it's uncomfortable on your side all the time, but you can spend time on your stomach, if you like. I should think, in about a week or so, you could lie on your back. We might even try getting you to sit up in a chair in a few days. We'll see how you're getting along, but sitting up some would help to relieve the monotony of having to stay on one side."

Once she was situated, she said, "Will you take a message back to Betsy from me?"

He laughed as he tugged his stethoscope from the black leather bag. "So I'm not only your doctor, I'm the message boy?"

"A mighty important part of making sure we get well, I should think." Sarah Emily grinned at him. Maybe Doc Werther didn't know she was Jack Gregory's daughter. "Tell her when we have our Skip to My Lou party, I've learned the proper way to eat rolls, if we have rolls, that is."

"A party? You're telling me you're planning another party after what happened at the last one you arranged? I'd have thought a party wouldn't be something you'd be considering, not for a good long while, in any case."

"It won't be right away. We both have to get well," she said with a lilt to her voice that even she found surprising with all she had facing her. It must have been her sheer joy in talking about Betsy.

She was quiet while Doc Werther listened to her lungs and heart and thought about some of what was ahead of her. She had to talk to the sheriff about what she had done. Robbery was a crime. Would she be punished? And Timothy—he must know by now that Jack Gregory is her pa. What must he think of her taking part with Marjorie in such a thing? Fatigue began opening its dark mouth to swallow her up. It didn't take much for her to be as weary as she used to be at the end of a long day of heavy chores.

By the time Doc Werther had finished listening and was pulling the instrument from his ears, Opal was standing at the foot of the bed with a breakfast tray.

"Well, let me get out of your way," Doc Werther said, snapping his bag shut. "I'll have a quick cup of coffee downstairs with Mr. Neal, and then I'm off to deliver a message about a Skip... what kind of party?"

"Skip to My Lou. Betsy will understand." Sarah Emily yawned.

Opal was getting ready to help her sip a little broth, but she wasn't sure she could hold her eyes open.

❦

"How about sitting in the chair today?" Doc Werther asked during his morning visit. "I understand each day you've been staying awake for longer periods. Do you think you could eat something more than just soup?"

"The answer is yes to both questions." After four days of being in bed, not to mention the three weeks she couldn't remember, and eating only soups and broth—delicious as they were—she welcomed the change.

"Ah, an eager patient," Doc Werther said, shutting his medical bag. "Well, let's start with some breakfast and see how you do. I'll tell Opal when I go downstairs. Don't be surprised, though, if you can't eat much to begin with."

Sarah Emily still hadn't seen Timothy since her days had been spent mainly sleeping, but she knew that he had continued to come around to check on her. She was hoping that maybe today she could see him.

Opal came in shortly after Doc Werther left with a tray. Sarah Emily expected oatmeal. What else? Oatmeal had been her breakfast for as long as she could remember, but when Opal set the tray on the bedside table, there wasn't a dab of the gooey gray cereal anywhere on it.

Chapter 23

ater that morning, Sarah Emily was sitting up, relaxing in the overstuffed chair with pillows at the small of her back so she wouldn't lean against the wound just under her shoulder blade.

The room was quiet; she was alone and reflecting on the happenings of the morning. Opal had brought her an egg—a poached egg, she had called it. It was warm, smooth and buttery tasting. Along with that were some peaches Mrs. Neal had put up last summer.

"Your stomach done shrunk up. But it'll stretch back out before you know it," Opal had told her when Sarah Emily realized Doc Werther had been right about her not being able to eat much.

Then Mrs. Neal came with a pitcher of warm water and soap that smelled like flowers and sunshine. She had been getting freshened up every day, but today Mrs. Neal helped her get a bath. Sitting now in the chair, in the warm sunlight, Sarah Emily put the back of her hand to her nose to smell the soap again. It was like no soap she had ever used before.

After she had dried off, Mrs. Neal handed her a beautiful pink nightgown. Its softness slipped through her fingers like liquid. The three buttons at the top were covered in satin, and a pink satin ribbon finished off the neck. It was the most beautiful thing

Sarah Emily had ever seen, let alone been able to wear.

Mrs. Neal tucked Sarah Emily's feet into warm, woolen slippers the same delicate pink as the gown. Opal returned to help change the sheets. First, she and Mrs. Neal led Sarah Emily to the big chair and propped her up. Then the two of them proceeded to change her sheets. At the orphan asylum, you changed your own sheets. Nobody did it for you, and those sheets weren't this white or anywhere near this soft.

Sarah Emily shifted in the chair, reaching back with her right hand, careful not to pull too far and involve her left shoulder where the bullet wound was. Her shoulder was slipping to the chair back, and that would be painful. She pushed one of the pillows up a little farther. There, that was perfect. She smoothed down the skirt of her gown and rested against the adjusted pillow. What a spectacular morning she'd had.

That was, until Mrs. Neal had reached into her pocket and pulled out the pearl hair clasp she'd given Sarah Emily the day they had found the letter. Sarah Emily had almost asked Mrs. Neal how she had it, but everything about the morning was so sweet smelling and wonderfully enjoyable that Sarah Emily didn't want to spoil it by inserting an anguishing subject.

It wasn't the hair clip anyway. Sarah Emily didn't want to know who else had seen the letter. *Coward,* she told herself. *You'll have to know sometime.*

Mrs. Neal had fluffed Sarah Emily's hair and stepped back to admire. "Don't you look pretty? Now one more thing to finish off your morning bath," she had said. Out of her other pocket she pulled an amethyst colored bottle. Mrs. Neal pulled the glass stopper out of the top and daubed perfume behind both of Sarah Emily's ears and another dab on each wrist.

When Mrs. Neal left her alone to relax in the chair, Sarah Emily had never in all of her life felt like more of a princess. But the more she sat there and thought about it, she knew she wasn't a princess. She was Jack Gregory's daughter. She had been involved in a robbery. Because of her, Cora could have been hurt or killed. If the hair clasp had been found, then so had the letter.

What had ever made her think it would be the answer to everything to know who she looked like? It couldn't have been a worse thing to know.

✦

Sitting in the chair, Sarah Emily dozed off. The next thing she knew, Mrs. Neal was singing, "You've got company," and patting her arm.

Emerging from her sleep-stupor, she found herself slumped down in the chair. Carefully hoisting herself up, getting repositioned and collecting her thoughts, she asked, "Company? Who?"

"It's Timothy," Mrs. Neal told her in a sparkly voice. "Let's get a robe on you, and then you'll be all ready to accept visitors." She opened the wardrobe door and took a robe off the hook that matched the gown Sarah Emily had on. She helped Sarah Emily into it and fastened the two dozen tiny satin covered buttons that went from neck to the floor-length hem. Mrs. Neal fluffed her hair again. "Ah, yes, lovely," she said. "I'll go get him."

Timothy—Sarah Emily was eager to see him, that she was sure of, but also a little apprehensive. Did he know about Jack Gregory?

The door opened. There he stood—tall, hair combed and slicked back and a lumpy parcel of some sort in his hands. And handsome. He was, without a doubt, the most handsome she had ever seen him. But it was when she became aware he was smiling at her with that lopsided, set-the-world-straight smile of his, that her toes began to twitch. Even his eyes were smiling! However he felt about Jack Gregory being her pa, he was smiling. However he felt about her going with Marjorie, he was smiling!

"I'm sure glad to see you," Timothy said, almost shyly, entering the room.

"You too," she said, almost as shyly. *Oh, for Pete's sake,* she thought, struggling with her toes. "You want to sit down?" she said, trying to step on her twitching toes with her other foot.

"Of course, he wants to sit down. He's going to have lunch with you." Mrs. Neal walked over to a narrow table under the window and began to remove the book, oil lamp and the doily it sat on, and set them over on the high bureau.

"How can I help?" Timothy said, laying his parcel on the bed.

"You can help me move this table."

They set it in front of Sarah Emily, and then Mrs. Neal said, "In the bedroom across the hall is a straight-backed chair. I think that would be more comfortable than the rocker for you to sit in while you eat."

"Opal is going to bring up lunch in just a few minutes. Now you two have a nice visit," she said, backing out of the room as soon as he returned with the chair.

"Did you know we were having lunch together?" Sarah Emily asked.

"Yes, Mrs. Neal had talked to me about it, but we wanted to make sure you were up to it, and then we decided to make it a surprise." His face suddenly flattened. "This is okay with you, isn't it?"

"Okay? It's a wonderful surprise!"

"Good. Well, then," he cleared his throat, "I'll sit down." And he settled in the chair he had put across the table from her.

She saw his eyes briefly light on the hair clasp and then move away. She'd wait and see if he mentioned the letter or how the hair clasp got here.

"How are you feeling?" he asked. "You sure look pretty and...you smell pretty too."

She lowered her eyes. "Thanks. I'm feeling better, but still about as frail as a glass house in a hailstorm. Doc Werther says I'm going to be fine."

"I'd say it's progress that you're sitting up in a chair."

All at once, it dawned on her that she was in a nightgown. She touched the top of the robe, self-consciously. "Yes, and it feels great to be up. Otherwise, I have to stay on my side in bed, and that gets uncomfortable after a while, so sitting up is a nice break."

"Lunch," Opal said, coming in with a heavily laden tray.

Immediately, Timothy stood to help her with it. There were two plates. One was heaped with thick slices of roast beef, browned potatoes and green beans.

"I talked to Doc Werther," Opal said, taking a pitcher of lemonade off the tray, and he said you could have a little of everything. It's important not to overdo, so I didn't put as much on your plate. Still, if you can't eat it all, just leave it." Then she set a basket of rolls next to a dish of preserves on the makeshift eating table. "Now don't you overdo on this either. You hear me?" She was smiling but looking at Sarah Emily, waiting for an answer.

"I won't, I promise," Sarah Emily said, breathing in the aroma of all the food.

"You two have a good time. I'll be back up later with dessert. Now, Timothy, you just let me know if either of you need anything else."

"Thanks, Opal," they both said as she left.

After they'd almost finished eating, talking the whole time, Timothy said, "Hey, did you hear why Cook was gone every afternoon for so long and why Mr. Wilbur's hair has been flying all over the place?"

"There's a lot I've missed out on." She took her last bite of a roll with preserves while he refilled her glass.

"Well, it seems that Cook decided to have new dresses made for all the girls for Christmas. That was just a made-up story about having one made for herself. That way she could show you the swatch of cloth to find out which color you liked. She had the most beautiful green one made for you, Sarah Em."

Her mind shot back to the day in the food line. It was the day Betsy came, and Cook had showed her the green swatch of fabric, asking so many times if she liked it.

"She thought green would look good on you with your beautiful green eyes."

Her green eyes! They came from Jack Gregory.

Timothy talked on, obviously unaware of her discomfort. "She's had that green dress hanging up in the dining room for everyone to see. Just waiting 'til you are well enough to wear it."

"How did she ever in a million years get enough money to have dresses made for all of us?"

"That's why she was gone every afternoon for so long. She took a job cooking for one of the rich families on the other side of the woods. Their cook had to go take care of a sick relative for a while. She didn't have the time to earn the money for the fabric and make the dresses, so she hired Miss Polly Fletcher to do it. You know, she's been having a rough time lately, and Cook was worried about her. The job helped her out a lot, from what I understand."

"That must be what Mrs. Hancock was referring to when we were listening from the upstairs storage room. Remember?"

"No, I have to admit, my mind was wandering while they were gossiping."

"That day, Mrs. Hancock remarked about how much fabric Polly Fletcher had bought, and they wondered what job could be so big." Sarah Emily couldn't wait to see the dress. Again, she was the recipient of the generosity of others. Life was confusing, to say the least.

"Okay, now on to Mr. Wilbur and his messy hair. He overheard some of the women from the Ladies' Aid Society talking about not being able to give you girls hair clasps for Christmas this year— something about needing new drapes for their meeting place. At any rate, he decided to buy hair clasps for all the girls, a toy for the younger boys and..." he proudly put his hand to his hair, "hair tonic for us older guys."

"That's why your hair looks so nice," she said, reaching over to touch his shiny hair.

"The only way he could afford to do all that was to go without buying hair tonic for himself." Timothy put his fork down and leaned back in his chair. "Aren't they some kind of terrific to do that for us? I'll tell you what, Sarah Emily, this would have been the best Christmas we'd ever had, with the presents from them, but with your being shot and unconscious and Betsy's being so sick, it was hard for anyone to enjoy their new things. Nettie even suggested that none of the girls wear their new dresses until you and Betsy were able to wear yours."

"That Nettie," Sarah Emily said, smiling.

"Everyone is sure glad you're going to be okay." He took her hand, "Some of us are glad for more reasons than just wearing a new dress." He grinned that lopsided grin.

Sarah Emily's toes twitched, and it felt wonderful. For the first time, she hoped the twitching never stopped.

"You want to see what's in that package I brought?" he said, getting up to get it.

She was so enthralled with Timothy, hearing about the gifts from Cook and Mr. Wilbur, that she couldn't imagine how there could be more.

He pushed her plate over and set the parcel in front of her. She untied the string, and when she opened it, there were two things—another wrapped something and Betsy's ma's lovely silver brush. "Where was it? How..." she traced the ornate design across the back and down the handle.

"When Sheriff Thornton arrested Jack Gregory, he found out where Gregory and Marjorie were hiding their stash of stolen things until it could be sold. We were told the reason they hadn't sold the brush yet was that Marjorie wanted it for herself. When Betsy knew I was coming here today, she asked me to bring it to show you. You should have seen her when the sheriff gave it back to her. I've never seen or heard such laughing and crying all at the same time. Mrs. Neal knew how you girls looked and looked for the brush, but no one suspected Marjorie. She said, 'That's the way it is with so many things; the questions are usually a lot more complicated than the answers.'"

"She's said some peculiar things to me too." Sarah Emily thought about being made in God's image.

"Well, at first you might think that they are, as you say, peculiar, but when you really listen to her and Mr. Neal, they make a lot of sense." He laid his hand on the unwrapped parcel still in front of her.

"You know, I've spent a lot of time over here waiting while you were unconscious. Mr. Neal and I did a lot of talking. He started telling me about God and the things like Mrs. Neal told you. Well, at first, I wasn't interested. I was only concentrating on you. But I listened to be polite. After all, I was staying here an awful lot and they were feeding me. But then, some of the things he was telling me started making sense. It made life make sense. Sarah Em, you know I've read every book I could ever get my hands on. But there was still something missing—a big piece of the big picture. Things like, why are we on this earth anyway? And how did it get here in the first place? Is there no justice for the things that happen to people? And lots more questions that I never could figure out no matter how many books I read or facts I learned."

Sarah Emily didn't say a word. Timothy was talking like an excited, happy child tumbling down a hill who can't be stopped until he reaches bottom.

"Mr. Neal told me about God and how he made everything—everything, Sarah Em. God created it all. Then he started telling me about his son, Jesus. Did you know that God loves you and me so much that he sent his Son to die for all the wrong things we do? To take our punishment for us? He told me how I can have that forgiveness, how to accept Jesus as my Savior. Oh," he rubbed his forehead, "I'm probably not explaining this very well. I just know that since I asked Jesus into my life, I feel different. I feel like my life has purpose.

"Mr. Neal gave me a Bible. That's the book Mrs. Neal read to you from. I took it back to the boy's dormitory and read it. I read it while I was waiting downstairs here for word about you. I read it from front to back. I couldn't stop 'til I'd read every line. It was the most wonderful book." He took a deep breath and sat back. "Open the package."

He had reached the bottom of the hill. She untied the coarse string, pulled back the crinkled brown paper and found a black book with gold printing on the cover that read, *Holy Bible.*

"I asked Mr. Neal," Timothy said, speaking slower now, but leaning forward, "if I could do some jobs around here, since I was here so much anyway. I wanted to earn the money to buy you a Bible. He said he'd be glad to give you one. I didn't have to work for it, but I wanted to. I wanted to be the one to give you the best book of all. Sarah Em, I want you to know about God and his Son, Jesus.

"Jack Gregory doesn't matter. Who you look like doesn't matter. *You* are made in God's image, Sarah Em. You're made in the image of goodness and love, and you have the ability to live forever with Him. Nothing else matters. Do you understand? Nothing else matters. You are special because God made you."

She let her fingers caress the leather cover. She opened the book. The delicate pages fluttered, their gold edges glittering. Was it possible that she just opened a plain, brown wrapper and found out that she really was the exquisite china?

Chapter 24

The next afternoon, Sheriff Thornton folded his long legs under the chair and pulled it up close to the edge of Sarah Emily's bed. His dark blue shirt made his eyes the color of navy blue marbles. "I'm sure I don't need to tell you how glad everyone is that you're going to be all right. I've come by every day, and there were always several others waiting around hoping for news. From what I saw, I don't think Timothy missed a day." He grinned, and his thick black moustache fanned out.

"So I've been told," she said trying to keep her voice even. "He came to see me yesterday, and we had lunch together. He said he'd be back today and is going to bring Ours. Everyone, simply everyone, has been extra kind," she quickly added.

"I assumed as much. That's good." The sheriff laced his fingers, propped his hands on the edge of the bed and leaned forward. "I've got to ask you some hard questions. Doc says you told him you feel up to it. Is that right?"

"I'm ready."

"If you get too tired, you just tell me."

She nodded.

"Well, of course, we talked to Marjorie before she was taken to Chicago."

"Chicago?"

"Yes, she's in jail there awaiting trial. And Gregory too. We found boxes and boxes of things they'd stolen from houses and stores all around Lander and surrounding towns, including Betsy's hairbrush. Timothy said he'd told you we found that."

"Yes, he did. I guess that explains all those nights when Marjorie wasn't in bed." Sarah Emily sighed and then asked, in a hesitating voice, "Was Jack Gregory really her boyfriend?"

"No, I don't see it that way at all. From what I can put together, she was helping with the robberies in exchange for part of the money. They'd been doing this for some time. It appears to me that she saw it as her way to have some money after she turned eighteen, which isn't far off." The sheriff pulled his lips together, his moustache bunching up, like he wasn't sure whether to be angry with Marjorie or feel sorry for her. "Marjorie evidently told Gregory that the Ladies' Aid Society was going to be at the orphan asylum the day of your Christmas party. He didn't just happen by."

Sarah Emily closed her eyes at this new information to let it settle in with all the rest.

"Cora told us what she knew, which wasn't much, only that Marjorie seemed to press you into going with her that night. Cora didn't know what was going on, but she heard Marjorie badgering you into something that didn't sound good. In her young mind, you had to be in trouble to do such a thing, so she was going to help you."

"Oh, Sheriff, I had no idea Cora would follow me. I never would have put her in that kind of danger. I didn't even consider that guns might be involved. Clearly, I didn't think any of it through very well." As soon as she was well, the first thing she would do is time a pot of water herself to see how long it took to boil.

"We're all thankful Cora wasn't hurt, but I know you feel guilty about what could have happened. What we really want to know is why you were with Marjorie. That just isn't like you." His voice was kind but firm.

Sarah Emily nibbled her bottom lip. She stared at the gold-framed lilac painting as if she'd find the answer among one of the thick, purple pyramids of blooms. What had Marjorie already told the sheriff? Would *she* be going to jail in Chicago like Marjorie? Should she tell him about her ma's letter? Should she tell him she knew Gregory was her father?

All at once, the whirl of questions came to a peaceful halt. The words *made in God's image* whispered at the chaos in her mind. Although she still didn't totally understand what they meant, they somehow seemed important—not only for today, but for the rest of her life.

"Sheriff, I'll tell you why I was with Marjorie. The day before the robbery at Melody's house, I read a letter for the first time that my ma wrote to me. I learned that Robert Butler is not my pa. And the worst part is, I'm pretty sure, almost positive now, that I'm Jack Gregory's daughter."

Sheriff Thornton squeezed her hand. "Go on."

"The day after I discovered the letter, Betsy nearly died. I felt like it was too terrible to imagine who I was, and if Betsy died—well, life was just plainly cruel. Then Marjorie overheard what was in the letter and said she'd tell everyone. I was so ashamed of who my pa is and how I came to be. Of course, then I didn't know it was Gregory, but I'd learned what had happened to Ma. I knew going with Marjorie was wrong. I never should have done it." Sarah Emily stared out the window at the late afternoon sun turning pink and purple. "And then when Cora came in and I saw that a gun was aimed . . ." She bit her lip and looked at Sheriff Thornton.

"That must have been terrible for you." He shook his head. "Timothy showed me the letter from your mother. I'd asked him not to say anything to you that he had until I talked to you. I wanted to see what you said first. He was very reluctant to let me read it because he'd promised you he wouldn't tell anyone. But after you were shot, he felt it would put the pieces together of all that had happened."

She could understand that. So, she thought, that's why Timothy hadn't commented on the hair clasp yesterday. He didn't want it brought up about the letter.

The sheriff said, "I'd already been piecing things together after Jack Gregory responded to Miss Percy's brooch like he did."

"So you knew right after the Christmas party?"

"I had a hunch that he was the man who attacked your mother. I didn't want to say anything to you because I was trying to locate Robert Butler. I hoped to talk to him before I came to you with just a hunch. But I didn't know Gregory was your father until I read the letter."

"Did you find Robert Butler?"

"No. I've sent telegrams to every sheriff within five hundred miles, but nobody's seen him. I don't know where he is."

"You said you'd read the letter?"

"Yes."

"Did you keep it?"

"Of course not. It's right there, in the mahogany box."

"Sheriff, I have a hunch too."

"About what?"

"About Miss Percy's brooch. I may be wrong, but I think the brooch Miss Percy has is the one that belonged to my ma."

The sheriff brushed his fingers over his glossy moustache. "You're not wrong. We're going to see to it that everything is set right before all this is over."

"Do you know how she got it or why?"

"No. She was shown the letter too. As soon as she read it, she had some kind of breakdown. There's still a lot of information we need to get from Miss Percy. I think she's getting better, but she's been in bed, hardly able to speak. We know that Butler gave her the brooch, and, of course, she knew your mother."

"Knew my mother?" That thought had never occurred to Sarah Emily and for some reason it disturbed her.

"Yes, you didn't know? They went to school together, along with Butler and me. But as far as the brooch goes, I still have it. Remember, I kept it after the robbery."

"What's going to happen to me?" Sarah Emily asked, fearing what kind of life she was going to have being Gregory's daughter and having a strange connection to Miss Percy.

"This was the first time you've ever done anything like this, and I've been talking to the judge. But you don't need to worry. Just get better."

He misunderstood her question, and it seemed easier to let it go.

"Okay, I'm going to leave now. You look mighty tired. I just needed to hear your story and see how it squared with everything else I knew. Thank you for being so completely honest."

That evening she lay in bed, the oil lamp spreading a long, lovely shaft of light. She wanted to enjoy the beauty of the room. She was getting used to its summer lilac scent, beautiful furniture and comfortable feeling, but she didn't know how much longer she would be able to stay. Going back to the orphan asylum hadn't been discussed with her.

Instead of relaxing and taking pleasure in her surroundings, her mind kept pushing around Jack Gregory. He was like something that washed up on the riverbank with a flood, debris clinging to his soggy mass in slimy strings. He was too bulky and heavy to heave back out. He was hers, forever.

"Do you feel up to talking for a few minutes before you go to sleep?" Mrs. Neal asked, sticking her head in.

"Yes," Sarah Emily said, welcoming the diversion from her present thoughts. "I'm surprised how wide awake I am after talking to the sheriff and Timothy's coming back for a short visit."

Mrs. Neal smiled and scooted the rocking chair close to the bed. "Timothy fairly floats down the stairs after being with you. I'm not sure his feet touch even one. He does seem to care so much for you."

As Mrs. Neal straightened the sheets, her expression turned serious. "Sarah Emily, everyone tells us you've never done anything like this robbery before. I have to tell you, Mr. Neal and I are worried that we played a part. Did finding the letter from your mother cause you to go with Marjorie?" She neatly folded the extra blanket toward the foot of the bed and then looked into Sarah Emily's eyes. "Could that be true?"

It was the letter. It was hearing that Betsy might not live. It was because Marjorie was going to tell that her ma had been raped. It had been so many things, a mixed-up combination of things.

"That's one reason why I went," she finally said. "I guess it was the start of most of the other reasons. You know, don't you," her stomach felt like a wet towel someone was wringing out, "I'm Jack Gregory's daughter? I've got his green eyes and turned-up nose. I'm going to be just like him." Her stomach twisted again.

Mrs. Neal put her warm palm to Sarah Emily's cheek. "It's wonderful when someone has a good earthly father, but not everyone does. But you do have a wonderful heavenly Father and His name is God. Your life is governed by what you choose to do about God, not what someone like Jack Gregory has done to you. Your green eyes and turned-up nose aren't nearly as important as the life God will give you.

"God has given you everything you need to be who He wants you to be. Dr. Werther told us that Timothy wants to become a doctor. Timothy doesn't know who his parents are, but God gave him a fine mind that easily learns and retains. He has a gentle spirit and cares about people. Don't you see that?"

"Of course, I see that. But maybe those were the kind of people his parents were."

"Sarah Emily, somehow you've gotten the idea that who you look like governs who you are. Do you know that some people go through their whole life measuring who they are by what others tell them or say about them or a failure they've had or where they live? That list of how people gauge themselves goes on and on. And the shame of that is men and women waste their lives on false ideas. Accepting Jesus and His boundless love for you—that's when you can know how truly special and valuable you are."

"Timothy told me he'd done that—accepted Jesus."

"Yes. That was a wonderful moment. Whenever you're ready, you can do the same."

Sarah Emily hesitated a minute. "I'll let you know." She wanted to think about all of this some more.

"It's your choice. God never forces Himself on anyone." Mrs.

Neal smiled. "But I'm praying you won't wait much longer. Now, there's one more thing I want to do tonight. I want to give you your mahogany box back."

"That was for you to get Betsy's medicine, and I understand you've had to buy a lot more than one dollars worth."

"From the beginning, I never intended to keep your box, sweetheart. But I knew if I hadn't that night, you wouldn't believe we'd get the medicine. And, quite frankly, the reason I asked you back to do chores was because I was looking for an excuse to have you visit me."

She leaned forward and kissed Sarah Emily's forehead. The kiss felt exactly like Sarah Emily always imagined a ma's kiss would feel like—sweet, soft and brimming with love.

Mrs. Neal pushed back the chair and stood. "Now you get some rest. Ring that bell if you need anything at all." She left the door slightly ajar.

Sarah Emily touched her forehead. The kiss was still there. She could feel it.

Then her gaze wandered to the window, and she watched clouds meander by. The sky had grown several shades darker. *False ideas cause people to waste their lives. Hollow fog.*

Sarah Emily looked at the bell and felt special. She had never had this much pampering. She studied the mahogany box and thought about her mother's prayers in the letter. *I pray for you, my precious Sarah Emily, that there will be someone in your life who will love you with a mother's love.*

She settled deeper into the smooth sheets; sleep came and she drifted off with it.

Chapter 25

*T*wo months after Sarah Emily had been shot, she stood in the Neals' parlor. Golden shimmering light snapped and danced on every surface, in every corner, off every face. The Skip to My Lou party was only about fifteen minutes away from starting.

"You look beautiful, simply beautiful!" Doc Werther's voice turned her around. He held a crystal cup with red punch, and his gray suit was pressed to a sharp crispness.

"It's the dress Cook had made that's beautiful," she said, lifting out the skirt and twirling around.

"Yes, the dress is beautiful, but it's you, my dear. You're lovely."

"Thank you. And thank you for giving permission for the party."

"Well, I had to relent. What man could stand up to you, Betsy and Mrs. Neal constantly begging and badgering?" He feigned a weary sigh. "You three women wore me down." He smiled and took a sip of punch. "Truthfully, Sarah Emily, I'm very pleased with the way you and Betsy have both recovered. If you hadn't been strong enough, I would have put my foot down, in spite of all the feminine charm you three put to use."

"We knew that; that's why we didn't mind being so persistent in our asking," Sarah Emily said, smiling. Then her smile faded and she said, "Is Miss Percy getting better?"

The doctor studied the red eddy of punch he twirled in his cup. "I'm afraid she and only she can determine that."

"Is she coming tonight?"

"I hope so. I told her it would do her good." He took a drink of punch. "Now, let's talk about Timothy. I'm sure you know he's told me of his interest in becoming a doctor. I couldn't have been more thrilled, and so, on his behalf, I've sent a telegram to my old alma mater. Now we're just waiting to see when we can go for some admission testing. As naturally smart as he is and with all the reading he's done, I feel confident he'll do well on those tests."

"He's always had a love of learning and now he gets to make use of all that time he spent with a book in front of his face. I'll admit, sometimes I thought he might be wasting his time," she laughed, "but of course, that never stopped him."

A group of men came in—Sarah Emily counted five—all dressed in black suits and bright white shirts and carrying musical instruments. They went directly to the small riser Mr. Neal had made just for this occasion. When they started tuning their instruments it was difficult to talk and Doc Werther excused himself to go find Mr. Neal.

Sarah Emily walked around the room touching the polished furniture, enjoying the warm light from the fireplace, and feasting her eyes on the trays and trays of food that sat on every available surface. In the dining room, she'd seen that the table was spilling over with more food. It would only be moments before everyone from the orphan asylum would be here. This room would erupt into a Skip to My Lou party with people darting everywhere like hummingbirds.

It was in here that she and Timothy had sat with the Neals the day she came to sell Ours and the box. That day, she would never have thought she would have spent two months at this house. She turned to get another sweeping view and saw a Bible on the edge of Mr. Neal's desk. She went to it, the band still honking and blowing behind her. They hadn't played one real song yet.

Sarah Emily knew that Betsy had talked to the Neals and was just as enthusiastic about God and Jesus as Timothy was. She lifted the black cover, then turned back a thick section of pages. Her fingers ran over the words. She wasn't reading, just touching. She had been reluctant to believe that God could love her, love who she was.

"Hey, there you are!" Betsy said above the mismatched notes of the musicians. Her new pink dress flowed around her in soft ripples. Her golden hair and curls were growing out to their former exuberance since Miss Percy hadn't been well and hadn't been cutting anyone's hair.

"Isn't this grand?" Betsy said, looking around the room. "Everyone is on their way."

"You're really excited about all of this aren't you?" Sarah Emily said, sweeping her hand over the Bible, forgetting the party for the moment.

"Yes. It's the best thing that's ever happened to me," Betsy said with confidence and a happier smile than Sarah Emily had seen on her before.

"Look here," Betsy flipped through the pages. "Remember when you were in the shed and I told you to say part of the Lord's Prayer?"

"Yes."

"Well, Faith must have gotten it mixed up because it's not the Lord's Prayer, it's the twenty-third Psalm. Here it is, right here—those very words Faith gave me to say."

Sarah Emily was amazed at how much Betsy had already learned about this strange book.

Cora darted in between Sarah Emily and Betsy. Sarah Emily could hear Ben and Nettie in the foyer. The party was getting ready to start.

"Mrs. Neal says I can stand on the stage with the musicians and tell everyone when it's time for Skip to My Lou." Cora was excited and talking as fast as her mouth could possibly form words. "Is that okay with you, Betsy? You'll have to give directions of what to do; I'm just going to tell everyone when it's time. Is that okay?"

"Of course it is. You can even stand with me to help me demonstrate. Why don't you pick a boy to help?"

"Timothy!" Cora made an immediate choice and ran off calling, "Timothy."

More voices wove together from the foyer in laugher.

Sarah Emily closed the Bible. "Is Miss Percy coming?"

"She was in her office when I left to come here, but she wasn't dressed yet."

"I haven't seen her since she went up to check on you, the night...I've got to talk to her. I'll be right back," she said, shouldering her way out against the thickening crowd coming in.

Sarah Emily wriggled into her coat as she hurried down Lilac Lane. She slowed when she neared the orphan asylum. Miss Percy was sitting on the front steps in her night robe, and her bun was uncinched, her long locks straggling down her back. Why ever was she outside in the cold?

The heavy iron letters on the sign that arched over the walkway, ORPHAN ASYLUM OF LANDER, threw odd-shaped shadows across Miss Percy in the moonlight. She looked fragile, almost as if she might crumble if someone were to touch her. Her hands were tightly wrapped together and lodged in her lap. Ours, lying at her feet, sat up and wagged her tail when she saw Sarah Emily.

Miss Percy slowly swiveled her head. "How's the party?" she said as though the past two months and all of its events had never existed.

"It was just getting started, but everything's beautiful. Why aren't you there? I thought you were coming."

"Did you want me to come?" Miss Percy looked pathetic and unguarded.

Sarah Emily shrugged. She didn't know what to say or for that matter, why she was there now.

"That's okay. You needn't say anything. Don't think I don't know how you and all the others feel about me." Miss Percy cocked her head to one side. "Listen," she said, her voice hushed. "You can hear the party music. That's why I came outside."

The music had started playing. They sat not saying a word, letting the happy party music ruffle around them. Sarah Emily saw a glint of something shiny between Miss Percy's fingers.

"I wish you liked me." Miss Percy's voice was flat, her eyes on the orphan asylum sign.

Sarah Emily's breath snagged in her throat. It had never occurred to her that Miss Percy cared how anyone felt about her, let alone liked her.

"I was your mother's schoolmate," Miss Percy said, as though that were the next logical part of their conversation.

"Yes, I know. Sheriff Thornton told me."

"Well, he may have told you that." Miss Percy let her gaze fall from the large, black orphan asylum letters to Sarah Emily. "But he didn't tell you everything, because I didn't tell him everything." Miss Percy didn't look angry or pleased; she looked vacant.

"I never knew who my father was." Miss Percy shifted slightly on the brick step. "My mother died when I was seven. After that, my grandmother took me in, and I felt more love from her than I ever had before—or since." She leaned down to pet Ours, long strings of her twine-looking hair bumped against her shoulders. When Miss Percy stirred, Sarah Emily was knocked back by the intense scent of her rosewater. She must have used the whole bottle.

"Grandmother even had a dog named Giggles that I adored."

"Giggles?" Sarah Emily repeated it to process the outlandishly absurd thought of Miss Percy being connected with anything named Giggles.

Miss Percy hesitated a moment as if she had to summon the details of that memory from a very long distance. "Grandmother named her that because she was such a happy dog and looked like she was always giggling." Miss Percy's words took on lightness, almost laughter. "I begged my grandmother to never leave me like my father and mother had, and she promised she wouldn't. Then one day when I was eleven years old, I came home from school and found her dead, slumped on the kitchen floor. Grandmother broke her promise," Miss Percy said, her tone turning frighteningly childlike.

"I was sent to live in the Lander Orphan Asylum when it was on the other side of town." Miss Percy continued to scratch Ours's head in that preoccupied way of not really seeing. "I never saw Giggles again. She was left alone too. I heard that a neighbor had killed her. I know Giggles wouldn't ever have left me if she'd had a choice."

Sarah Emily drew her coat tighter around her. At that point, she couldn't have said if it was the chill of the night air or Miss Percy's words.

"When I was moved to the orphan asylum, I met your mother. We didn't have our own school, so we went to the same one. *She* had a mother and a father, a home and such nice clothes—beautiful colorful dresses with bows and ribbons. In the orphan asylum we wore plain, drab gray dresses every single day.

"Your mother was so pretty. She had light brown hair that floated around her shoulders." Miss Percy closed her eyes and tilted her head back, making her stringy black hair swish around her own shoulders. Sarah Emily saw that it was matted and gummy. "The headmistress cut our hair off," Miss Percy said.

"Didn't any of the other girls have pretty hair?" Sarah Emily asked, the question sounding stupid even to her.

"Yes, but not as pretty as your mothers. I wanted to be like Anna. Anna's mother always wore a beautiful brooch. I dreamed of having a mother who had such a beautiful thing.

"Then when I was seventeen," she continued informatively as if notifying her of the next day's menu or chores. "I fell in love with a tall boy a grade ahead of us. One day, I heard him say he liked the scent of rosewater. So I did odd jobs in town to make enough money to buy some. But even wearing the rosewater, he didn't notice me. His eyes only saw Anna." She said the name like acid hit her tongue.

Sarah Emily sat motionless, almost afraid to breathe, watching Miss Percy who seemed like a small, battered mouse.

"Robert Butler is who it was."

Robert Butler. Sarah Emily had trouble absorbing the thought. The music from the party kept coming in lively waves. It made a bizarre backdrop for the conversation.

"When I finished school, I stayed on working at the orphan asylum doing different jobs. At the time, there weren't many other options, and I wanted to stay in Lander because I hoped that Robert would notice me. Then, they finally asked me to be headmistress because they couldn't find anyone else. I wasn't their first choice. Do you know what I had been all my life?"

"No," Sarah Emily said softly.

"I was a small pebble dropped into a huge, raging river. It didn't make the river stop or even hesitate to see what had been dropped in. Being an orphan makes you invisible, insignificant."

In that instant, Sarah Emily saw Miss Percy's heart and knew it was as shriveled as her bony body. *False ideas. Wasted lives.* Mrs. Neal's words took form and life, right then, in the shape of Miss Percy.

"Sarah Emily, when your grandparents died, Robert came to me, begging me to take you. The state wouldn't pay for you since it appeared you had one parent alive."

It made sense now—Sarah Emily's name never on the list from the state agency—the number of rations always one short.

"In exchange, Robert offered me the brooch and a monthly payment," Miss Percy said. "That brooch—the one I'd wanted for so long. So, of course, I agreed to take you. I also felt that if I did this for him, he might take notice of me as a woman. After all, Anna was dead."

Miss Percy's bitterness had turned rancid. Sarah Emily could see the maggots and smell the stench.

"Through the years, he came a couple of times to ask for the brooch to use as collateral for business deals, but I knew that if I gave it to him, I'd never see it again. He was a poor businessman after your mother died. He just couldn't get his life together again, and he knew I wouldn't keep you without support money."

Things were starting to come clear to Sarah Emily—disturbing things.

"The last time Robert came," Miss Percy said, "when you saw him outside the school house, he again wanted the brooch for collateral and said he couldn't pay me any more money. It was his money I'd used to buy the extra things I wanted. I already had several new cups and saucers ordered at the mercantile, so I had to dip into the supplies allotment sent to them from the state. The Mitchells let me do that without turning me in because I offered them as much free labor as they wanted from some of the boys. I substituted what Robert gave me by making the boys work at other paying jobs too. It's funny, but in all these years, Robert never told anyone that you weren't his. I guess he was still trying to protect Anna."

Sarah Emily's stomach curdled at the web that had snared both Miss Percy and her together.

Miss Percy's usually rigid shoulders had sagged into limp lumps. "My mother didn't have a brooch to hand down to me, but she had a beautiful collection of china cups and saucers. My grandmother and I had tea every morning with them. And she'd serve treats to me on her beautiful pink plate; the cinnamon buns were my favorite. It was a special time of day, time with Grandmother and using my mother's cups and saucers." Miss Percy straightened up and looked intently into the night and across the years. "I can scarcely remember being that girl." Then she sagged again.

"The day I was taken to the orphan asylum, I was only able to get the pink plate and one cup and saucer—the one with tiny yellow flowers. I dropped the cup trying to get it into my satchel quickly, and a chip broke off. I pledged to build my own collection, which I've done, with the money Robert sent me each month to take care of you." She lifted her head, her voice full of pride.

Sarah Emily thought about the one possession she had of *her* mother's—her mahogany box. Betsy also had one possession of her mother's—the hairbrush. People are so much alike, at the core; she saw that now. For the first time ever, Sarah Emily felt compassion for Miss Percy and laid her hand on top of Miss Percy's clenched ones.

Miss Percy seemed to soften at her touch. A tear fell on Sarah Emily's hand. *Miss Percy crying?*

"When I heard you'd blocked that bullet for Cora, I was stunned. I came to the Neals' and saw you right before Dr. Werther did surgery to remove the bullet. I stood there and looked at you and kept thinking, *An orphan would do something like that for someone else?* I have to tell you, Sarah Emily," Miss Percy hesitated as though struggling to speak, "I admire that, but I don't know how or why you did it. You know, I've never hit one of you with my leather strap."

Sarah Emily's mind lurched. Had she missed a transition? If she had, it was too late to find it; Miss Percy wasn't stopping.

"I've whirled it through the air. I've threatened with it. I've slapped it against your bed rails. But I've never hit one of you with it."

Sarah Emily searched for memories with the strap. Miss Percy was right! She and the others believed it had happened because Miss Percy said it and brandished it often enough. That revelation rose to an astonishing jolt in Sarah Emily's mind. How had she never seen that?

"I didn't want to hit you," Miss Percy said in a surprisingly soft tone. "Do you know why I made you all walk on the rope 'til you were sixteen?"

"No."

"Because I needed all of you to be humiliated and belittled. I felt I had to keep an iron heel on your throats to be in control. The older you all got, the harder it was for me to have authority. That's why I wouldn't let Mr. Wilbur tear down the shed. I had to have that too, or so I thought."

Miss Percy shook off Sarah Emily's hand and unlocked her fingers.

Sarah Emily saw the brooch and the deep imprints in both of Miss Percy's palms from holding it so hard.

"I should have treated you like my grandmother treated me, but instead I treated you with the anger I had for being left alone. I know you won't believe me, but I really wanted you all to love me."

"You did?"

"Yes."

Miss Percy let the brooch lie in her left hand while she lifted the other to the sky. With her palm up, she said, "If you close one eye, you can hold a star on the tip of your finger."

Sarah Emily held her hand up to the heavens. She closed one eye and suddenly she was balancing a shiny star on the tip of her finger.

"My grandmother taught me this," Miss Percy said. "She used to say, 'hold a star on your finger and determine to make your life as bright as that star.'"

Miss Percy's hand fell with the weight of a brick back to her lap. "I didn't do that." Her fingers curled like claws around the brooch. She breathed deeply.

"Why didn't you?"

"I don't know. It's the same as if you were sitting in a room on a scorching hot day, knowing a cool breeze is blowing outside, but the windows are closed and you won't get up and open them. So you just sit there and stifle in the heat."

At that moment, Sarah Emily knew exactly what Mrs. Neal meant. *Your life is determined by what you decide to do about God, not what someone does to you.* "You don't have to stay this way, Miss Percy. I don't know much about God, but I'm learning that He loves me, and He loves you too."

"Maybe. But I doubt it." Miss Percy took a deep breath and licked her lips. "I'm going to a sanitarium in Chicago."

"A sanitarium? When?"

"Tomorrow. The state has someone new coming in."

"Will you be back?"

"I'm not sure." Then, slowly and deliberately, Miss Percy twisted on the brick step to face Sarah Emily and pinned Anna's jeweled brooch on her dress. "I asked Zeke to let me give you the brooch. If you hadn't come tonight, I was going to send for you. This brooch is yours. Now go back to the party and to the Neals."

Sarah Emily put her arms out toward Miss Percy, wanting to hug her. "Thank—"

"I said go back to the party." Miss Percy pulled away, leaned down, her hair covering her face, her rosewater so strong it was almost a stench, and patted Ours.

Sarah Emily watched, desperately wanting to say something— something that would make the awful pain in Miss Percy go away. It was unmistakable that she had let bitterness and jealousy occupy a very large space in her life.

"Go back to the party. Leave me alone," Miss Percy finally said, still crouched over.

Moments later, Sarah Emily walked back to the party, stroking her brooch—her mother's brooch. The events of the past half-hour poured through her mind.

She looked up to the sky and spoke softly, "God, I don't really know how to talk to you yet. But Miss Percy is sorry for the way she treated us. She doesn't know you or how to get rid of the hate and hurt that's filled her for so long. Could you let her know that you love her and she needs you? Opal told me those were the two most important things to know, and I can see that now. Please let Miss Percy understand that too.

"Thank You for putting Mrs. Neal in my life to answer my mother's prayers that someone would love me like a mother, and thank You that I have her brooch. I really want to thank You for letting me find out that You're my Father. It's been a difficult lesson, but I think I've learned that looking like Jack Gregory doesn't matter. I don't want to waste my life by believing false notions. I want to understand what being made in Your image means. But, please, don't forget Miss Percy. Help her."

At the white and green house, music and laughter glided outside. As she approached the front porch steps, Timothy was standing there. Timothy's hair was shiny and slicked back with the hair tonic from Mr. Wilbur. He had on a new suit that fit him perfectly. Light shone through the partly open door, shooting rods of bright yellow into the night. "I was waiting for you. Betsy said you'd gone to talk to Miss Percy."

"Yes, I did."

"Whatever for?"

"I'll tell you all about it later. Let's go into the party, but before this night is over, I want to talk to you and Mrs. Neal about letting Jesus into my life."

"Oh, Sarah Em that is the best news. I'm so glad you realize that who you are or who you look like doesn't matter; it's who He is." His eyes lit on the brooch. "You've got it. Wow! It looks like it belongs on you." He leaned over and brushed her cheek with a tiny kiss. "I still say," he whispered, "if you're a bean, you're a lima bean 'cause they're my favorite. My very favorite."

Her toes twitched.

She touched her cheek and smiled. The words of the one prayer in her ma's letter that hadn't been answered yet came to her: *I pray that you will find a godly husband.* Could Timothy…?

She felt his arm slip around her waist and guide her toward the front door. The honking of geese flying overhead split the air. They both looked up. The geese were flying in a perfect triangular formation.

"Geese," Timothy said, "have an internal compass that's sensitive to a magnetic field in the earth. They calibrate their compass by the sunlight and stars. That's how they know who they are and where to go. Just think, if God put that in geese, what's in us since we're made in His image?"

Betsy stuck her head out the door. "Come on, you two; we're about to begin the first round of Skip to My Lou, and Cora is looking for Timothy."

Just before she stepped inside, Sarah Emily turned around, lifted her hand to the sky and balanced a star on the tip of her finger.

SARAH EMILY'S LIFE LESSONS APPLIED TO YOUR LIFE

The life-lessons that Sarah Emily learned apply to all of us. These questions can be explored on your own, or they would be excellent for group discussion after everyone reads the book.

1. The false idea that Sarah Emily latched onto about identifying her real self was from a misunderstanding of a snatch of overheard conversation: "It's who you look like; that's who you'll be." As ridiculous as we see that, we all have our own misguided perception of ourselves. List your good qualities and your faults as you see yourself.

2. Now, go back through the list and look at all the negative ones. Find the ones that are sins—for instance, lying. Lying is a sin and must be dealt with as such. Go through your list and ask God to forgive you of those. Now, cross those off, and what should be left are ones like: "I feel inadequate to accomplish much" or "I'm unworthy of people liking me."

   Whatever your ideas are, do you know where they came from? If you don't, that's fine. All that matters is for you to know that they aren't from God. They are false ideas ultimately from Satan to keep you from being what God intended you to be and from living the life He redeemed for you.

3. Who is the "Miss Percy" in your life? This is someone who irritates or frightens you by his/her actions and/or words. Do you know why his/her behavior is so severe? If you don't, ask God to give you a compassionate heart, realizing that almost everyone's annoying behavior comes from a place of hurt. However, if someone is actually abusing you, although you may pray for compassion, *don't* allow yourself to be abused.

4. Sarah Emily's mother prayed for Sarah Emily years before she was aware of the prayers. Was God negligent to allow Sarah Emily to experience those years in the orphan

asylum? Name a time(s) in your own life when God has been at work behind the scenes on your behalf.

5. Name a time(s) when your prayer was not answered immediately, but in God's time you saw the completion of your prayer.

6. Cook, Mr. Wilson and the Neals all had a spirit of giving, even to the point of self-sacrificing. Has there ever been a situation in your life when you gave to someone in that manner, or someone gave to you? What benefits did you receive from giving?

7. Betsy's terrible experiences with the basement hole made her able to help Sarah Emily with her day in the shed. How has a difficult situation made you able to help someone else? Or did the situation make you so bitter that you can't reach out to others?

8. There is the long-standing debate of heredity versus environment and which has the most influence. How does the grace of God play into or supercede either of those? The Bible tells us we are made in God's image. What does that mean to you?

*Go to www.ThatEndOfLilacLane.com
to download these questions and for more material.*